DEMOGRAPHY IN ARCHAEOLOGY

Demography in Archaeology is a review of current theory and method in the reconstruction of populations from archaeological data. Starting with a summary of demographic concepts and methods, the book examines historical and ethnographic sources of demographic evidence before addressing the methods by which reliable demographic estimates can be made from skeletal remains, settlement evidence and modern and ancient biomolecules. Recent debates in palaeodemography are evaluated, new statistical methods for palaeodemographic reconstruction are explained, and the notion that past demographic structures and processes were substantially different from those pertaining today is critiqued. The book covers a wide span of evidence, from the evolutionary background of human demography to the influence of natural and human-induced catastrophes on population growth and survival. This is essential reading for any archaeologist or anthropologist with an interest in relating the results of field and laboratory studies to broader questions of population structure and dynamics.

ANDREW T. CHAMBERLAIN is Reader in Biological Anthropology at the University of Sheffield.

CAMBRIDGE MANUALS IN ARCHAEOLOGY

General Editor
Graeme Barker, *University of Cambridge*

Advisory Editors
Elizabeth Slater, *University of Liverpool*
Peter Bogucki, *Princeton University*

Books in the series
Pottery in Archaeology, Clive Orton, Paul Tyers and Alan Vince
Vertebrate Taphonomy, R. Lee Lyman
Photography in Archaeology and Conservation, 2nd edition, Peter G. Dorrell
Alluvial Geoarchaeology, A. G. Brown
Shells, Cheryl Claasen
Zooarchaeology, Elizabeth J. Reitz and Elizabeth S. Wing
Sampling in Archaeology, Clive Orton
Excavation, Steve Roskams
Teeth, 2nd edition, Simon Hillson
Lithics, 2nd edition, William Andrefsky Jr.
Geographical Information Systems in Archaeology, James Conolly and Mark Lake
Demography in Archaeology, Andrew T. Chamberlain

Cambridge Manuals in Archaeology is a series of reference handbooks designed for an international audience of upper-level undergraduate and graduate students, and professional archaeologists and archaeological scientists in universities, museums, research laboratories and field units. Each book includes a survey of current archaeological practice alongside essential reference material on contemporary techniques and methodology.

DEMOGRAPHY IN ARCHAEOLOGY

Andrew T. Chamberlain

CAMBRIDGE
UNIVERSITY PRESS

CAMBRIDGE UNIVERSITY PRESS
Cambridge, New York, Melbourne, Madrid, Cape Town, Singapore, São Paulo

Cambridge University Press
The Edinburgh Building, Cambridge CB2 2RU, UK

Published in the United States of America by Cambridge University Press, New York

www.cambridge.org
Information on this title: www.cambridge.org/9780521596510

First published 2006

Printed in the United Kingdom at the University Press, Cambridge

A catalogue record for this publication is available from the British Library

ISBN-13 978-0-521-59367-0 hardback
ISBN-10 0-521-59367-0 hardback

ISBN-13 978-0-521-59651-0 paperback
ISBN-10 0-521-59651-3 paperback

To Clive and Stephen, who pointed the way.

CONTENTS

FIGURES

TABLES

PREFACE

The original impetus to write this volume emerged nearly a decade ago. It stemmed from a dissatisfaction, in fact a cognitive dissonance, between on the one hand the need to instruct graduate students in the available procedures for the reconstruction of past populations from skeletal remains, and on the other hand a profound unease at the results generated by such exercises. Fortunately it turned out that several researchers were simultaneously trying to square the same circle, and although the gestation of this book has been inordinately long, it has benefited from the insights provided by the combined endeavours of a new generation of anthropologists, archaeologists, population geneticists and biostatisticians whose research has reinvigorated the science of palaeodemography. In this book I have attempted to summarise and evaluate some of these exciting new developments, as well as to revisit some of the older and more established procedures for inferring population parameters from archaeological evidence.

Many individuals and organisations have knowingly or unwittingly contributed to the production of this book. Thanks are due first of all to the stimulating intellectual environment provided by colleagues and students at the University of Sheffield, and to the long-standing policy of the Department of Archaeology to resource periods of study leave for some of its academic staff. Some of the ideas expressed in this book have been trialled on successive cohorts of students enrolled on the Human Osteology masters training programme at the University of Sheffield. A few of those students have helped me substantially by contributing to the research reported here through their graduate and postdoctoral studies, in particular Dr Rebecca Gowland of the University of Cambridge and Dr Jo Buckberry of the University of Bradford. Other colleagues have been generous with their data, ideas and opinions – too many to name them all individually, but a particular debt of thanks is owed to Professor Charlotte Roberts of the University of Durham who sensibly reminded me of the inverse correlation between health and mortality! And quietly watching from the sidelines have been my editors at Cambridge University Press, whose enduring patience and support, flavoured with occasional gentle cajoling, have been invaluable.

Funding for some of my research has been provided by the Arts and Humanities Research Council, and several individuals and organisations have facilitated the study of unpublished skeletal remains. Louise Humphrey (Natural History Museum) and Eugenia Cunha (Coimbra) permitted access to their collections of known-age skeletons, and James Vaupel (Director of the Max Planck Institute of Demographic Research) kindly invited me to participate in some of the research projects sponsored by his Institute.

Introduction

1.1   THE PRINCIPAL CONCERNS OF DEMOGRAPHY

1.1.1   What is a population?

The term 'population' refers to a bounded group of living individuals, but the concept of a population is fluid depending on whether it is used in a biological or a sociocultural context. In biology, a population is a group of interbreeding organisms, or more formally a cluster of individuals which have a high probability of mating with each other compared to their probability of mating with members of some other population (Pianka, 1978). Biological populations have many properties, only some of which are the primary concern of demography. For example, the interaction between a population and its environment is the concern of ecology, while the variation of genes within and between populations is the concern of population genetics and evolutionary biology. Demography considers the population as a singular object for quantitative analysis, and seeks to explain variations in population size, structure and dynamics.

An alternative definition, more frequently encountered in the human sciences, views the population as a social unit in which individuals are linked by their common linguistic, cultural or historical experience. This kind of population, sometimes labelled a 'community', a 'culture' or a 'people', refers to a group of individuals united by their mutual social recognition of ancestry and kinship, by other cultural affinities and by co-residence or geographical proximity (Kreager, 1997). This definition emphasises socioeconomic and sociocultural factors in the formation and maintenance of human populations.

In considering archaeological populations both the biological and the social perspectives are important. Economic factors are often deeply implicated in the determination of patterns of migration and in an individual's reproductive decisions, while at the same time the constraints of biology are evident in regular patterns of fertility and mortality that are common to all human and animal populations.

1.1.2   *Population characteristics*

The following characteristics or attributes of populations are important in demographic analysis (Daugherty and Kammeyer, 1995: more formal quantitative definitions of these attributes are provided in Chapter 2).

- Population size: the number of individuals in the population
- Population structure: the distribution of the individuals across designated categories, principally those of age and sex
- Population dynamics: the growth or decline in the size of the population or of its component parts over time
- Population density: the number of individuals resident per unit area of territory
- Fertility: the number of offspring produced by an individual in a given time interval
- Mortality: the likelihood of death occuring to an individual in a given time interval
- Migration: the proportion of individuals entering or leaving the population, other than through fertility or mortality.

Changes in the first four of these attributes (size, structure, dynamics and density) can in principle be predicted for a particular population if fertility, mortality and migration rates for that population are known. However, in real examples of living populations fertility, mortality and migration rates vary substantially across age and sex categories, and they also change over time. As a result, quantitative demographic models of real populations are often complex and population characteristics occasionally change in a counter-intuitive fashion.

1.1.3   Demographic data: from individual life histories to population parameters

Life-history variables are chronological properties of an organism's life cycle, such as gestation period, time to maturation, frequency of reproduction and longevity (Roff, 1992; Stearns, 1992). In all successful groups of animals individuals are born, move around their environment, potentially reproduce and eventually die. These four classes of life-history events, which are fundamental to the lives of all animals, generate the data for demographic analysis. Within every population individuals vary in their probability of death, in their fertility and in their participation in migration. In the case of mortality and fertility, these events are strongly age structured, with the probability of death usually being much higher in the very young and in the very old, while fertility is usually at a maximum during the early and middle part of adult life. Age and sex differences in migration are observed in most animal species and are also characteristic of many human groups, as the propensity to migrate is strongly conditioned by socioeconomic circumstances and by cultural norms.

The demographic properties and behaviour of a population are therefore a summation and an average of the characteristics and behaviour of its constituent members. The total number of individuals in a population will vary over time if the number of births, deaths, immigrants and emigrants do not balance to zero over the relevant time period. The structure of a population can also change over time independently of the size of the population, and short-term changes in size and structure may be hidden from view by temporal averaging if the data are accumulated over a series of lifespans or generations (such as may happen when vital records are aggregated or when cemetery data are analysed).

1.2   DEMOGRAPHY IN ARCHAEOLOGY

1.2.1   *Archaeology and people*

In seeking to reconstruct the cultures and societies of the past, archaeology primarily investigates the material remnants that survive in the present-day environment. This evidence consists typically of the more robust elements of material culture, supplemented by the organic evidence for past environments and to a lesser extent by the surviving skeletal remains of the people themselves. There is no quick and easy route by which population size and structure can be inferred from these kinds of archaeological data. A multitude of confounding factors, including the differential deposition, preservation and recovery of archaeological remains, conspire to render samples incomplete and unrepresentative, while indirect evidence for population numbers (such as settlement size) is amenable to a variety of conflicting interpretations. However, the following examples outline some of the ways in which demographic models and data can play an important role both in underpinning the theoretical basis of archaeology and in aiding the interpretation of particular sites and assemblages.

1.2.2   *Population pressure: cause or effect?*

Qualitative demographic models have frequently played an important role in theoretical archaeology, as they have more widely within social history. Significant increases in population seem to have accompanied major technological advances such as the invention of Upper Palaeolithic blade industries (Shennan, 2001), the origins of food production (Hassan, 1973; Bronson, 1975; Cohen, 1977) and the onset of industrialisation in western Europe (McKeown, 1976). One general explanation for these episodic rises in population numbers, presented by Childe (1936) and endorsed by subsequent generations of economic historians and prehistorians, is the neo-Malthusian axiom that under normal circumstances the size of a population approaches an upper limit determined by the availability of critical resources. According to this viewpoint, technological, social and/or ideological change brings about the conditions under which a population is free to expand beyond these restraints until it is limited by a new barrier to growth. The recurring resource 'problem' is solved through a succession of sociocultural innovations, including change in land use, novel patterns of exploitation of resources, technological advance, specialisation, increased economic exchange and so on, enabling the population to periodically increase in size and density.

Set against this view is the theory, first articulated by Boserup (1965) and Dumond (1965), and taken up with enthusiasm during the rise of New Archaeology by Binford (1968), Carneiro (1970) and Renfrew (1973), that cultural change is primarily a *consequence* of population growth rather than a trigger for growth. It is perhaps noteworthy that Boserup's model not only appealed to Processual Archaeologists as a plausible exemplar of the theorised ecological basis of cultural change, but it also coincided with wider concerns about the possible economic and social consequences of unconstrained twentieth-century global population growth (Ehrlich, 1968). Population growth has been invoked as a prime mover in prehistoric cultural change, e.g. in the replacement of Neanderthals (*Homo neanderthalensis*) by anatomically modern *Homo sapiens* (Zubrow, 1989), in the rapid peopling of the Americas (Martin, 1973) and in the wave of advance model for the spread of agriculture in Europe (Ammerman and Cavalli-Sforza, 1973).

Case Study 1.1 Colonisation and population growth in the Late Pleistocene Americas

The Americas constitute the last continental land mass to be colonised by humans. This event took place in the Late Pleistocene, and although there is sporadic evidence for earlier settlement the main colonisation event probably occurred towards the end of the last Ice Age and involved the migration of hunter-gatherers into North America from eastern Siberia. The timing and rate of spread of this major colonisation event is controversial, and several lines of evidence have been pursued in order to investigate the early demographic history of the Americas including linguistic diversity amongst present-day native Americans (Nettle, 1999), genetic diversity in modern and ancient native populations (Torroni et al., 1994; Stone and Stoneking, 1999), morphological comparisons amongst human skeletal remains (Jantz and Owsley, 2001), chronological patterning of archaeological sites (Meltzer, 1995) and computer geographical modelling of population dispersal routes (Anderson and Gillam, 2000).

The colonisation process in the initial inhabitation of the Americas is believed to have been very rapid, based on the near contemporaneity between the earliest dated Palaeoindian sites in North and South America and the abundance of archaeological sites that emerge across North America at around 12,000 years BP. The colonisation of an unoccupied space is relatively easy to simulate mathematically, and several authors have generated numerical models that reconstruct the colonisation process. These models, which incorporate high average rates of population growth (increase in numbers of 1% to 3% per annum) and rapid geographical migration (up to 300km per generation), show that the Americas could have been occupied to carrying capacity within 2,000 years starting from a relatively small initial founding population (Young and Bettinger, 1995; Steele et al., 1998; Anderson and Gillam, 2000; Hazlewood and Steele, 2004). The demographic models rely on the assumption that hunter-gatherer populations migrating through unoccupied territory can pursue the option of long-distance 'leap-frog' colonisation movements to ensure that unexploited and productive foraging territory is immediately available for population expansion.

1.2.3   Population structure

Quite apart from the importance of overall numbers and rates of population growth, the analysis of population structure can also provide significant insights into past lifestyles and processes. Both human and animal populations exhibit a restricted range of age–class structures and sex ratios under natural circumstances. These structures of the living community translate into regular mortality profiles which can be reconstructed from assemblages of skeletal remains (see Chapter 2). Mortality profiles provide two key lines of information about past communities and processes. If a mortality profile reconstructed from archaeological evidence bears a close resemblance to a previously established profile derived from a present-day population, then it is reasonable to assume that the attributes of the modern population also apply to the archaeological sample. In contrast, the extent to which the age structure of an archaeological sample departs from the mortality profile of the modern population can provide the investigator with evidence about specific cultural and natural (taphonomic) processes that may have biased the composition of the archaeological sample.

1.2.4   Health and disease

Palaeopathology (the study of disease in past populations: Roberts and Manchester, 1995; Larsen, 1997) provides important evidence for past lifestyles and adaptations. Population statistics are now recognised to be crucially important in studies of medical history and palaeopathology (Waldron, 1994), as the prevalences of many diseases are age and sex dependent, and morbidity from infectious disease in particular is strongly dependent on population size and density. The demographic structure of a population, in turn, is influenced by the cumulative effects of the current and historical experience of health and disease in that population.

In some circumstances demographic data may provide evidence of a particular cause of death (Margerison and Knüsel, 2002; Dutour et al., 2003; Gowland and Chamberlain, 2005). Catastrophic mortality, occurring as a result of a natural mass disaster or from an outbreak of disease with high infectivity and mortality, will generate a mortality profile that reflects the living-age structure of the population at risk, whereas chronic malnutrition and ill health will tend to have a greater impact on the youngest and oldest age classes. Human migration and colonisation have had a profound effect on the global distribution of disease, with catastrophic consequences for many aboriginal populations (Verano and Ubelaker, 1992; Larsen and Milner, 1994).

Case Study 1.2 Impact of European contact on aboriginal North American populations

When Europeans began to colonise the New World in the late fifteenth century they encountered native aboriginal populations who lacked immunity to some infections such as measles, smallpox and scarlet fever, diseases that were common in Old-World communities. Following the arrival of European colonists outbreaks of these diseases became frequent amongst the native New-World populations, and although estimates of precontact aboriginal population numbers vary widely there is little doubt that contact-induced infectious disease was a major contributor to the decline of the native-American populations. The cumulative effects of repeated outbreaks of epidemic disease could be very great, as individual epidemics often killed more than 50% of the exposed native population.

Detailed studies of archaeological settlement data, combined with historical demographic records have provided clear evidence for the timing and cause of this 'crisis' mortality in native northeastern North America during the seventeenth century (Snow, 1996; Warrick, 2003). These studies indicate that there was a delay of about one century between initial European colonisation of North America and the arrival and spread of pandemic European diseases in the native populations. Warrick (2003) has attributed this delay to the small size of the original colonising populations and the fact that subsequent waves of European immigrants included larger numbers of children who were more likely to carry contagious diseases.

1.2.5 *Migration*

Hypotheses of human migration are often central, if controversial, in reconstructions of culture change. The physical migration of populations is sometimes put forward as a competing hypothesis to set against non-migrational models of cultural diffusion and indigenous development. Culture change may itself result in demographic change, thus the demographic signature of migration, particularly in prehistory, may be unclear. Nonetheless, there exist a wide range of historical and ethnographic studies of migration that can provide the theoretical basis for understanding the importance of migration in archaeology and the circumstances under which it takes place (Adams et al., 1978; Anthony, 1990). Information about the history of residence of individuals represented in the archaeological record can also be obtained from the chemical analysis of human skeletal remains.

Case Study 1.3 Isotopic evidence for prehistoric migration in Europe

Stable isotopes are non-radioactive, chemically similar forms of an element that can be detected and discriminated through small differences in their physical properties. Stable isotopes can be used in studies of migration, because individuals who are born and live in a specific geographical region will have an isotopic signature in their skeleton that is characteristic of the local sources of ingested nutrients (i.e. food and water) found in that region (Katzenberg, 2000). The presence of migrants in past populations can be detected by unusual isotopic values in their skeletal remains: this is normally undertaken using stable isotope ratios of bone-seeking elements such as strontium and lead, although in some regions of the world the isotopic ratios of oxygen can also be used to infer place of residence.

Migration has been invoked to explain the origin and rapid spread of various prehistoric cultures in Europe, including the early Neolithic Linearband-keramik (LBK) and the late Neolithic Bell-Beaker culture. Price et al. (2001) used the ratio of ^{87}Sr to ^{86}Sr in the tooth enamel of skeletons from LBK cemeteries in Flomborn and Schwetzingen in the Upper Rhine Valley, Germany, to distinguish locally born individuals from people who had migrated into the Rhine Valley from elsewhere. Tooth enamel, which is formed during infancy and early childhood, retains the isotopic signature of the early years of an individual's life, whereas bone which is continually remodelled throughout the lifespan has isotopic values that reflect approximately the last decade of life. At the Flomborn LBK cemetery 7 (64%) of the 11 individuals were classified as migrants on the basis of their elevated strontium isotopic ratios (indicating that they had grown up outside the region), while at the Schwetzingen cemetery 33% of 21 individuals were classified as migrants. At both cemeteries females were over-represented amongst the migrants, a finding that is consistent with genetic evidence for historically higher migration rates in females than in males (Seielstad et al., 1998).

Grupe et al. (1997) sampled tooth enamel and bone from 69 skeletons from Bell-Beaker cemeteries in southern Bavaria, Germany, and identified 17 immigrants (25% of the sample) on the basis of discrepancies between the strontium isotope ratios of enamel when compared to the isotopic ratios in bone from the same skeleton. As with the study of LBK cemeteries, a higher proportion of females than males exhibited residential mobility as evidenced by their isotopic ratios. In both studies these estimates of migration frequency are minimum values, as it is not possible to detect individuals who move between regions that have the same underlying geology.

1.3   SOURCES OF EVIDENCE

1.3.1   Theoretical models

As is the case in many areas of archaeological research, uniformitarian models play a very important role in palaeodemography. Certain life-history parameters such as age at reproductive maturation, age at menopause and longevity are subject to evolutionary constraints and are relatively invariant across human populations, and patterns of age-specific fertility and mortality tend to vary in predictable and easily modelled ways (Coale and Trussell, 1974; Coale and Demeny, 1983).

The application of the uniformitarian principle in palaeodemography is still controversial, as there are persistent claims that the human populations of the past differed systematically from present-day populations in their structure and dynamics. For instance, there is a durable belief that people in the past aged more rapidly, died at a young age and that few individuals survived beyond what would today be regarded as middle age. This belief has been sustained by a combination of systematic bias in skeletal-age estimation (which has generated mortality profiles with too few old-adult individuals) coupled with a tendency to confuse *average* age at death, or life expectancy, with *maximum* age at death, or longevity.

The theoretical basis for the study of palaeodemography is explained in detail in Chapter 2, while the use of uniformitarian models to inform Bayesian approaches to the reconstruction of mortality profiles is addressed in more detail in Chapter 4.

1.3.2   *Ethnographic and historical evidence*

Ethnographic studies have provided a very important body of historical demographic data for hunter-gatherer and subsistence-agriculture communities. Unfortunately, reliable data for hunter-gatherers is exceedingly sparse, particularly for periods that antedate full contact with modern western civilisations. Nevertheless, the available data for hunter-gatherers can be compared to 'model' life tables, which are theoretical population structures designed to represent a broad spectrum of real-life sedentary populations. Such comparisons show that the structures of mobile hunter-gatherer and pastoralist communities resemble those of more sedentary populations.

Historical sources for demography include systematic records of vital events (births, marriages and deaths), cross-sectional enumerations of living populations (censuses and taxation records) and an assortment of other records including commemorative inscriptions. In Europe there are few systematic records of vital events before the sixteenth century AD, but census data is sometimes available from much earlier periods (Wiseman, 1969; Ball, 1996). This evidence is discussed further in Chapter 3.

1.3.3   *Archaeological evidence: skeletal remains, settlements and site catchments*

Hollingsworth (1969) published a list of written and material sources for historical demography. Ranked nineteenth, and therefore least important, on this list were cemetery data, which he regarded as 'most unreliable sources for making any demographic estimate' (Hollingsworth, 1969: 43). This attitude has sometimes been endorsed by archaeologists, but skeletal remains, together with evidence of the size of settlements and calculations of carrying capacity, constitute essential sources of evidence for archaeological demography. Although skeletal remains are the primary source of data for palaeodemography, the demographic analysis of skeletal remains can be problematic, partly because of the potential for error in estimating age at death and sex, and partly because of the confounding effects of cultural and taphonomic factors that may introduce bias both when bones enter the archaeological record and during their subsequent detection and recovery.

Analyses of house size, settlement size and of the area, accessibility and productivity of land surrounding settlements ('site catchment analysis') can provide independent estimates of the size of local and regional populations (Hassan, 1978; Roper, 1979). Such estimates often depend on ethnographic parallels that allow population density to be inferred from the floor space of buildings and sustainable population size to be calculated from the availability and distribution of arable land and pasture. Where a cemetery is known to serve a particular settlement the average size of the population can also be estimated from the size, age structure and period of usage of the cemetery (Acsádi and Nemeskéri, 1970), which can serve as an independent check on population estimates derived from settlement size or site catchment analysis. The nature of archaeological evidence for past populations, and problems in its interpretation, are discussed in further detail in Chapter 4.

1.3.4   Genetic and evolutionary evidence

There is a wealth of information about the demographic history of the human species contained in the genome, and an understanding of human life histories can be gained from comparative analyses of other closely related species and from the fossil record of human evolution. Studies of the human genotype, including analyses of allele and haplotype frequencies, karyotypes and mitochondrial and genomic DNA sequences, provide a fertile source of information about past population history (Cavalli-Sforza et al., 1994). Modern human genetic diversity has arisen through the cumulative effects of the process of population expansion, subdivision, migration and extinction, and both recent and ancient demographic events have left a signature in the genetic record. Analysis of this diversity can be extended to past populations through the techniques of biomolecular archaeology which allows the extraction and characterisation of genetic material from ancient remains, and through biometric studies of the morphological variation in ancient skeletal remains.

A fundamental question in demography is whether the distinctive aspects of human-population structure and dynamics, such as increased generation length and longevity or survival, are the consequence of recent historical events or whether they reflect a deep evolutionary history. This question can be addressed through comparisons of human-population data with other animal species (especially non-human primates) and through the elucidation of life-history data obtained from fossil hominids. These questions are reviewed in Chapter 5.

1.3.5   Evidence from disease

Age-specific patterns of mortality are a direct reflection of the differential risk of fatal disease and injury throughout the life cycle. Palaeopathological and palaeoepidemiological studies are therefore central to gaining an understanding of the demography of past populations. Infectious disease is believed to have been a major determinant of mortality in the past, and with increased population density and the development of more sedentary and nucleated settlement following the transition to agriculture new opportunities emerged for the evolution and spread of new infectious diseases. The presence of disease in past populations can be identified from a range of evidence, including morphological changes in bones and teeth, textual and pictorial representations of disease and the biomolecular signature of disease organisms. Epidemic diseases that cause mass mortality can also be identified through the demographic structure of the mortality sample. However, as only a minority of individuals affected by disease will manifest skeletal changes, the application of biomolecular methods is a particularly important approach in the detection and diagnosis of disease in past populations. The nature of the interaction between disease and demography is explored further in Chapter 6.

Demographic concepts, theory and methods

2.1 POPULATION STRUCTURE

2.1.1 Age categories and age distributions

The age structure of a population refers to the distribution of numbers of individuals according to their instantaneous age at the time when the population is censused. Age structures can be recorded either for living populations or for a sample of deaths from a living population. It is important to note that the age-at-death structure of a mortality sample will generally differ from the age structure of the living population within which the deaths occur. In most populations the risk of death varies significantly with age and this results in proportionately greater numbers of deaths in the higher-risk age categories.

Although population and mortality profiles can be treated as continuous distributions of ages, the curves of survivorship and mortality contain multiple inflections and therefore they require the determination of several parameters in order to describe them as continuous mathematical functions (see Section 2.3 below). It is a long-standing demographic convention to aggregate age distributions into discrete age intervals, which in the case of humans are usually measured in units of months, years or multiples of years since birth. For example, in human historical demography age distributions are often determined by summating the number of individuals within five-year or ten-year age classes (Figure 2.1).

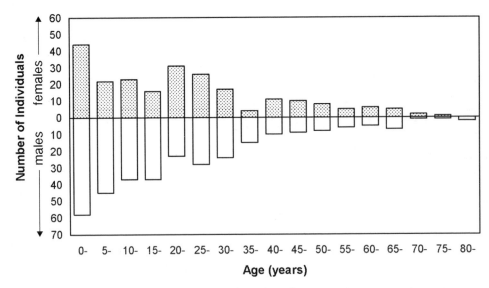

Figure 2.1 Age distribution in the Ache, a hunter-gatherer group in eastern Paraguay. Females are shown as shaded bars above the horizontal axis, males are below the horizontal axis. The data form a classic 'population pyramid' with large numbers of children, substantial numbers of young adults and reduced numbers of older adults. This pattern of survivorship is generated by the cumulative effects of attritional mortality as the members of the population progress through the successive stages of life. Data taken from Hill and Hurtado (1995: Figure 4.8), ages are in 5-year intervals.

In fact, five-year age categories may represent too fine a subdivision for some historical datasets in which inaccuracies in age recording are evident from the patterns of 'age heaping' (see Section 3.1.1. below). For archaeological samples precise estimates of chronological age are usually not available, and instead rather broad age categories may be adopted that reflect the imprecision with which ages at death are estimated from skeletal remains.

One of the simplest subdivisions by age, and one that is applicable to both human and non-human species, is to divide the lifespan into three intervals: juvenile (i.e. pre-adult), prime adult and old adult (Stiner, 1991). These age stages may be of unequal length when expressed in chronological years, but the boundaries between the intervals reflect important physiological and behavioural transitions in the life history of the individual. Juvenile organisms are physically and socially immature, and in some species including humans are highly dependent on adults for subsistence and protection: in most vertebrate species juveniles experience the highest levels of mortality of any age class. The boundary between the juvenile and the prime-adult stages may differ between the sexes, and as a general rule the onset of fecundity in females and of sexual maturity in males are the appropriate markers for the attainment of adulthood, as both of these life-history stages coincide approximately with the cessation of somatic growth. Prime adults are physically and reproductively mature, and usually experience the highest fertility and the lowest levels of mortality. The transition from prime adult to old adult is less well defined biologically, but is marked by a decline in (female) fecundity and an increase in levels of mortality in both sexes as individuals become increasingly vulnerable to senescence, disease and predation.

Stiner (1991) has used a three-age system for distinguishing patterns of animal mortality that are attributable to different predation strategies (Figure 2.2). In human demography a socioeconomic version of the three-age system is utilised in calculating a population's Dependency Ratio, which is defined as the sum of the numbers of persons under 15 years of age plus those over 65 years of age, expressed as a percentage of the number of persons aged between 15 and 65 years (Daugherty and Kammeyer, 1995: 85). In palaeodemography the transition between the human prime-adult and old-adult categories is sometimes placed at 45 or at 50 years of age, which corresponds to the upper limit of female fertility as well as being the approximate limit of conventional macroscopic methods for determining adult age at death (see Chapter 4).

There has been some discussion in the historical and anthropological literature concerning the ages at which individuals are considered to enter and leave socially defined life stages such as childhood and old age (Ariès, 1962; Shahar, 1993). To a certain extent, such age categories are based on physical maturation and the timing of biological senescence, which exhibit limited variation across populations and cultures (see Section 3.3 below).

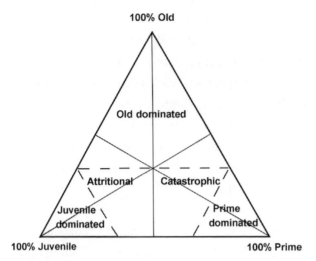

Figure 2.2 Triangular graph of mortality depicting the relative proportions of juvenile, prime-adult and old-adult individuals. The axes of the graph run from the middle of the sides of the triangle to the opposite apex. The expected proportions of the age categories for attritional and catastrophic mortality regimes are also indicated.

However the social status, rights and responsibilities associated with the achievement of any particular age horizon are culturally determined.

2.1.2   *Sex distributions*

In humans and nearly all other vertebrates there are two sexes, with the female defined as the sex that produces the larger gamete (Short and Balaban, 1994). The sex composition of a population is conveniently expressed by the sex ratio, which is calculated as the number of males divided by the number of females. The sex ratio generally varies with age as a consequence of sex differences in mortality (migration can also have a profound effect on sex ratios).

In modern human populations the sex ratio at birth usually averages close to 1.05, that is about 105 males are born for every 100 newborn females. One explanation for the slight numerical bias towards males at birth is that postnatal mortality in all age classes is usually higher in males than in females, so that the sex ratio at the age of first reproduction is closer to unity. However, higher sex ratios at birth are found in some human populations, particularly hunter-gatherers (Hewlett, 1991; Hill and Hurtado, 1995). It has been argued that this may occur because under certain conditions parental investment can make a greater contribution to the reproductive success of offspring when it is directed towards male children rather than female children (Sief, 1990: 27). The same factor may also take effect through sex-biased infanticide (Daly and Wilson, 1984).

In archaeological skeletal samples sex determination may be difficult or impossible to achieve, particularly in the pre-adult age classes, and sex distributions are often available only for adults. There are alternative methods for estimating sex that rely on sex-specific sequences of DNA (Brown, 1998). These can be applied to human skeletal remains from archaeological sites where there is exceptionally good preservation of the organic constituents of bones and teeth.

2.1.3   *Other structuring categories*

Age and sex are the principal variables which are used to characterise population structure, but other physical parameters such as spatial location and genotype, as well as social categories such as marital status, employment, religious affiliation, ethnic identity, socioeconomic and health status are sometimes important in the demographic analysis of modern human populations.

2.2   POPULATION GROWTH AND DEMOGRAPHIC TRANSITION

2.2.1   *Geometric and exponential growth*

The change through time in the number of individuals in a population depends on the balance between births, deaths and migration into and out of the population. Births and deaths are sometimes referred to as intrinsic or vital events, while migration is an extrinsic factor. Births, deaths and out-migration are usually density dependent: that is, the numbers born, dying and out-migrating are usually dependent on, and a positive function of, the size of the parent population. In-migration may depend partly on the size of the receiving population (for example, a large settlement might be expected to attract and accommodate more migrants than a small settlement), but will also depend on the size of the potential donor populations. The partial or complete density dependence of the intrinsic and extrinsic factors that determine the total number of individuals in a population gives rise to the property of geometric growth. Populations increase or decrease in size geometrically rather than arithmetically, because at a given rate of population growth or decline a fixed *proportion* of the total (rather than a fixed *number*) is added to or subtracted from the population in each time interval.

The rate of geometric increase r can be modelled as the proportion of the original population that is added in unit time: if P_0 is the initial size of the population at time $t = 0$, and P_t is its size at time t, then

$$rt = \frac{P_t - P_0}{P_0}$$

or by rearranging terms

$$P_t = P_0 (1 + rt)$$

When the population is decreasing, P_t is less than P_0 and r is negative. When population numbers are stable P_t is equal to P_0 and $r = 0$.

However, because populations grow continuously rather by a sudden increment at the end of a discrete time interval, the above formulas are better replaced by the formulas for instantaneous or exponential growth:

$$rt = \ln(P_t) - \ln(P_0) \quad \text{or} \quad P_t = P_0 \exp(rt)$$

[note that $\exp(rt)$ is the limit of $(1 + rt/j)^j$ as $j \to \infty$]

From the equations for exponential growth we can derive a useful quantity known as the population doubling time, which is achieved when

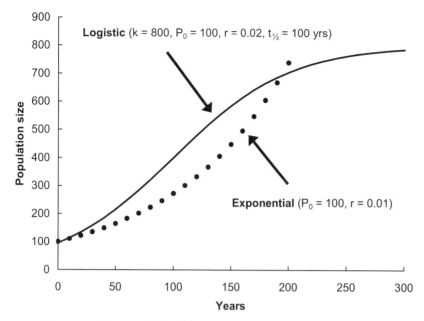

Figure 2.3 Exponential and logistic growth. The dotted line depicts a population growing exponentially at a rate of $r = 0.01$ per annum. The solid line depicts a population growing logistically with growth rate $r = 0.02$, carrying capacity $k = 800$, and with maximum growth rate occurring at $t = 100$ years.

$\exp(rt) = 2$, so that $t = \ln(2) \div r = 0.693 \div r$. Thus for a population growth rate of 1% per annum, $r = 0.01$ and the doubling time is 69.3 years. At higher rates of growth the doubling time is proportionately shorter: a population growing exponentially at a growth rate of 3% per annum will double in size in just 23 years, which is somewhat less than the average length of a human generation. Exponential growth is depicted in Figures 2.3 and 2.4.

2.2.2 *Logistic growth*

The formula for exponential growth implies that there is no limit to the ultimate size of the population, which therefore will increase inexorably and ever more rapidly with time. In practice, natural populations tend to

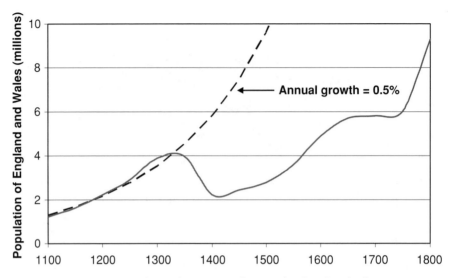

Figure 2.4 Estimated population growth in England and Wales between
AD 1100 and 1800 compared to an annual exponential growth rate of 0.5%.
The population decline in the fourteenth century is associated with the Black
Death and its aftermath.

be limited by competition for limited resources, and the rate of increase in
population size will level off as the population approaches the maximum
possible size, which is sometimes denoted the carrying capacity k. This
pattern of population increase can be modelled by the logistic growth
curve, which is described by the formula:

$$P_t = \frac{k}{1 + \exp(-rt)}$$

where t is measured from time of maximum growth rate

The logistic growth curve is S-shaped, with P close to 0 for very negative
values of t, $P = k \div 2$ for $t = 0$, and P approximating to k for large positive
values of t (Figure 2.3).

The logistic growth equation has been applied extensively in human
demography because it provides a reasonable model for the pattern of
population size increase that has occured historically during demographic
transitions, when populations move from conditions of high fertility and

Table 2.1 *Changes in population parameters during the demographic transition*

Stage	Death rate	Birth rate	Growth rate	Population age structure
Stage 1	High	High	Low	Low average age of living population, high proportion of children
Stage 2	Falling	High	High	Low average age of living population, highest proportion of children
Stage 3	Low	Falling	Falling	Increasing average age of living population, falling proportion of children
Stage 4	Low	Low	Low	High average age of living population, low proportion of children

high mortality to low fertility and low mortality (see Section 2.2.3 below). However, it is arguable whether any human populations (with the possible exception of hunting/foraging societies, and perhaps some groups confined to oceanic islands) are limited by an ecologically determined maximum population size.

2.2.3   *Demographic transition*

Demographic transition is the name given to a widespread and consistent pattern of change in birth and death rates, with its consequent impact on rate of population growth, that has occurred during the last few centuries in regional human populations undergoing economic development. The transition is manifest as a decline in mortality followed, usually after a delay of several generations, by a parallel decline in fertility (Notestein, 1945). The demographic transition is made up of a sequence of four stages, each with a characteristic mortality and fertility experience (Table 2.1). A typical outcome of a demographic transition is a doubling of the average duration of life and a halving of the number of children born to each female

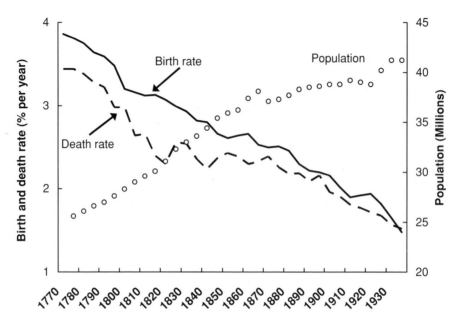

Figure 2.5 Population transition in France, eighteenth and nineteenth centuries. During the first half of the nineteenth century the crude death rate fell faster than the crude birth rate, generating a rapid increase in the size of the national population. Towards the end of the nineteenth century birth and death rates converged and the rate of population increase levelled off (data taken from Bourgeois-Pichat, 1965).

(Figure 2.5), and the pattern of population growth during the transition resembles the logistic growth curve (Figures 2.3 and 2.5).

There has been considerable discussion about the causes of demographic transition, which is often attributed to some aspect of social or economic modernisation. Populations exhibiting the transition have often had recent experience of industrialisation, urbanisation, technological advance and increased access to health care and education, any or all of which may serve to reduce both mortality and fertility. However, demographic transitions have also occurred in populations that are not undergoing socioeconomic development (Coale and Watkins, 1986; Kirk, 1996), and anthropologists have demonstrated that the initial conditions of high fertility/high mortality are not always characteristic of pre-industrial aboriginal populations (Binford and Chasko, 1976).

2.3   MORTALITY, SURVIVORSHIP AND LIFE TABLES

2.3.1   *Mortality*

The mortality or death rate is defined as the proportion of a population that dies within a specified interval of time. In most biological species the probability of dying is not constant with age: in humans and many other organisms the age-specific mortality is high in juveniles, falls to a minimum in late adolescence and early adulthood, and thereafter rises steadily with increasing age (Caughley, 1966). Mortality rates also vary with sex and socioeconomic status and with other population parameters. Therefore valid comparisons of the mortality experience of different populations may require that these parameters are controlled by means of standardisation (see Section 2.6 below).

The crude death rate (CDR) is obtained by dividing the number of deaths D by the product of the size of the population at risk P and the time period t during which the deaths occur.

$$CDR = \frac{D}{Pt}$$

This formula assumes that the population is of constant size during the period when deaths are recorded. The CDR can be decomposed into a vector of age-specific death rates provided that the age structure of the population is known. Then, for a given age category x, the age-specific death rate (ADR) is D_x (the number of deaths at age x), divided by the product of P_x (the size of the population of age x) and the time period t.

$$ADR = \frac{D_x}{P_x t}$$

2.3.2   *Survivorship*

Survivorship is a useful demographic concept that expresses the probability that an individual will survive to a specified age. Individuals have a maximum probability of 1.0 (or 100%) of being born, i.e. of achieving an age of zero, and a minimum probability of 0 of exceeding the greatest longevity recorded for the population. At intermediate ages the probability of survivorship is between 1.0 and 0, and by definition the survivorship function decreases monotonically with increasing age. An alternative way of thinking of survivorship is to consider a cohort, or group of individuals all born in the same year, and then to record, for each successive time interval, the proportion of this original cohort that is still alive at the end of the time interval.

Survivorship is a cumulative function in which the value of the function at a specified age is dependent on the values of survivorship at all preceding ages. Thus points on a survivorship curve are not independent data, a fact that has implications for the statistical comparison of survivorship patterns in different populations.

2.3.3   Stable populations

In a population that is closed to inward and outward migration the age and sex distribution is determined by the population's current and recent history of mortality and fertility. If age-specific birth and death rates are constant over a period of time the population will eventually converge on a stable age structure with population size increasing or decreasing at a constant rate (this property of a stable population was shown mathematically by Sharpe and Lotka (1911), and can be demonstrated empirically using Leslie matrices, see Table 2.3 and Section 2.4 below). In a stable population the numbers of individuals in each age category increase or decrease at the same rate as the whole population. It takes a few generations, typically 50–100 years, for the age distribution of a human population to achieve stable structure (Coale, 1957), and in practice any given closed population will show in its age structure the cumulative effects of up to a century of intrinsic demographic events.

Stable populations are idealised constructs because no real population maintains unchanging fertility and mortality schedules for long periods of time (and few real-life populations are truly closed to migration). However, pre-industrial human populations may approximate stable populations, as the rapid changes in fertility and mortality rates associated with demographic transitions appear to be a recent historical phenomenon.

A special case of stable structure is the stationary population, in which crude birth and death rates are equal and the population is therefore neither increasing or decreasing in size. Demographers sometimes use the concept of a quasi-stable population, in which fertility is approximately constant but mortality rates continue to fall, a situation which characterises some present-day populations. Quasi-stable populations approximate quite closely to the ideal of stable structure because fertility has a much greater impact on age distribution than does mortality. As a general rule, both increasing fertility and decreasing mortality tend to shift the age structure of a living population towards a higher proportion of juveniles, but the effect of changes in fertility on age structure is much more marked because fertility affects a single age cohort (the birth cohort) whereas mortality is distributed across the complete range of lifespans (Coale, 1957). This leads to a counter-intuitive property of populations, that an aggregate parameter of the age structure of a population, such as mean length of life (i.e. life expectancy at birth) is more influenced by fertility than it is by mortality (Sattenspiel and Harpending, 1983).

2.3.4   The life table

Introducing the life table

The life table, sometimes known as discrete time survival analysis, is a mathematical device for representing the mortality experience of a population and for exploring the effects on survivorship of age-specific probabilities of death. One reason why life tables have been ubiquitous in demography is that mortality cannot easily be modelled as a single equation or continuous function of age (see Section 2.3.5 below for continuous modelling of mortality with hazard functions). Instead, the cumulative effects of age-specific mortality on a succession of discrete age classes are determined under the assumption that age-specific mortality rates do not change during the lifetime of an individual. The calculation of a life table by hand is tedious, time consuming and prone to error, but the widespread availability of computer spreadsheets now makes the necessary calculations simple and straightforward.

The central concepts in life-table analysis are mortality and survivorship. A cohort of individuals of a given age will experience a predictable number of deaths during a finite interval of time, with the proportion dying depending on the length of the time interval and on the population's age-specific probability of death. The number of survivors at the end of the time interval will equal the original cohort minus the individuals who have died. Thus survivorship decreases at each successive age interval, from a maximum value at birth to zero at the age at which the last survivor dies. By convention, life tables are standardised so that the original cohort is equal to a large round number such as 100,000 but in the following examples survivorship is treated as a probability of survival to a given age, starting from a maximum value of 1.0 at birth.

There are two approaches to constructing a life table. A *cohort* life table requires observations over at least one maximum lifespan, and is based on records of the collective mortality experience of an entire group of individuals born at the same time. An *instantaneous* life table is constructed by determining the effects of fixed age-specific mortality rates on a hypothetical cohort of individuals, and it is this type of life table that is illustrated in the following example (see also Table 2.2).

Calculating the life table

The life table is based on a tabulation of the age-specific probability of death q_x for a series of discrete age categories x. The age categories can vary in the length of time that they represent, but for convenience the examples that follow use five-year age categories, beginning with the interval 0 to 4 years. The value of x refers to the age of the individual at the *start* of a particular five-year age interval, thus $x = 0$ refers to the age interval 0 to 4 years, $x = 5$ refers to 5 to 9 years and so on.

Table 2.2 *Life table for Northern Ache females. The table is calculated from survivorship data in Hill and Hurtado (1995). x = age at start of 5-year interval, Lx = average years per person lived within age interval, Tx = sum of average years lived within current and remaining age intervals, l_x = survivorship, d_x = proportion of deaths, q_x = probability of death, e_x = average years of life remaining (average life expectancy).*

x	l_x	d_x	q_x	L_x	T_x	e_x
0	1.00	0.27	0.27	4.34	37.35	37.35
5	0.73	0.09	0.12	3.45	33.01	44.97
10	0.64	0.04	0.05	3.13	29.57	45.91
15	0.61	0.02	0.03	2.99	26.43	43.40
20	0.59	0.03	0.06	2.86	23.44	39.86
25	0.56	0.01	0.02	2.75	20.58	37.09
30	0.54	0.04	0.07	2.62	17.84	32.78
35	0.50	0.01	0.01	2.50	15.22	30.19
40	0.50	0.03	0.07	2.40	12.71	25.58
45	0.46	0.04	0.10	2.21	10.31	22.27
50	0.42	0.02	0.05	2.04	8.11	19.35
55	0.40	0.05	0.13	1.86	6.07	15.24
60	0.35	0.07	0.19	1.57	4.20	12.11
65	0.28	0.03	0.11	1.32	2.60	9.41
70	0.25	0.11	0.45	0.97	1.31	5.27
75	0.14	0.14	1.00	0.35	0.35	2.50
80	0.00	0.00	–	0.00	0.00	0.00

The survivorship l_x for each age category is defined as the probability that an individual from the hypothetical birth cohort is still alive at the start of the age category (as all members of the birth cohort are alive at the beginning of the first age category, $l_0 = 1$). The value of l_x declines through the life table as survivorship is successively depleted by the proportion of deaths d_x occurring in each successive age interval, so that $l_{x+i} = l_x - d_x$ for an age interval of length i. The proportion of the total deaths that occur in each age interval is given by the equation

$$d_x = l_x q_x$$

Thus during the first age interval ($x = 0$), the proportion of total deaths (d_0) is $l_0 q_0$, and the proportion of the population surviving and entering the next age interval (l_{x+i}) is $l_0 - d_0$. The proportion of total deaths in the next age interval is given by $d_{x+i} = (l_{x+i}) (q_{x+i})$, and so on.

Additional calculations are used to calculate age-specific average life expectancy, that is the number of years of life remaining to the average individual on entering a particular age category. First is calculated the number of years that an average person will live within each age interval, designated L_x. This is found by averaging the proportion of individuals at the beginning and end of each interval, multiplied by the length of the interval in years (this assumes that individuals tend to die at a constant rate during the age interval, an assumption that may need to be modified for the initial age interval in the life table when probability of death is changing rapidly). The values of L_x are then summed cumulatively from the bottom of the column, to give the total person-years of life remaining to the cohort entering each age category T_x. This total is divided by the proportion of individuals entering the age interval to give the age-specific average life expectancy $e_x = T_x \div l_x$.

The average life expectancy at birth e_0 is an often quoted but somewhat misleading figure, as it takes a value that is typically in the range of ages when probability of death is a minimum. Probability of death in animal and human populations subject to attritional mortality is bimodally distributed with respect to age, and most individuals therefore die either when they are very young or when they are old, rather than in the middle years of life. However, life expectancy at birth is important as a single parameter that summarises the mortality experience of the entire population, and it is a useful measure when comparing different model life tables (see 'Model life tables' below).

Because d_x, l_x and q_x are directly related to each other a life table can be constructed starting either from a set of age-specific deaths (d_x), or a set of age-specific probabilities of death (q_x), or indeed the age-specific survivorship (l_x). However, in a population that is not stationary (i.e. in which the number of births exceeds the total number of deaths, or vice versa) the individuals of different ages will belong to birth cohorts of different sizes, and therefore both d_x and l_x must be known in order to calculate q_x. In most archaeological applications of life-table analysis the primary demographic data is in the form of age-specific deaths (d_x), and age-specific survivorship and probability of death can only be calculated indirectly by making additional assumptions about the stability or stationarity of the population. If the life table is constructed assuming zero population growth, but the birth rate actually exceeds the overall death rate (i.e. conditions of intrinsic population growth) then there will be an expansion of birth cohort size in the younger age categories and this will result in proportionately more subadult deaths. Paradoxically, the apparent effects of intrinsic population growth are a *decrease* in survivorship at all ages and *reduced* average life expectancy at birth.

Although non-stationarity has been raised as a substantial problem in palaeodemography (Wood et al., 1992b), it is easily dealt with under the assumption of stable population structure. It is straightforward to convert the d_x values for a stable population into the equivalent values for a stationary population if the growth rate r of the stable population is known or can be estimated over the duration of the lifespans included in the life table. In this case d_x for the stationary population is approximated by d_x $(1 + r)^x$.

Model life tables

A model life table summarises the mortality experience of a typical or ideal population. A model life table is constructed by averaging the age-specific mortality data for a series of historical populations with broadly similar mortality rates. Individual real-life populations may approximate to a model life table, but will show irregular deviations from the model as a result of stochastic variations in age-specific fertility and mortality. Model life tables are particularly useful when the investigator wishes to reconstruct the life table of a population for which reliable data is available only for some of the age categories. For example, using the appropriate model life table one can estimate infant and child mortality for a population in which only the adult deaths have been recorded.

The most widely used model life tables are those compiled by the Office of Population Research at Princeton University (Coale and Demeny, 1983). These regional tables are based on over 300 censused populations, although the sample is mainly from developed countries and with an emphasis on European populations. The tables are grouped into four regions, designated 'North', 'South', 'East' and 'West', to indicate the areas within Europe where different mortality patterns were typically found. The average mortality pattern, and the one which is most widely and frequently used in human palaeodemography, is given by the Coale and Demeny 'West' model life tables. The West model life tables are thought to give the most reliable results at the high levels of mortality that characterise present-day populations in some developing countries (Coale and Demeny, 1983: 25) and by extrapolation are appropriate for modelling historical and prehistoric populations.

The Coale and Demeny tables are organised according to differing levels of average female life expectancy at birth, with the lowest life expectancy set at 20 years (Level 1) and the highest at 80 years (Level 25). Each increment in level corresponds to an increase in average female life expectancy at birth of 2.5 years. Most of the differences between the mortality levels are accounted for by variation in infant and childhood mortality.

2.3.5   Hazard functions for modelling mortality and survivorship

Hazard functions express the instantaneous risk of death as a continuous function of time, and therefore provide the basis for modelling demographic structure as a continuous function, rather as a series of discrete values (Wood et al., 1992a). Hazard functions provide some advantages over life tables, particularly when exact ages at death are known, as they enable the maximum amount of information to be used in the analysis of deaths in a population.

The basis for calculating a hazard function is to consider length of life in a sample of individuals as a continuous random variable T, whose variation with age t can be described by the Survivor Function, or $S(t)$, defined as:

$$S(t) = p(T > t) \text{ the probability that an individual survives}$$
$$\text{to at least time} = t.$$

Note that $S(t)$ is the continuous time equivalent of the life-table quantity l_x (survivorship to age x).

The Probability Density Function of T, or $f(t)$, expresses the instantaneous rate of change of the Survivor Function:

$$f(t) = -\frac{d}{dt}S(t)$$

The negative sign ensures that $f(t)$ is positive even though S always declines with increasing t. Note that $f(t)$ is equivalent to the life-table quantity d_x (proportion of deaths in age-interval x).

The Hazard Function, $h(t)$, is then defined as the Probability Density Function of T conditional on survival to age t, and is thus the Probability Density Function divided by the Survivor Function:

$$h(t) = -\frac{1}{S(t)} \times \frac{d}{dt}S(t)$$

Note $h(t)$ is equivalent to the life-table quantity q_x (probability of death in age interval x).

As noted above, the risk of death is not constant with age and the usual pattern across the entire lifespan is for $h(t)$ to decline from a high level at birth to a minimum around the age of maturity, and then to increase steadily with advancing adult age. This pattern can be matched by a competing hazards model, in which the total age-specific hazard is the combined sum of three hazards: one hazard acting mainly on juveniles, one acting mainly on adults, and a constant hazard that is age

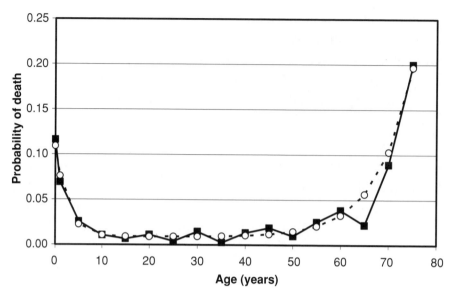

Figure 2.6   Age-specific mortality in female Ache hunter-gatherers (solid line, q_x data from Table 2.2) modelled with a five-parameter Siler model (dashed line). The parameters of the Siler model are: $a_1 = 0.1$, $b_1 = 0.4$, $a_2 = 0.009$, $a_3 = 0.000006$, $b_3 = 0.138$.

independent (Siler, 1979, 1983; Gage, 1990: see Gage, 1989 and Wood et al., 2002 for detailed discussions of competing hazards and other mortality models).

In the Siler model the hazard function is

$$h(t) = a_1 \exp(-b_1 t) + a_2 + a_3 \exp(b_3 t)$$

The parameters a_1 and b_1 describe the shape of the juvenile portion of the mortality curve when $h(t)$ is decreasing with age, with a_1 setting the initial (neonatal) mortality hazard and b_1 determining the rate of decrease. The parameter a_2 describes the constant hazard when mortality is at a minimum, while a_3 and b_3 describe the senescent portion of the curve when $h(t)$ is increasing with age. By adjusting the values of all five parameters the Siler model can be fitted reasonably well to historical and ethnographically documented mortality profiles (see Figure 2.6).

2.4   FERTILITY AND POPULATION PROJECTION

2.4.1   *Fertility*

In demographic terminology *fertility* refers to the number of children born to an individual, whereas *fecundity* refers to the physiological ability to bear children. As with mortality, natural patterns of fertility characterise human and animal populations. However, whereas mortality has the potential to affect all sectors of a population, births are confined to those individuals who are fecund. Furthermore, human fertility (to a much greater extent than mortality) is directly influenced by individual reproductive behaviour, so that parameters such as age at first marriage and deliberate birth spacing have strong effects on population fertility rates.

There are several ways of quantifying the fertility rate for a population The simplest is the crude birth rate, CBR = (number of births ÷ population size) per unit time, the calculation being analogous to that used to determine the crude death rate. In a stationary population,

$$CBR = CDR = 1 \div e_0,$$

where e_0 = average life expectancy at birth.

A quantity that partially controls for the age and sex structure of the population is the general fertility rate,

GFR = (number of births ÷ number of fecund women) per unit time.

It is usually assumed that women are fecund between the ages of 15 and 49. Population age structure is more comprehensively accounted for by calculating age-specific fertility rates, ASFRs, using the same age categories that are employed in the calculation of a life-table. Typically ASFRs are calculated for the seven five-year age categories beginning with 15–19 and ending with 45–49 years. Human ASFRs show a characteristic pattern of change with age, peaking in the decade 20–29 and declining rapidly after 40 years of age (Figure 2.7). The population age-specific fertilities for five-year age categories can be aggregated to give the total fertility rate, TFR

$$TFR \sum (ASFR \times i)$$

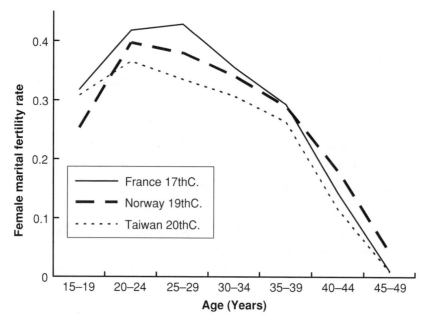

Figure 2.7 Examples of the general pattern of age-specific variation in human female fertility. The fertility rates (average number of births per year) are calculated for 5-year age-intervals. Data taken from Wood (1994: Table 2.1).

where i is the length of the age-interval in years. In population-projection calculations (see Section 2.4.2 below) the number of daughters born to mothers, rather than the total number of children of both sexes, provides a more accurate basis for predicting population trends: the term *reproductivity* designates the rate at which mothers produce of female offspring.

2.4.2 Population projection

Having established age-specific rates of mortality and fertility the dynamical behaviour of a closed population can be modelled through time in simple manner by using matrix arithmetic (Lewis, 1942; Leslie, 1945, 1948). For simplicity the analysis of population projection is confined to females distributed across equal-length age categories and assumes fixed age-specific rates of reproduction and mortality. The age distribution of the female

Table 2.3 *Leslie matrix for Northern Ache females. The matrix was calculated from mortality and fertility data in Hill and Hurtado (1995: Tables 6.1 and 8.1), aggregated into 5-year age intervals. Reproductivity values (first row of the matrix) were derived from female age-specific fertilities divided by 2.05 to account for a probable male-biased sex ratio at birth. Survival probabilities (sub-leading diagonal of the matrix) were calculated as $1 - qx$ from female life-table probabilities of death. The matrix models the Ache population with a growth rate of 2.5% per annum. Both axes are in 5-year age categories.*

x	0	5	10	15	20	25	30	35	40	45	50	55	60	65	70	75	80
0	–	–	0.02	0.37	0.67	0.73	0.78	0.68	0.53	0.17	–	–	–	–	–	–	–
5	0.73	–	–	–	–	–	–	–	–	–	–	–	–	–	–	–	–
10	–	0.88	–	–	–	–	–	–	–	–	–	–	–	–	–	–	–
15	–	–	0.95	–	–	–	–	–	–	–	–	–	–	–	–	–	–
20	–	–	–	0.97	–	–	–	–	–	–	–	–	–	–	–	–	–
25	–	–	–	–	0.94	–	–	–	–	–	–	–	–	–	–	–	–
30	–	–	–	–	–	0.98	–	–	–	–	–	–	–	–	–	–	–
35	–	–	–	–	–	–	0.93	–	–	–	–	–	–	–	–	–	–
40	–	–	–	–	–	–	–	0.99	–	–	–	–	–	–	–	–	–
45	–	–	–	–	–	–	–	–	0.93	–	–	–	–	–	–	–	–
50	–	–	–	–	–	–	–	–	–	0.90	–	–	–	–	–	–	–
55	–	–	–	–	–	–	–	–	–	–	0.95	–	–	–	–	–	–
60	–	–	–	–	–	–	–	–	–	–	–	0.87	–	–	–	–	–
65	–	–	–	–	–	–	–	–	–	–	–	–	0.81	–	–	–	–
70	–	–	–	–	–	–	–	–	–	–	–	–	–	0.89	–	–	–
75	–	–	–	–	–	–	–	–	–	–	–	–	–	–	0.55	–	–
80	–	–	–	–	–	–	–	–	–	–	–	–	–	–	–	0.00	–

population at time t is represented by a column vector $P(t)$ containing the numbers of individuals P_x in each age category x. The age-specific female reproductivity data (f_x) and survival probabilities (s_x) are contained in a square projection matrix M (sometimes known as a Leslie matrix, see Table 2.3) in which each row and column corresponds to a single age category. The first row of the projection matrix contains the age-specific reproductivities, or rates of production of female offspring f_x (these rates are set at zero for the age categories outside the reproductive years of 15 to 49). The sub-leading diagonal of the projection matrix contains the age-specific probabilities of survival ($s_x = 1 - q_x$), calculated from the life-table values of q_x, for each age category up to the penultimate category (individuals in the last age category do not contribute to the future population). Then the population at future time $t' = t + i$ (where i is the duration of a single age category) is given by the matrix multiplication $P(t') = M \cdot P(t)$. The operation can be repeated to give the projected population at time ($t + 2i$), ($t + 3i$) and so on.

2.5   MIGRATION AND COLONISATION

2.5.1   *Migration*

Migration refers to the process whereby individuals enter or leave a population other than through birth and death. As with fertility and mortality, migration is influenced by age and sex but in a less consistent fashion. The analysis of migration requires that the population has recognisable boundaries, usually defined for human populations in terms of the individual's place of permanent residence. Migration also implies the existence of two populations (donor and recipient) and as migrants' mortality and fertility characteristics may differ from those of both donor and recipient populations it is likely that migration will have an effect on population structure.

Migration is a special instance of spatial mobility, and it is distinct from the regular movements within a territory that are undertaken by nomadic peoples, itinerant workers and the like. The latter are more appropriately termed 'circulation' (Pressat, 1985). The rate of migration is also usually an inverse function of the distance migrated, and some demographers have developed gravity models in which migration is proportional to the size of the donor and recipient populations and inversely proportional to a

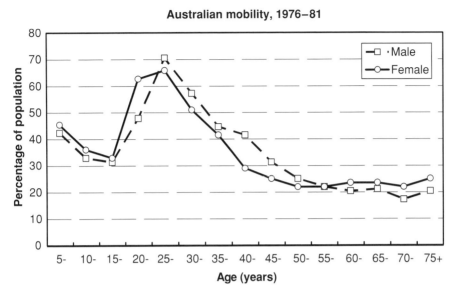

Figure 2.8 Age-specific migration rates in Australia (data from Jones, 1990), ages are in 5-year intervals.

function of intervening distance between donor and recipient populations (Lowe and Morydas, 1975; Plane and Rogerson, 1994).

Human migration is difficult to model and predict because it depends on individual decision making as well as the fluctuating demographic, economic and political circumstances in both donor and recipient populations. Stimulants to migration include increased employment opportunities, improved living conditions, and the desire to escape from objective hazards such as conflict and epidemic disease. Furthermore, unlike birth and death which are singular and irreversible events, an individual can participate in more than one migration event. Migration tends to be age structured, with people in their early twenties together with their dependent infant offspring exhibiting the highest mobility and hence the highest probabilities of migration (Figure 2.8). An additional effect, observed in some present-day urbanised populations, is that secondary peaks of migration can occur in the elderly, either at the time of retirement from full-time employment or when a marital partner dies (Rogers, 1988).

Crude migration rates are expressed as the ratio between the number of individuals migrating in a given period and the size of the population against which the migration rates are measured:

$$\text{Out-migration rate} = O \div P$$
$$\text{In-migration rate} = I \div P$$
$$\text{Net migration rate} = (O - I) \div P$$

where O = number of emigrants, I = number of immigrants and P = size of population donating or receiving the migrants. Note that strictly speaking these equations express only the out-migration rate in probabilistic terms, as the size of the donor population(s) from which the immigrants are derived is not specified. As migration is often strongly age structured the crude migration rates are usually replaced by age-specific migration rates where the data allow these to be calculated.

A more sophisticated approach to quantifying migration makes use of a two-dimensional migration matrix to characterise the unidirectional migration rates between all the pairs of populations that are involved in exchanging migrants. In the migration matrix the donor populations are represented as rows in the matrix and the receiving populations as columns, designated by the subscripts i and j respectively. Then the migration rate (proportion of population migrating during the census interval) from population i to population j is defined as $M_{ij} \div P_i$, and this value is entered in the appropriate cell at row i and column j in the migration matrix. The diagonal elements of the migration matrix contain the 'endemicities', i.e. the proportions of the donor populations that continue to reside in the same place for the duration of the census interval.

2.5.2   Colonisation

Colonisation is a special case of migration in which the recipient population is numerically zero, i.e. the migration is effectively into an unoccupied region. Mathematical models of colonisation typically take account of both the growth rate and the diffusion rate of the colonising population, and in some cases also the carrying capacity of the colonised region (Young and Bettinger, 1995; Steele et al., 1998) or of physiographic barriers to movement (Anderson and Gillam, 2000).

2.6 POPULATION STANDARDISATION AND COMPARISON

2.6.1 *Population standardisation*

Standardisation is a statistical technique that weights average values of vital rates to allow valid comparisons to be made among populations with different demographic structures. For example, in comparing the overall death rate in two populations we need to take account of age structure: a population which has a large proportion of very old or very young individuals will normally have a higher crude death rate than a population of predominately young adults. Standardisation is also an important technique in epidemiology, as the likelihood of contracting disease is often found to be correlated with age and sex.

Direct age standardisation uses the age structure of an arbitrarily chosen population as a weighting standard. An appropriate standard age structure might be the average age structure of all of the populations under study, alternatively the standard age structure can be selected from a family of model life tables. For each population to be compared the age-specific rates of the test population are multiplied by the number of individuals in each age category in the standard population, thereby allowing the calculation of an average rate for the test population that is weighted according to the standard population age structure:

$$\text{Directly Standardised Rate} = \sum \frac{R_{x,t} P_{x,s}}{P_s}$$

where $R_{x,t}$ is the age-specific rate in the test population, $P_{x,s}$ is the size of age cohort x in the standard population, and P_s is the total size of the standard population.

In some situations the crude overall rate but not the age-specific rates are known for the test population. In this case *indirect standardisation* can

Table 2.4 *Comparison of mortality in the Early Period (AD 300–550) and the Late Period (AD 550–700) at the Tlajinga 33 site at Teotihuacan, Mexico (data taken from Storey, 1985). D_x = number of deaths, d_x = percentage of total deaths.*

Age (years)	D_x Early	d_x Early	D_x Late	d_x Late
0	28	28.9	24	32.4
0.2	2	2.1	5	6.8
1	3	3.1	2	2.7
3	7	7.2	3	4.1
5	2	2.1	8	10.8
10	5	5.2	4	5.4
15	6	6.2	5	6.8
20	4	4.1	6	8.1
25	8	8.2	3	4.1
30	10	10.3	2	2.7
35	9	9.3	2	2.7
40	2	2.1	6	8.1
45	2	2.1	3	4.1
50+	9	9.3	1	1.4
Total	97	100.0	74	100.0

be used, provided that the age structure of the test population is known or can be estimated. Indirect standardisation applies a standard set of age-specific rates to the test population age structure to give an expected overall rate for the test population. The ratio of the actual to the expected overall rates in the test population is then multiplied by the overall rate for the standard population to give the standardised overall rate for the test population:

$$\text{Indirectly Standardised Rate} = \frac{R_s R_t}{\sum (R_{x,s} P_{x,t}) \div P_t}$$

where R_t = crude rate for the test population and R_s = crude rate for the standard population.

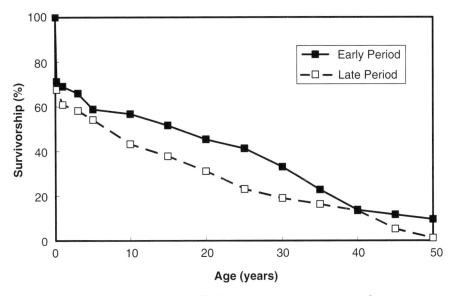

Figure 2.9 Survivorship at the Tlajinga 33 apartment compound at Teotihuacan, Mexico. The Early Period is represented by the solid line and the Late Period by the dashed line. The difference in survivorship between the chronological periods, when examined by the Wilcoxon-Mann-Whitney test, is of marginal statistical significance.

2.6.2 *Population comparison*

In some instances it may be desirable to demonstrate whether populations differ significantly in their age or sex distributions. Sex is a binomial vari-able, and therefore the difference in sex ratio between populations can be tested in a straightforward manner using the Chi-squared statistic. Age is recorded as a continuous or a discrete ordered variable, but age distri-butions are often multimodal and it is therefore preferable to use a non-parametric or distribution-free statistic for testing differences in age struc-ture between samples. A further consideration is that age categories may not be equal in length, especially adult age categories where the oldest recorded category may in fact be open ended.

Appropriate nonparametric tests for comparing age distributions are the Kolmogorov-Smirnov test, which tests the maximum divergence in the shapes of the cumulative frequency distributions of the two population samples, and the Wilcoxon-Mann-Whitney test, which determines whether the summed ranks of individual ages are significantly different between the samples (Zar, 1999). The Wilcoxon-Mann-Whitney test is the more powerful of these statistical tests and it is generally preferred for this reason. Both tests are available in computer statistical packages such as SPSS.

As an example of population comparison, Table 2.4 shows the age-specific mortality derived from chronologically distinct samples of skeletal remains excavated from the Tlajinga 33 locality, an apartment compound within the urban Mesoamerican site Teotihuacan, Mexico (Storey, 1985). Survivorship at all ages appears to be higher in the Early Period at Tlajinga 33 (Figure 2.9), but the difference in survivorship between the two periods is only of marginal statistical significance when subjected to the Kolmogorov-Smirnov test ($p = 0.093$) and the Wilcoxon-Mann-Whitney test ($p = 0.057$). Note the lower p-value associated with the greater power of the Wilcoxon-Mann-Whitney test.

Historical and ethnographic demography

3.1 DOCUMENTARY SOURCES OF DEMOGRAPHIC DATA

3.1.1 *Vital registration*

Vital registration refers to the collection of data on individual life-history events, such as births, marriages and deaths. In most countries in the present day some form of registration of vital events is mandatory. In England, for example, systematic ecclesiastical records of baptisms, marriages and burials began to be collected in every parish from 1538, and civil registration of births and deaths became a statutory civic requirement in 1837 (Hollingsworth, 1969). In Japan the Buddhist temples maintained registers of deaths from the sixteenth century onwards (Janetta and Preston, 1991). Less frequently, and only in a minority of present-day countries, a population register is maintained with individual records for each citizen which are revised following each vital event. These registers also record citizens' changes of permanent residence, and therefore such registers can provide comprehensive data on internal and external migration.

A common problem with data that are collected in vital registration is that of age heaping, with exact ages being rounded up or down usually to the nearest five or ten years. This may occur where individuals do not know their exact age, or when the age of a deceased individual is reported by a surviving relative or estimated by the person registering the death. Age heaping is often accompanied by an avoidance of ages ending in certain

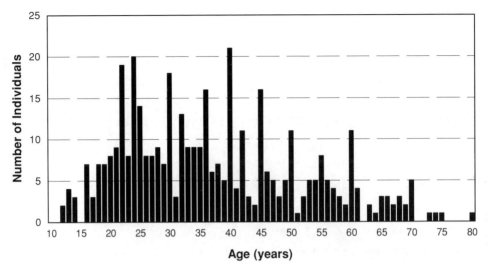

Figure 3.1 Age heaping and year avoidance in the burial registers from a nineteenth-century hospital. The small number of burials of juveniles reflects the hospital's policy of normally admitting only adults as patients. Note the large number of individuals whose age is recorded as 30, 40, 45, 50, 55 and 60 years and the deficits of individuals aged 31, 41 and 51 years. Data are taken from transcriptions of the Newcastle Infirmary burial registers for 1803–15 and 1822–45 (Nolan, 1998).

digits, such as the ages 31 years, 41 years and so on. Both age heaping and age avoidance are demonstrated clearly in data taken from the burial registers of a nineteenth-century hospital in England (Figure 3.1). Various objective measures of bias in age reporting are available (Newell, 1988), and the effects of reporting biases on the calculation of age distributions can be mitigated by substituting a three-year moving average in place of the reported number of individuals of a given age.

3.1.2   Censuses

A census is the systematic collection of demographic and (usually) socio-economic data for an entire population at a designated point in time. The earliest censuses for which records survive were conducted in Mesopotamia in the third millennium BC (Alterman, 1969; Ball, 1996), and were under-taken in order to establish the size of the taxable population. The censuses carried out in republican Rome from the sixth century BC were initially for assessing citizens' liabilities for military service, but were subsequently used to levy taxes and to assign voting rights (Wiseman, 1969). As a result of the political and fiscal motives that underpin many censuses there is an understandable tendency for the less economically visible categories of a population to be under-enumerated, while some individuals may actively evade enumeration as a tax-avoidance strategy or because of reli-gious or ethnic persecution. For sound logistical reasons censuses focus on interview and questionnaire data obtained from permanent households, and therefore vagrants and migrant workers may be omitted from census returns.

The first reliable modern censuses of national populations were con-ducted in Quebec in 1665 and in Iceland in 1703 (Hollingsworth, 1969; Tomasson, 1977) and from the end of the eighteenth century many western countries have conducted a regular national census, usually at intervals of ten years. Each census provides an instantaneous demographic profile of a living population, so the comparison of data from consecutive cen-suses separated by a fixed interval of time allows estimates to be made of demographic parameters such as the intercensal population growth rate and survivorship ratios (Preston, 1983; Gage et al., 1984).

3.1.3 Commemorative inscriptions

As a durable record of vital events, inscriptions on tombstones and other commemorative artefacts can provide a useful source of demographic data. However, there are considerable difficulties in using simple aggre-gations of data from tombstone inscriptions because of the selectivity involved in creating memorials. A typical finding is that children, and especially young infants, are heavily under-represented among tombstone inscriptions, while various biases can affect the age and sex distribution among commemorated adults. As Hopkins (1966: 262) aptly commented, 'tombstones are a function not only of the mortality of the commemorated, but also of the survival of the commemorator'.

Several studies (e.g. Henry, 1959; Hopkins, 1966) have found an excess of young-female adult deaths in the age range 15 to 45 years represented on tombstones, in comparison to official registers of actual deaths and when compared to model life-table predictions of age-specific mortality. Early authors attributed the apparent excess female mortality to the hazards of childbirth, but Hopkins has argued convincingly that in the case of Roman tombstone inscriptions dating to the first to third centuries AD, women were more likely to be commemorated if they predeceased their husbands, and with husbands being on average nine years older than their wives most of the commemorated women were necessarily relatively young when they died. Mortality distributions calculated under the assumption that deaths recorded on Roman tombstones are unbiased show anomalous peaks in the young-adult age categories for both males and females (Figure 3.2), reflecting the fact that older adults were less likely to have a surviving spouse and hence they had a lower probability of being commemorated. The bias is accentuated for females because of the sex difference in average age at marriage.

3.1.4   Other written sources

Wrigley (1966) and Hollingsworth (1969) have reviewed a wide range of documentary sources from which the researcher can extract demographic data of varying quality. Taxation returns are widely available in all parts of the world where tax-collecting governments have been empowered, confirming Benjamin Franklin's aphorism that 'in this world nothing can be certain, except death and taxes'. Certain categories of people were often exempt from taxation (most obviously children and paupers) but these can be allowed for in computing population numbers from taxation records. As with census data, tax collection often focused on households (e.g. hearth taxes) and a coefficient for numbers of people per residence must be introduced in order to estimate population size from the numbers of residences taxed. Archaeological and historical evidence for the dimensions of

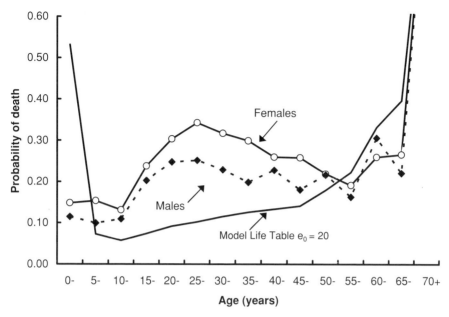

Figure 3.2 Age-specific probability of death calculated from Roman
tombstone inscriptions, compared to probability of death in the West Level 1
female model life table in which average life expectancy at birth (e_0) = 20
years. Note the effects of under-enumeration of young children (ages 0–4
years) and the over-representation of young and prime-aged adults (ages 15 to
45 years) in the tombstone inscriptions. Data taken from Hopkins (1966).

domestic buildings provide the basis for an independent estimator of
household size (see Section 4.5 below).

Genealogies – the recording of patterns of marriage and descent within
families – are important in many societies in determining the inheritance of status and wealth and in negotiating the privileges and obliga-
tions conferred by kinship. Historical records of genealogies tend to be
more complete for families with high social position, but some religious
groups such as the English Quakers have traditionally maintained accurate
and comprehensive genealogies for all of their members (the Quakers also
recorded births, rather than baptisms, providing more reliable data for the
estimation of perinatal mortality). Genealogical records tend to be more
complete for families that survive to the present day: records may be lost
when lineages become extinct with no surviving descendants, but in some

circumstances genealogies can be reconstructed from documentary records through the method of family reconstitution.

3.2   FAMILIES AND HOUSEHOLDS

3.2.1   *Family units*

Families are kinship units, minimally defined as a married couple and their dependent offspring (a conjugal unit). Extended families include more than one conjugal unit; if these are distributed across successive generations the unit is a stem family, and if there are multiple conjugal units per generation the unit is referred to as a joint family (Skinner, 1997). The members of a family typically participate in a single cooperative domestic economy, but the additional requirement of close kinship distinguishes family members from those that constitute a household (see Section 3.2.3 below).

3.2.2   *Family reconstitution*

Family reconstitution is a method of record linkage that assembles information on the vital events affecting a single individual or married couple, together with similar information on their parents and offspring, in such a way that the demographic history of a family can be reconstructed across multiple generations. Family reconstitution was formalised as a method in the 1950s by the French demographers Fleury and Henry, and the technique has been applied extensively by historical demographers working with parish registers and census data. The method is based around the family reconstitution form, a record on which information relating to a single marriage is collated (Table 3.1). Each family reconstitution form is allocated a unique identification number, and the preceding generations of a single family are cross-linked to it via the identification numbers of the forms relating to the marriages of the husband's and wife's parents.

The advantage of family reconstitution is that it facilitates longitudinal (cohort) studies of life histories, whereas only cross-sectional (period)

Table 3.1 *Data recorded on a family reconstitution form (FRF).*

Family Member	Name	Date of Baptism	Date of Marriage	Date of Burial	Place of Baptism	Place of Marriage	Place of Burial	Occupation at Marriage	Occupation at Burial	Linking FRF Number
Husband	✔	✔	✔	✔	✔	✔	✔	✔	✔	
Wife	✔	✔	✔	✔	✔	✔	✔	✔	✔	
Husband's Father	✔					✔		✔		✔
Husband's Mother	✔									✔
Wife's Father	✔					✔		✔		✔
Wife's Mother	✔									✔
Children	✔	✔	✔	✔						
:	:	:	:	:						
:	:	:	:	:						

studies are otherwise possible using vital registration data. In particular, reproductive parameters such as age-specific fertility and birth intervals can be readily calculated. However the records on which family reconstitution are based are often incomplete, most frequently because one or other of the marriage partners has migrated from an adjacent or distant location, and often the records for several contiguous areas must be consulted in order to complete a satisfactory number of forms.

3.2.3   *Household size*

A household is defined as one or more persons who make common provision for food, shelter and other living essentials (Pressat, 1985). Households figure prominently in historical demography because they often form the unit of assessment in censuses, taxation and other exercises in enumeration. Household size can vary substantially and depending on family structure (e.g. conjugal versus extended families), completed family size, age at marriage of offspring and other factors such as population density and subsistence practice a range of estimates of numbers of persons per household are possible. Estimates of household sizes based on ethnographic observations of agricultural communities tend to fall within the range three to seven individuals with a median value of five (Hassan, 1981: 73; Kolb, 1985), and similar values have emerged from historical studies of census data from rural communities (e.g. Drake, 1969; Laslett, 1969; Bagnall and Frier, 1994). Estimates of total fertility and completed family size are often much higher than this, but the conditions of relatively high infant mortality in pre-modern populations ensured that at any given time families and hence households were usually limited in size.

3.3   LONGEVITY, MENARCHE AND MENOPAUSE

3.3.1   *Perceptions and misperceptions of longevity*

Longevity is a general term that refers to the length of life, and there are several ways in which this attribute can be quantified. *Lifespan* designates the maximum age to which an individual may live, whereas *life expectancy* captures the central tendency of longevity in a population (Daugherty and Kammeyer, 1995: 137). Life expectancy and lifespan are therefore quite different, the first measuring the centre of a range of variation and the second the upper extreme of that range. Life expectancy is usually quantified as an arithmetical average, but as ages at death are often distributed bimodally in a population the modal (i.e. most frequent) length of life may differ substantially from the average life expectancy. As an illustrative example, for females in the United States in 1988 average life expectancy at birth was 75 years, modal age at death was 85 years and the verified longest-lived individual was aged 120 years (Olshansky et al., 1990: 635). Clearly the maximum observed length of life is likely to be influenced by sample size: as the United States population includes over 250 million individuals, the maximum age recorded in this population is likely to be an extreme outlier that is wholly unrepresentative of the norm.

A commonly expressed view is that in medieval and Renaissance Europe individuals aged more rapidly than in modern times, and that people were considered to be old in their fifth decade of life. By implication, lifespan would have been reduced prior to the modern era. Shahar (1993) has compiled an array of historical evidence that indicates that this is a mistaken perception, based partly on the confusion between the concepts of lifespan and average life expectancy and compounded by the uncritical reading of contemporary autobiographical texts. Shahar makes the forceful argument that in the Middle Ages, as it does in modern times, physical competence began to become limited, on average, in the seventh decade of life and this was the age at which medieval people were exempted from military service and other forms of obligatory work. A similar exemption from military service after the age of sixty was operative in Republican Rome (Harlow and Laurence, 2002: 118). There is thus no clear historical evidence that maximum lifespan was reduced in earlier historical times. Ethnographic studies of hunter-gatherer populations which experience moderate or high levels of mortality also confirm that some individuals in these populations survive into their seventies or eighties (see below, Section 3.5.1). Taken together, the historical and ethnographic data thoroughly refute the notion that ageing progressed more rapidly in past populations.

Despite Shahar's evidence, Crawford (1999: 114) has argued that the impact of low average life expectancy would have resulted in high rates of orphancy and a lack of grandparents in medieval England, and she quotes a figure of only 2.3% of medieval children as having a living grandparent, based on data collected by the Cambridge Group for the History of Population and Social Structure (Laslett, 1972: 148). However, this low estimate of grandparental survival seems to derive from a misunderstanding of the nature of the Cambridge Group's household data, in which children were only defined as 'grandchildren' if they were actually living in a household containing one or more grandparents. By ignoring the unknown (but potentially large) numbers of grandparents living outside the child's household, Crawford has inevitably underestimated the proportion of children whose grandparents were still alive. Simulation studies show that even in a population with relatively high rates of mortality, with average life expectancy at birth of 30 years, 84% of newborn children and 62% of 10-year-old children have at least one living grandparent (LeBras and Wachter, 1978: see also Saller, 1994, for evidence of high proportions of children with surviving grandparents in Roman families).

3.3.2   Menarche and menopause

Menarche and menopause designate respectively the commencement and cessation of menstruation in women, and to a first approximation they define the limits of the female reproductive span. Menarche is followed by a short period (one to two years) of adolescent sub-fecundity, reflecting a delay in the commencement of regular ovulation, and menopause is similarly preceded by several years of sub-fecundity (Pavelka and Fedigan, 1991; Wood, 1994).

The age at menarche varies amongst populations but is closely correlated with developmental maturity and nutritional quality. Median age at menarche is approximately 12.5 to 13.5 years in modern western populations, but median ages as high as 18 years have been recorded in some foraging communites (Eveleth and Tanner, 1990). Historical data for European countries show a secular decline in the average age at menarche during the last two centuries, with most of the decline occurring in the first half of the twentieth century, and it is believed that this may be attributable to improvements in nutritional status (Wood, 1994: 416–17).

Average age at menopause is close to fifty years in modern western populations, and is likely to be invariant as similar values have been established in ethnographic surveys of hunter-gatherer populations (Howell, 1979; Hill and Hurtado, 1995). Studies of historical datasets (e.g. Amundsen and Diers, 1970, 1973; Post, 1971) provide closely comparable estimates and confirm that there has been little change in the age of onset of menopause in human populations over the last two millennia. As female longevity generally exceeds menopause by at least a decade there has been some speculation about the function and role of post-menopausal survival in women, which is best explained by the reproductive benefits to daughters and other genetically related kin from the care-giving assistance provided by grandmothers (Hawkes et al., 1997; Blurton Jones et al., 2002).

3.4   HISTORICAL EVIDENCE OF MIGRATION AND COLONISATION

3.4.1   *Migration in pre-industrial Europe*

Sparse historical accounts, together with more extensive place-name and material cultural evidence suggest that substantial population movements took place in early medieval Europe following the collapse of the western Roman empire. It is difficult to quantify the numbers of people involved in these migrations, and there is controversy over the extent to which the cultural changes that marked this period were consequent on wholesale population replacement or whether they reflect elite transfer followed by cultural emulation (Burmeister, 2000: 548). Recent genetic studies of British and northwest European populations have helped to resolve these issues (see Section 5.3 below).

From the late medieval and early modern periods many historical documents are available that record the place of origin and/or residence of individuals, thus providing a quantitative basis for inferring patterns of migration. However, such sources record migration incidentally rather than by design, and the evidence may therefore need to be treated with circumspection (Whyte, 2000). For example, in parish registers the place of residence recorded for partners at the time of their marriage may post-date the movement of one or both of the partners into the parish, and thus the extent of migration at marriage may be underestimated.

In late medieval and early modern pre-industrial Europe migration mainly occurred over short distances, typically between contiguous parishes or between a rural hinterland and its urban centre (Tilly, 1978: 65). Migration at marriage has been studied intensively, mainly because of the wide availability of marriage registers, notwithstanding the fact that the migration of hired labour was also a significant component of population movement. In rural England during this period the incidence of endogamous marriages (both partners resident within the same parish) averaged between 30% and 70%, and in exogamous marriages the partners tended to move only short distances (Whyte, 2000).

Population turnover – the proportion of individuals still present in a community after a given time interval – also provides a basis for estimating out-migration rates, after accounting for losses through mortality. Turnover rates of around 4–6% per annum, of which 2–3% typically represents mortality with the balance attributable to migration, have been estimated for a sample of English rural parishes in the sixteenth century (Kitch, 1992). Somewhat higher in-migration rates of up to 10% per annum have been established for pre-industrial cities in seventeenth-century Europe (Moch, 1992: 44). From the mid-eighteenth century onwards Britain experienced burgeoning population growth, developing industrialisation, accelerating urbanisation and improved communications, all of which contributed to a substantial increase in the volume of migration – though the distances travelled were still short, with much of the migration being from rural areas to the nearest urban centre.

Colonisation events are often alluded to in accounts of ethnogenesis, but nonetheless they are poorly documented in the classical and medieval eras. The settlement of Iceland by Norse peoples in the ninth century AD constitutes one of the few such events for which statistics can be reconstructed. Perhaps twenty to thirty thousand settlers migrated to the previously uninhabited island from Scandinavia and the British Isles between AD 870 and AD 930, and continued migration and indigenous population growth resulted in Iceland having an estimated population of 60,000 by AD 965 (Tomasson, 1977). Genetic studies of present-day Icelanders have confirmed the predominant Norse and British source of Iceland's founding populations (Williams, 1993; Helgason et al., 2000).

3.4.2 Mass migration and colonisation in the modern era

The development of long-distance trade and global routes of communication at the beginning of the sixteenth century initiated a process of large-scale European migration and colonisation, together with forced migration of subjugated peoples, that continued for the next 400 years. During the sixteenth century about 250,000 people migrated from Spain to the New World, and perhaps twice that number left Britain for the American colonies during the seventeenth century (Canny, 1994). While substantial, these numbers are small compared to European transatlantic migration in the nineteenth century. For example, nearly three million people emigrated from Ireland in the decade following the great famine and epidemics of 1847, and by 1900 the rate of emigration from Europe was about one third of the rate of natural growth of the population of the continent.

The Atlantic slave trade of the eighteenth and nineteenth centuries resulted in the forced migration of many millions of people from West Africa to the colonies of the New World. The demand for slaves in the colonies was fuelled both by the expansion of plantation agriculture and by the fact that mortality amongst the captive slave populations was exceptionally high and usually exceeded their reproductivity (Sheridan, 1985; John, 1988), necessitating continual augmentation of the plantation workforce through importation of fresh slaves. The effect of the Atlantic slave trade on the indigenous West African population is not easy to determine, but a simulation study has indicated that the preferential selection of slaves in their prime reproductive years resulted in a marked reduction of fertility in the indigenous African populations (Manning and Griffiths, 1988).

3.5   HUNTER-GATHERER DEMOGRAPHY

3.5.1   *Population structure in hunter-gatherers*

Human life-history traits evolved hundreds of thousands of years ago when all members of our species pursued a foraging lifestyle, so it is logical to regard the world's few surviving hunter-gatherer communities as potentially rich sources of information about ancestral human demographic patterns and processes. Unfortunately ethnographers had only a fleeting opportunity to study such communities from a demographic perspective before irrevocable changes in health and subsistence practice were imposed on hunter-gatherers as a consequence of their contact with peoples from industrialised nations. Very few anthropological surveys of hunter-gatherers provide census and vital registration data of sufficient quality to allow reliable reconstruction of age and sex structure and patterns of mortality and fertility. Lack of written records, uncertainty concerning the chronological age of individuals and the dates when vital events occurred and sometimes the difficulty of obtaining information about deceased individuals have complicated the task of the anthropological demographer.

Data obtained from four hunter-gatherer communities (the Ache, the Agta, the Hadza and the !Kung) have been assembled here to provide a comparative baseline for the analysis of prehistoric populations (Table 3.2). The Ache were formerly a foraging population inhabiting the tropical forests

Table 3.2 *Population structure from census data for hunter-gatherer and subsistence-farming populations (numbers of males and females are combined). Sources of census data: Northern Ache: 1970 census, annual growth rate = +0.7% (Hill and Hurtado, 1995); Casiguran Agta: 1984 census, annual growth rate = −0.2% (Headland, 1989); Eastern Hadza: 1985 census, annual growth rate = +1.3% (Blurton Jones et al., 1992); Dobe !Kung: 1968 census, annual growth rate = +0.2% (Howell, 1979).*

Age (years)	Ache	Agta	Hadza	!Kung
0–4	102	75	112	70
5–9	67	64	84	58
10–14	60	72	79	38
15–19	53	67	67	54
20–24	54	59	61	38
25–29	54	63	48	49
30–34	41	49	47	56
35–39	19	34	39	39
40–44	21	24	32	46
45–49	19	28	27	28
50–54	16	26	27	27
55–59	11	15	21	22
60–64	11	17	24	20
65–69	12	11	20	10
70–74	3	4	12	9
75–79	2	1	6	5
80+	2	0	0	3
Total	547	609	706	572

of eastern Paraguay. An intensive ethnographic study of the Ache commenced some ten years after the hunter-gatherers' first sustained contact with sedentary Paraguayans, following which the hunter-gatherer bands were encouraged to leave the forest and were thereafter largely confined to reservation settlements. The census data used here are for the Northern Ache population in 1970, the last year when they were still subsisting as forest-dwelling hunter-gatherers (Hill and Hurtado, 1995). During the last decade of forest life the Ache population was growing in size at an average rate of about 1% per year.

The Agta were semi-nomadic hunter-gatherers living in the rainforests along the eastern coast of Luzon Island in the Philippines. Unlike the Ache they had maintained peaceful trading contact with neighbouring indigenous farming communities since prehistoric times. The Casiguran Agta were studied ethnographically from 1962 onwards by Thomas and Janet Headland, who conducted two censuses of the Agta population in 1977 and 1983–84 during a period when the Agta were becoming integrated into rural Filipino society (Headland, 1989; Early and Headland, 1998). The data used here are from the 1984 census, which showed that a slight decline in population size had occurred since 1977 corresponding to an annual growth rate of −0.2%.

The Hadza are foragers occupying savanna woodland in northern Tanzania. Despite multiple attempts during the twentieth century to encourage the Hadza to abandon their foraging lifestyle, in the 1980s a significant proportion of the Hadza were still either full-time hunter-gatherers or supporting themselves through a mixture of foraging and farming. The Eastern Hadza were partially censused in 1966–67 and in 1977, and were more comprehensively studied in 1985, and it is data from the 1985 census that are used here (Blurton Jones et al., 1992). From 1967 to 1985 the Hadza population growth rate was estimated to be 1.3% per year.

The final group of hunter-gatherers for which high-quality demographic data are available are the !Kung San, an indigenous people who occupy the Kalahari desert in southern Africa. A subpopulation of the !Kung, living in the Dobe area on the border between Botswana and Namibia, was surveyed by R. B. Lee and Nancy Howell from 1963 to 1973, and those members of the Dobe !Kung who were resident in the area in 1968 constitute the censused sample used here (Lee, 1979; Howell, 1979: 45). It should be noted that in order to estimate the chronological ages of individuals in the Dobe !Kung sample Howell initially placed the individuals in rank order of age, and then assigned each woman in the sample to a particular five-year age category according to the age distribution interpolated from the Coale and Demeny

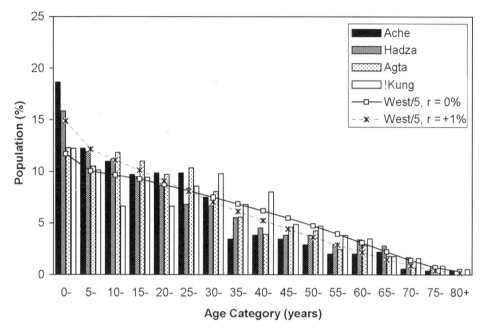

Figure 3.3 Age structures of four hunter-gatherer populations compared to
the age profiles in the Coale and Demeny (1983) 'West' Level 5 model stable
populations with growth rates of 0% and 1% per annum. Numbers of males
and females are pooled. Estimated annual growth rates at the time of census
were +0.7% (Ache), –0.2% (Agta), +1.3% (Hadza) and +0.2% (!Kung).
Sources of the hunter-gatherer data are given in Table 3.2.

'West' Level 5 female stable population models with a growth rate of 0.7%
per year. Males were then assigned to age categories via their age ranking
with respect to the females. As there are several alternative stable population
models that could have been used to assign the age-ranked sample to
discrete age categories there is inevitably some uncertainty about the true
age structure of the Dobe !Kung (Hill and Hurtado, 1995: 485). According
to Howell (1979: 214), population growth rate in the Dobe !Kung prior to
1950 appeared to be very low, about 0.26% per year.

   Figure 3.3 shows the pooled-sex age structures of these four hunter-
gatherer populations compared to the age profiles in the Coale and Demeny
'West' Level 5 model stable populations with growth rates of 0% and 1% per

annum. The Agta and the !Kung, both of which had estimated population growth rates close to zero, show a moderately good match to the stationary 'West' Level 5 model population (female $e_0 = 30$ years), particularly in the age categories 0–4 and 5–9 years for which the age estimation is likely to be most accurate. In contrast, the Ache and Hadza were expanding populations at the time of census, and in the subadult age categories these populations are closely approximated by the 'West' Level 5 model population with 1% per annum growth. All of the hunter-gatherer populations have a small proportion of individuals surviving to 70 years or above, confirming that maximum lifespan in these communities is similar to other populations with comparable levels of mortality.

3.5.2   *Mortality and fertility in hunter-gatherers*

Estimation of mortality in populations for which records are few or nonexistent is problematic because for each age and sex category two quantities must be estimated: the number of deaths and the size of the age cohort at risk of death. The same problems occur in the estimation of age-specific fertility, where the quantities of interest are number of births and number of fertile females of a particular age. The typically small size of ethnographically studied hunter-gatherer populations leads to relatively few observations within each age category, and as a consequence there can be a substantial random error component to estimates of age-specific mortality and fertility for these populations.

Age-specific mortality data are available for three of the censused hunter-gatherer populations, the Ache, Agta and !Kung, based on deaths that occurred during the period when they sustained a foraging lifestyle (Table 3.3; Figure 3.4). Age-specific mortality in these populations follows the expected pattern with high infant mortality, a minimum risk of death in the second decade of life and steadily rising mortality risk with increasing age during adulthood. As was found for the age structures of their living populations, the mortality profiles of these hunter-gatherers are closely

Table 3.3 *Age-specific risk of death in hunter-gatherer populations. Probabilities are expressed as average risk of death per annum within each age interval, with the sexes pooled. Sources of mortality data: Northern Ache: deaths during the foraging period prior to 1970 (Hill and Hurtado, 1995: 196–198); San Ildefonso Agta: deaths during the foraging period 1950–64 (Early and Headland, 1998: 102); Dobe !Kung: deaths during the foraging period prior to 1969 (Howell, 1979: 81).*

Age (years)	Ache	Agta	!Kung
0–1	0.115	0.369	0.202
1–4	0.032	0.032	0.044
5–9	0.020	0.010	0.015
10–19	0.010	0.006	0.008
20–29	0.010	0.010	0.009
30–39	0.011	0.034	0.023
40–49	0.015	0.029	–
50–59	0.026	0.053	–
60–69	0.033	0.051	–
70–79	0.100	0.100	–
80+	–	–	–

matched by the Coale and Demeny (1983) 'West' Level 5 model life table (Figure 3.4).

The pattern of age-specific fertility of hunter-gatherer women is distinctive in that the peak of fertility may occur in the late twenties or early thirties (Figure 3.5), rather than in the early twenties as is the case in many sedentary agriculturalist populations practising natural fertility (see Figure 3.8). Hunter-gatherer women also tend to reach sexual maturity at an older age, and the period of sub-fecundity following menarche may therefore extend into the early twenties in these women (Wood, 1994: 39). In the !Kung, age-specific fertility reaches a maximum in the early twenties, but fertility at higher ages is reduced as a consequence of extended

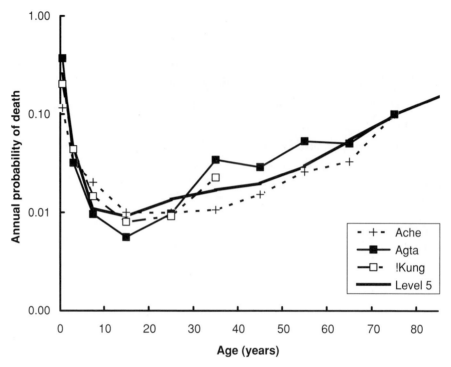

Figure 3.4 Age-specific probability of death in three hunter-gatherer populations, compared to the probability of death in a model life table (Coale and Demeny 'West' female model with Level 5 mortality, $e_0 = 30$ years). Probabilities of death for the hunter-gatherers are calculated from the average risk of death per annum within each age interval, with males and females combined (probability of death is plotted on a logarithmic scale). Sources of the hunter-gatherer data are given in Table 3.3.

inter-birth intervals following the birth of the first child and the !Kung have a low Total Fertility Rate compared to most other hunter-gatherer populations (Pennington and Harpending, 1988; Bentley et al., 1993).

3.6   DEMOGRAPHY OF AGRICULTURAL POPULATIONS

3.6.1   Population structure in agricultural populations

It is widely believed that sedentary populations are able to sustain higher fertility rates than mobile populations, and this would be expected to be

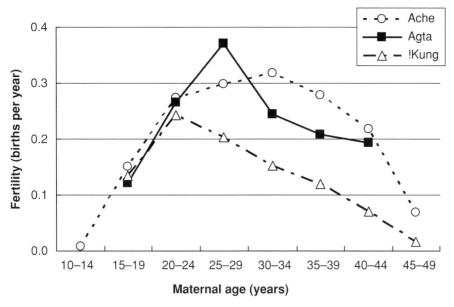

Figure 3.5 Age-specific fertility in hunter-gatherer women. Sources of the hunter-gatherer data are given in Table 3.2.

reflected in population structure, with proportionately larger cohorts of infants and juveniles due to rapid population growth. Some agricultural populations show the effects of high fertility, such as the Cocos Islanders who were censused in 1947 after nearly three decades of high intrinsic population growth (Smith, 1960). This population grew in size from 782 individuals in 1921 to 1802 individuals at the time of census in 1947, which equates to an exponential growth rate of 3.2% per year. The age structure of the Cocos Islanders corresponds closely to the West Level 5 stable population with an annual growth rate of 3% (Figure 3.6).

Such high growth rates are unusual, however, and more moderate growth rates are probably more typical of agricultural populations, as exemplified by a census of a rural community at Otmoor, England in 1851 which matches a West Level 5 stable population with a growth rate of 1% (Figure 3.6). This population had grown from about 2800 to 3800 between censuses conducted in 1801 and 1831, although the annual numbers of baptisms and

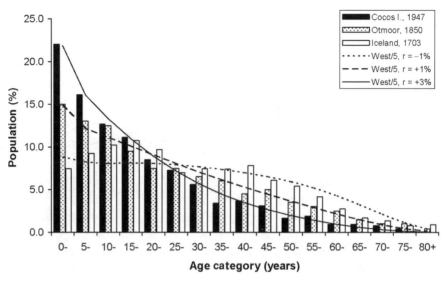

Figure 3.6 Age structure in agricultural populations with a wide range of growth rates, compared to age structures in model stable populations with annual growth rates of –1%, +1% and +3%. Male and female values are averaged. Sources of data: Cocos Islands: Smith, 1960; Otmoor: Harrison, 1995; Iceland: Tomasson, 1977.

burials had stabilised by the census date in 1851 after which time the population size declined, probably due to increasing rural–urban emigration (Harrison, 1995).

The census of Iceland in 1703 provides an example of the age structure of a population in long-term decline (Tomasson, 1977). The 1703 census shows the relatively flat age structure that characterises populations in which mortality exceeds fertility (Figure 3.6). Although the background level of attritional mortality in Iceland was relatively low, the island was vulnerable to a succession of natural catastrophes that ensured that average mortality remained high compared to other European countries (Tomasson, 1977: 417).

As these examples demonstrate, agricultural populations *can* show high intrinsic population growth but they do not *necessarily* do so. The continued expansion of a region's population must eventually be limited by

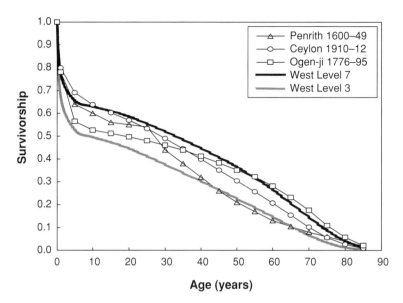

Figure 3.7 Survivorship in agricultural populations. Data are taken from the Ogen-ji temple death register, Japan, 1776–95 (Janetta and Preston, 1991); vital registration records for Ceylon, 1910–12 (Sarkar, 1951); and family reconstitution data for females in Penrith, England, 1600–49 (Scott and Duncan, 1998).

available resources, so it is likely that agricultural populations will vary in growth rate depending on how closely they approach their regional carrying capacity, with excess numbers being removed either by increased mortality or by increased out-migration.

3.6.2   *Mortality and fertility in agricultural populations*

Vital registration data for samples of other agricultural populations confirm the pattern seen in the census data. Survivorship curves calculated from mortality data for agricultural communities in England, Ceylon and Japan show relatively high levels of mortality that resemble West Level 3 to Level 7 model life tables (Figure 3.7). These levels and patterns of mortality do not differ substantively from those observed in hunter-gatherer populations, however the pattern of female marital fertility in agricultural

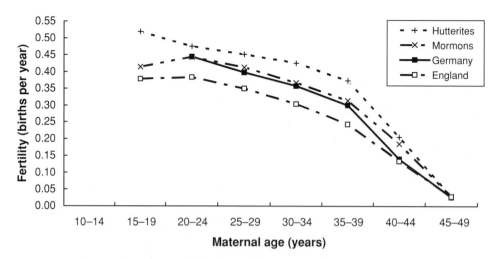

Figure 3.8 Age-specific fertility in women from agricultural populations. Hutterites: marriages pre-1921 (Wood, 1994, after Eaton and Mayer, 1953); Mormons: marital fertility in Utah 1840–69 (Mineau et al., 1979); German villages: marital fertility pre-1750 (Knodel, 1978); English rural parishes: marital fertility 1550–1849 (Wilson, 1984).

populations is distinctive (Figure 3.8). Compared to fertility in hunter-gatherers (Figure 3.5), the peak in natural fertility in agricultural communities tends to occur at younger maternal ages and the peak fertility rate is higher, typically 0.4–0.5 births per year compared to maximum values of around 0.3 births per year in hunter-gatherers.

The pattern of higher total fertility in agricultural groups has been confirmed in carefully constructed studies using ethnographic data from a wide range of populations (Bentley et al, 1993; Sellen and Mace, 1997). There are a diverse set of explanations for the higher average fertility in agriculturalists, including the direct effects of sedentism on maternal fertility (through reducing the need to carry dependent offspring between temporary campsites: Sussman, 1972), increased food availability and security of food supply under agricultural-subsistence regimes (Boserup, 1965), increased availability of suitable weaning foods (Lee, 1972), and earlier net contributions of children to household energy budgets (Kramer and Boone, 2002).

3.7   CONDITIONS OF HIGH MORTALITY

3.7.1   *Crisis mortality and natural disasters*

Model life tables, such as those published by Coale and Demeny (1983), are designed to provide stable age distributions for the full range of mortality and fertility patterns likely to be encountered amongst self-sustaining populations, but it is recognised that extraordinary causes of death such as warfare, famine, large-scale natural disasters and outbreaks of epidemic disease can cause deviations from stable structure. Crisis mortality is believed to be responsible, in part, for the observation that long-term population growth rates tend to be much lower than short-term growth rates, with the average rate of growth being curtailed by the occurrence of episodic events of high mortality in a so-called 'boom and bust' pattern (see Watkins and Menken, 1985, for discussion of this theory).

Episodes of high mortality can be catastrophic, with all age categories experiencing the same elevated risk of mortality, or they can be essentially attritional, with proportionately elevated mortality across all age categories but with the highest death rates occurring in the youngest age and oldest age categories. Short periods of famine, episodes of adverse climate, imposition of harsh working conditions and exposure to new disease environments all tend to produce an elevated attritional pattern of mortality. For example, the deaths experienced by emigrants in the Donner Party of 1846 and the Willie Company of 1856 were attritional in nature, although the overall crude death rates in these natural disasters were very high at 45% and 16% respectively (Grayson, 1990, 1996). Extreme attritional mortality rates have also been reported for plantation slaves in nineteenth-century Caribbean colonies (Roberts, 1952; John, 1988) and amongst American emigrants to West Africa (McDaniel, 1992).

The demographic effects of large-scale natural disasters, including earthquakes, volcanic eruptions, floods and extreme storms, have been reviewed by Seaman et al. (1984). Deaths in earthquakes are caused mainly by the collapse of buildings, although rockfalls and landslips in steep terrain and tsunami ('tidal waves') in coastal locations may also contribute to mortality.

There is some evidence for variation in age- and sex-specific risk of death in earthquakes, with a consistent pattern of young adults and very young infants having lower mortality rates than children and the elderly, and men having lower mortality than women (Seaman et al., 1984; Armenian et al., 1997; Chan et al., 2003). This has been attributed to the protection afforded to young infants by their mothers, and to the greater agility/mobility of young adults (especially men) which enhance their likelihood of escaping from buildings on detection of the first tremors in an earthquake. The AD 79 explosive eruption of Vesuvius that buried the Roman city of Pompeii in pyroclastic volcanic sediments killed an estimated 1600 victims, based on the human remains recovered from the excavated portions of the city (Luongo et al., 2003). The proportion of women and children amongst the victims at Pompeii was substantially higher than the proportion of adult men, perhaps indicating that the men had a greater probability of escaping alive from the city.

In the case of catastrophic flooding there is frequently little advance warning of impending disaster and victims may have limited ability to mitigate their individual risk. The age pattern of mortality in such events tends toward a catastrophic age profile (i.e. risk of death being independent of age), though there is evidence for some additional risk amongst children and the elderly and, as with earthquakes, young adults tend to exhibit the lowest risk of death (Figure 3.9).

3.7.2   Famine

Famine can be defined as extreme hunger, starvation and malnutrition affecting a substantial proportion of a population and resulting in a demographic crisis characterised by excess mortality, reduced fertility and inter-regional migration (Scrimshaw, 1987; Maharatna, 1996). Although famines are known to have great social impact, historical demographic data even for famines of the recent past are of variable quality, as the social breakdown that accompanies famine is inimical to the maintenance of accurate records, and estimates of mortality may be confounded with population

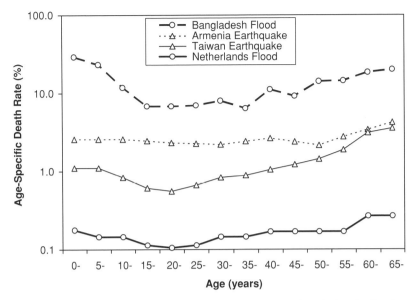

Figure 3.9 Age-specific mortality in catastrophic floods (Netherlands 1953, Bangladesh 1970) and in earthquakes (Armenia 1988, Taiwan, 1999). Data are taken from Seaman et al., 1984; Armenian et al., 1997, and Chan et al., 2003. Although the mortality rates differ by up to a factor of 100, all of these natural disasters show a partially catastrophic mortality profile, with reduced variation in age-specific mortality rates compared to standard models of attritional mortality. Note that the age-specific death rates are plotted on a logarithmic scale.

losses due to migration (Watkins and Menken, 1985; De Waal, 1989). The excess deaths that occur during famines are usually not attributed directly to malnutrition and starvation, but are instead mainly due to increased susceptibility to infectious diseases such as measles, malaria and diarrhoeal conditions (de Waal, 1989; Moore et al., 1993).

Maharatna (1996) undertook a detailed analysis of patterns of mortality in four large-scale famines that affected extensive areas of the Indian subcontinent during the last quarter of the nineteenth century. Figure 3.10 shows the age-specific pattern of mortality during the famines that occurred in Berar province of central India during 1896–97 and 1889–1900, compared to the pre-famine baseline years of 1891–95 (Maharatna, 1996).

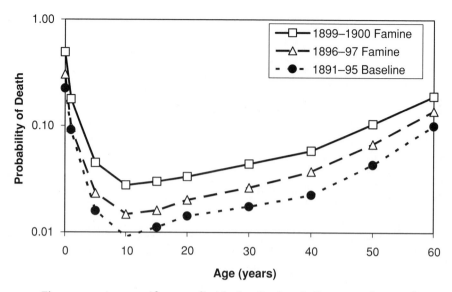

Figure 3.10 Age-specific mortality during famines in Berar province, India compared to a pre-famine baseline (data from Maharatna, 1996: Table 2.8). Note that the age-specific death rates are plotted on a logarithmic scale.

The data indicate that overall mortality rates increased above baseline rates by about 50% in 1897 and 150% in 1900, and that there was a proportionate increase in mortality across all of the age classes with the exception of infants and young children, in which smaller increases were observed. Relatively small increases in infant mortality were also observed in other regions of India during the late nineteenth-century famines. These findings may indicate that infants and young children were given preferential access to food during the Indian famines, or that these age categories were less susceptible to the disease outbreaks that caused many of the famine-related deaths or that infant disease rates were already high prior to the onset of famine. Crude birth and death rates for Berar province during the two decades from 1891 to 1911 are shown in Figure 3.11. The impacts of the 1896–97 and 1899–1900 famines are seen most clearly in the sharp peaks in crude death rate, but are also evident in declines in the birth rate one year after each famine, with a compensating increase in birth rate above baseline levels two years after the end of the famine.

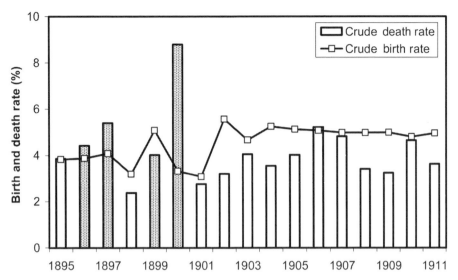

Figure 3.11 Crude birth and death rates in Berar province, India from 1895 to
1911 (data from Maharatna, 1996: Table 2.2). Shading indicates death rates in
famine years.

The demographic impact of a famine in Darfur, western Sudan, in 1984–
85 has been reported by De Waal (1989). As in the Indian famines studied by
Maharatna, increases in age-specific mortality during the famine in Darfur
occurred across all age categories except for infants, in which mortality did
not rise significantly above the pre-famine baseline rate. Fertility declined
significantly in the year following the famine in Darfur, and reduced birth
rates were also recorded during the severe 1984–85 famine in Ethiopia
(Kidane, 1989).

Fertility decline followed by a compensating fertility rebound appears to
be a regular feature of famines, and may be attributable to a combination of
biological and social causes (Watkins and Menken, 1985: 656–57). Recovery
of fertility, together with the removal of frail individuals from the population, can result in population numbers returning to pre-famine levels
within a few years. Watkins and Menken (1985) have simulated the effects
of an extremely severe famine of two years' duration, in which mortality
increased by 110% and fertility declined by 33%. The simulation showed

that with an average annual growth rate of 0.5% the famine-affected population returned to its original pre-famine size within 12 years, even though the simulation did not include post-famine fertility rebound. Watkins and Menken argue that although the social impacts of famines may be severe, they have relatively small long-term demographic effects because of the ability of human populations to recover from mortality crises by intrinsic growth.

3.7.3   *Epidemic disease*

An epidemic is defined as a mass outbreak of disease, typically confined to a geographical locality and constrained in time (Pressat, 1985). Epidemics are contrasted with endemic disease (disease that is present with constant frequency in a population) and with pandemics, which are epidemics that lack geographical confinement and thus spread throughout an entire population. An epidemic of infectious disease can arise through several mechanisms including changes in the infectivity and susceptibility of hosts, increases in virulence and transmissibility of infective organisms, and interactions between the life cycles of infective organisms and host population size. Disease outbreaks can also vary in their demographic impact: an infective agent may cause low mortality in a population whose individuals have been exposed to the disease organism and have therefore built up immunity, whereas the same infection may result in high mortality in a so-called 'virgin soil' population which lacks prior immunity (Crosby, 1976). Disease organisms may also become resistant to therapeutic treatments through the mechanism known as drug resistance (Anderson and May, 1991).

The pattern of age-specific mortality in an epidemic may be attritional, catastrophic or a mixture of both. In the pandemic of influenza A virus, which spread across the world in 1918–19, the age-specific mortality rates in Britain followed an approximately attritional pattern up to age 30 years, but in adults older than 30 years the age-specific mortality was reduced, perhaps because older cohorts of the population had been exposed to earlier

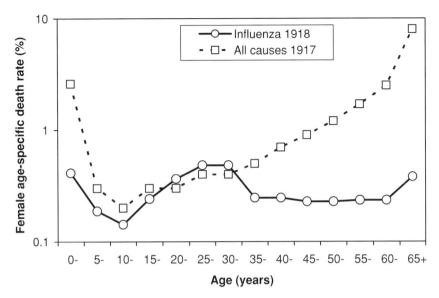

Figure 3.12 Age-specific death rates from influenza in females in 1918, and from all causes of death in 1917. Data are for females in England and Wales (Langford, 2002).

outbreaks of the same virus and these older individuals may therefore have acquired some immunity to the influenza virus (Langford, 2002). Overall, the mortality pattern in this outbreak of influenza was quite distinct from the attritional mortality from all causes of death in the year preceding the outbreak (Figure 3.12).

Catastrophic mortality occurs in outbreaks of bubonic plague (*Yersinia pestis*), an endemic infection of rodents that is transmitted by fleas and occasionally causes epidemics in human populations. Bubonic plague is thought to be the agent responsible for the Black Death which swept across Asia and Europe in the fourteenth century (Ziegler, 1991), although alternative causative agents have also been proposed for this pandemic (Twigg, 1984; Wood and DeWitte-Aviña, 2003). Prior to the modern era there were no effective antibiotic treatments for bubonic plague and outbreaks resulted in very high rates of mortality (Benedictow, 1987). There is little reliable historical data on mortality in the Black Death pandemic, but

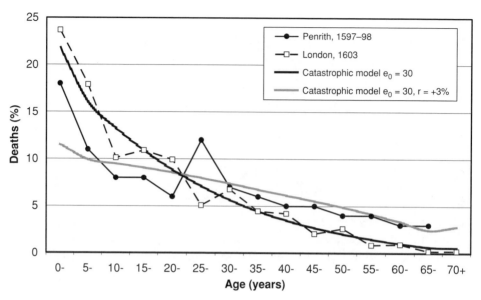

Figure 3.13 Distribution of deaths from plague in Penrith, 1597–98 (Scott and Duncan, 1998) and London, 1603 (Hollingsworth and Hollingsworth, 1971), compared to the age structures of living populations (West Level 5, e_0=30) with growth rates of 0% and 3% per annum.

anthropological analyses of skeletal remains obtained from mass graves of victims of the Black Death in Europe show the characteristic catastrophic mortality profile (Signoli et al., 2002; Margerison and Knüsel, 2002; Gowland and Chamberlain, 2005). Detailed records are available for episodes of plague in Europe in the sixteenth and seventeenth centuries (Hollingsworth and Hollingsworth, 1971; Ell, 1989; Scott et al., 1996). The mortality profiles of deaths in plague outbreaks in Penrith, 1597–98 and in London, 1603 are shown in Figure 3.13. Both plague episodes produced catastrophic mortality profiles that follow the living-population age structures represented by the Coale and Demeny West Level 5 models. The London-plague mortality shows higher proportions of children and lower proportions of adults, and corresponds to a Level 5 population with annual growth of 3%, which is the estimated growth rate for London during this time.

3.7.4   *Conflict mortality*

Armed conflict unsurprisingly leads to an increase in mortality amongst both military and civilian populations. Hostile actions amongst combatants typically cause a minority of deaths in recorded episodes of warfare, and most deaths are instead attributable to hostility directed by combatants against civilians and to the disruptions that inevitably occur to food supplies, health care and hygiene amongst civilian populations. Data on civilian deaths in conflicts are often uncertain, even for military actions conducted during the last 100 years, but in modern (post-World War II) warfare civilian deaths can amount to 90% of total conflict-related mortality (Spiegel and Salama, 2000; Roberts et al., 2004). For example, in the Vietnam War from 1964 to 1973 over one million Vietnamese civilians died, but less than 50,000 US military deaths were attributable to hostile action. In the recent conflict in Iraq, unofficial estimates of Iraqi civilian deaths due to military action range from many thousands (Iraq Body Count, 2004) to over 100,000 (Roberts et al., 2004).

From ethnographic data on non-literate societies a mixed picture emerges, with an estimated one quarter of surveyed societies targeting non-combatants in warfare (Otterbein, 2000 – but see Keeley, 1996, for higher estimates). The extent to which prehistoric warfare resulted in deaths of non-combatants is largely unknown, but in a recent analysis, samples of human skeletal remains from eleven prehistoric mass burial sites were studied to determine if they exhibited the demographic characteristics of combatant warfare (Bishop and Knüsel, 2005). These sites all showed skeletal evidence of fatal trauma inflicted at the time of death. The demographic measures included the ratio of subadult to adult mortality and the adult sex ratio. None of the mass-mortality sites fitted the demographic structure expected of combatant mortality, instead these assemblages were found to contain substantial proportions of children, adolescents and adult females. The authors of the study concluded that the burials represented either massacres of non-combatants, or a mixture of combatant and non-combatant deaths, suggesting that the targeting of non-combatants may have formed a common element of prehistoric warfare strategies.

Civilian deaths are numerically high during conflict for several reasons. Firstly, much use of force during conflicts is indiscriminate in nature rather than targeted specifically against combatants. Put crudely, combatants tend to be far fewer in number than civilians and, when encountered, combatants are harder to kill: on average they are physically stronger and they are better trained in defensive tactics than are their equivalents in the civilian population. Thus indiscriminate application of force inevitably results in high civilian mortality, even if civilians are not specifically targeted. Secondly, during conflicts armed combatants are often able to secure vital resources such as food, shelter, and health care, to a much greater extent than are civilians within the conflict area who are therefore more exposed to the effects of disease and malnutrition. During the 1998–99 conflict in Kosovo crude rates of civilian mortality amongst Kosovar Albanians increased by a factor of 2.3 above a pre-conflict baseline, with war-related trauma being responsible for two thirds of the civilian deaths (Spiegel and Salama, 2000). Much greater increases in civilian mortality are seen during conflicts in less developed countries, where elevated mortality from famine and disease are the principal causes of death (Guha-Sapir and van Panhuis, 2003).

Distinguishing between civilian and military deaths in modern conflicts is problematic, and official military records may either ignore civilian deaths (Herold, 2002) or they may deliberately disguise massacres of civilians by recording these events as engagements with opposing armed forces (Rainio et al., 2001). However, combatant and non-combatant groups are demographically highly distinguishable. The age structures of military organisations are typically dominated by young adult males with a modal age at death in the early twenties, whereas civilian groups have age structures that reflect the distribution of ages in the living population, and these very different age structures result in quite distinct mortality patterns. Figure 3.14 shows the age structure of recent conflict-related violent deaths in samples of adult (>15 years old) male civilians from Palestine and from Bosnia in the former Yugoslavia. The Palestinian sample consists

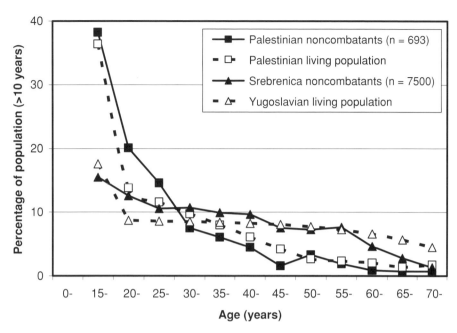

Figure 3.14 Age distribution of civilian deaths in Srebrenica, 1995 (Brunborg et al., 2003) and Palestine, 2000–02 (Radlauer, 2002) compared to the age structures of the populations living in the conflict areas.

of 693 non-combatants who died in 2000–02 during the Al-Aqsa uprising (Radlauer, 2002). The sample of non-combatants from Srebrenica in Eastern Bosnia includes 7,570 male Bosnian Muslim civilians judged to have been massacred by Bosnian Serbs in July 1975, based on well-corroborated informant records compiled by the International Committee of the Red Cross and the humanitarian organisation Physicians for Human Rights (Brunborg et al., 2003; see also Komar, 2003). Both the Palestine and the Srebrenica samples show age distributions that approximate those of their source (i.e. living) populations, with the exception that the age category 20–30 years is slightly over-represented in both samples of deaths indicating greater exposure of younger adults to conflict-related death. These age distributions contrast strongly with the age distribution of military personnel and combat deaths in modern and historical conflicts, in which

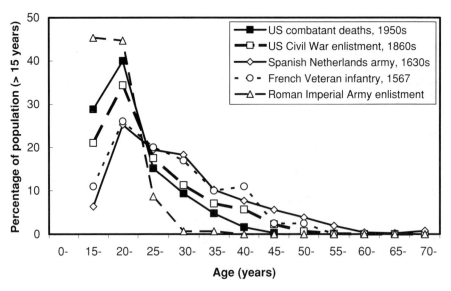

Figure 3.15 Age distribution of combatant deaths in a modern conflict, and distribution of ages at enlistment and at muster in military organisations from various periods. Sources of data are McKern and Stewart, 1957 (US combatants, Korean War), www.shepherd.edu/gtmcweb (US Civil War enlistment), Parker, 1972 (Spanish Netherlands army in 1630–34), Wood, 1996 (Brissac Company Veteran Infantry in 1567), and Scheidel, 1996 (Roman Imperial Army enlistment).

a marked peak is observed in the age category 20–24 years, with very few deaths of individuals aged above 45 years (Figure 3.15). Thus the age distributions of samples of conflict deaths can provide an indication of whether the deaths are likely to be those of combatants or of non-combatants.

Archaeological demography

4.1 PAST POPULATION STRUCTURE

4.1.1 Background to the palaeodemography debate

Prior to the 1930s most studies of human palaeodemography relied on historical records such as commemorative inscriptions and censuses as sources of mortality and survivorship data. Following pioneering work by T. W. Todd (1920, 1924) on the timing of age-related changes in the adult human skeleton there emerged new opportunities to utilise anthropological data in palaeodemography (Acsádi and Nemeskéri, 1970: 51–57). Early applications of skeletal evidence for estimating age at death in palaeodemography include the demographic analysis of skeletons from Pecos Pueblo (Hooton, 1930) and a study by Vallois (1937) of longevity in European Palaeolithic and Mesolithic populations. During the second half of the twentieth century there was a proliferation of publications on the age structure of skeletal samples, and palaeodemographic studies became almost a routine aspect of the laboratory analysis of large series of large assemblages of excavated skeletons.

In this early phase of palaeodemography methodological concerns focused on ensuring that skeletal samples were representative of the deaths that had occurred in the population, and that procedures for estimating sex and age at death were accurate (Angel, 1969; Acsádi and Nemeskéri, 1970: 57–58). The problem of under-representation of infants in skeletal samples was well recognised (e.g. Goldstein, 1953: 5; Howells, 1960: 167) and some workers also noted that young-adult deaths appeared to be over-represented in cemetery samples, most likely as a result of systematic bias in adult-age estimation (Goldstein, 1953: 5; Weiss, 1973: 59; Masset, 1976).

In 1977 Lovejoy and co-workers published the results of their palaeode-mographic study of the Libben ossuary population, a Late Woodland skele-tal sample of 1327 individuals, of which 1289 skeletons were included in their life-table analysis (Lovejoy et al., 1977). Claiming that their sample con-stituted 'the largest and most comprehensively censused North American prehistoric cemetery', they drew attention to contrasts between the Libben mortality experience as inferred from estimating skeletal age at death and the demographic pattern established from ethnographic censuses of post-contact aboriginal populations. The Libben population had an average life expectancy at birth of 20 years, but it apparently exhibited lower infant mortality and higher adult mortality than comparable living populations. In Figure 4.1 the age-specific mortality (% of total deaths) in the Libben sample is compared with mortality from the model 'West' Level 1 life table of Coale and Demeny (1983) which has the same estimated life expectancy at birth of 20 years. Compared to the model life-table profile, the Libben mortality distribution clearly shows reduced numbers of deaths between 0 and 5 years of age, a marked excess of adult mortality between 25 and 45 years, and a truncated age-at-death distribution with no individuals surviving beyond 60 years.

Lovejoy et al. (1977) rejected under-enumeration of the infants and erro-neous age estimation of the adult skeletons as possible explanations for the divergence between the Libben mortality profile and the mortality profiles of contemporary 'anthropological populations'. They argued that infants must be adequately represented in the skeletal population because the Libben site showed excellent bone preservation and had been carefully and totally excavated. Also they claimed that their estimates of adult age were reliable because they had been achieved using a combination of seven mor-phological age indicators. Lovejoy et al. proposed that it was the modern anthropological populations which were abnormal as they were exposed

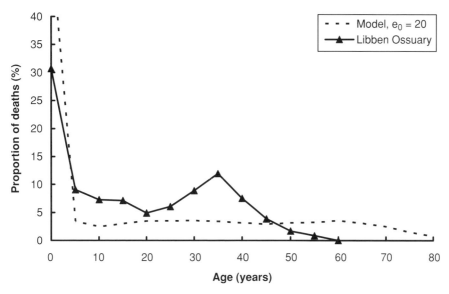

Figure 4.1 Age-specific mortality (percentage of deaths) in the Libben cemetery (Lovejoy et al., 1977) versus mortality in the model West Level 1 female life table with average life expectancy at birth (e_0) of 20 years (Coale and Demeny, 1983).

to 'the selective influence of a battery of novel pathogens', resulting in high levels of infant mortality and a consequent reduced adult mortality of those individuals who survived the high risks of early childhood.

Nancy Howell noted that while the Libben mortality profile was frequently seen in demographic analyses of skeletal material, the Libben pattern had 'never been observed in an on-going or historically documented population' (Howell, 1982: 264). Howell modelled the age distribution of the hypothetical living population that would have generated the distribution of deaths observed in the Libben cemetery. She demonstrated that the Libben population would have had a very high proportion of dependent children, and as a consequence of high mortality among young adults many of the children would have been orphaned. Furthermore, nearly all families would have been restricted to two generations and less than 5% of children would have had living grandparents. Howell concluded that either the prehistoric mortality pattern implied an extremely heavy work load for adults in order to provide subsistence for large numbers of dependent children, or that the life table had been distorted by the effects of differential preservation of skeletal remains and inaccurate estimation of age at death from skeletal indicators.

4.1.2   *The challenge by Bocquet-Appel and Masset*

In the same year that Howell published her critique of Lovejoy et al.'s analysis, Bocquet-Appel and Masset (1982) presented a more wide-ranging attack on traditional palaeodemographic techniques. Starting from the observation (c.f. Howell, 1982) that mortality patterns derived from skeletal samples differed systematically from age at death profiles recorded in a wide range of historically documented populations, Bocquet-Appel and Masset explained how the use of imprecise skeletal age indicators coupled with statistical procedures for age estimation led to the age structure of reference series being superimposed on series of skeletons from excavated cemeteries. They illustrated this effect by constructing two sub-samples of a known-age skeletal reference series in which the extent of cranial suture closure had been recorded previously. One of these sub-samples had a mean age at death of 26 years, while the other had a mean age of 51 years. Bocquet-Appel and Masset showed that while the *mean stage* of cranial suture closure for a *given age* did not vary appreciably between the two sub-samples, the *mean age* for a *given stage* of closure was profoundly dependent on the mean age of the sub-sample of the reference series. They pointed out that most biological anthropologists used inverse regressions with age at death as the dependent variable and skeletal indicator stage as the independent variable to establish standards for the estimation of age from the skeleton, rather than the biologically more appropriate regression of skeletal indicator stage on age (statistically it is the skeletal morphology that depends on chronological age, not *vice versa*). Bocquet-Appel and Masset showed that when inverse regression is employed the age structure of the reference series is effectively superimposed on any skeletal sample which is assessed using the reference series as an ageing standard.

Bocquet-Appel and Masset also drew attention to the generally low correlation between skeletal-age indicators and actual age at death, which resulted in unacceptably large standard errors of estimation. Typical correlation coefficients between single age indicators and actual age at death were within the range r = 0.5 to 0.7, while multiple-correlation coefficients based on combinations of two or more age indicators ranged from r = 0.7 to 0.8. Bocquet-Appel and Masset argued that for an indicator with a correlation coefficient of r = 0.7 the 95% confidence interval for a single estimate of adult age at death is approximately 30 years, and they regarded this as being much too imprecise to be of any use in palaeodemographic analysis.

One palaeodemographic parameter which can be estimated reliably from skeletal samples, according to Bocquet-Appel and Masset, is the juvenility index i.e. the ratio D_{5-14} / D_{20+}, which expresses the number of deaths in older children (aged 5 to 14 years) as a ratio of the number of adult deaths (aged 20 years or greater). This ratio is unaffected by the preservation and recovery bias that frequently causes under-representation of infants and young children in skeletal samples, and furthermore it avoids the problems discussed above in assigning adult skeletons a specific age at death (see Figure 4.2). Bocquet-Appel demonstrated that in historically documented populations the reciprocal of the D_{5-14}/D_{20+} ratio had a high correlation (r > 0.9) with standard life-table parameters including average life expectancy at birth and the overall birth and death rates. However, the application of this ratio to published European and North African cemetery samples gave a relatively narrow range of estimates of average life expectancy at birth (e_0 typically close to 25 years), which Bocquet-Appel and Masset suggested was evidence for another kind of reference series bias: in this case superimposing the age structure of the historically documented populations from which the ratio had been derived. In overall conclusion Bocquet-Appel and Masset stated that while the aim of obtaining unbiased age estimates from skeletal remains was a valuable one, the current application of demographic methods to skeletal age at death data was futile.

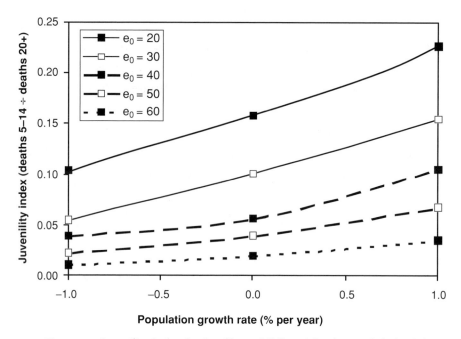

Figure 4.2 Juvenility index (ratio of later childhood deaths to adult deaths) in stable populations with different mortality levels and rates of population growth. Data are from model West female life tables (Coale and Demeny, 1983). The juvenility index increases with decreasing average life expectancy at birth (e_0) and with increasing rates of population growth.

In a direct response to Bocquet-Appel and Masset's article, Van Gerven and Armelagos (1983) cited empirical evidence to justify the usefulness of skeletal-age estimation in palaeodemography. They pointed out that the skeletal series from Kulubnarti and Wadi Halfa in Sudanese Nubia, that had been assigned ages at death primarily using the Todd pubic symphysis method, showed significant differences in mortality profile both from each other and from the age distribution of the reference series on which the Todd system was based. Van Gerven and Armelagos also claimed that age at death distributions for skeletal series could be validated by examining the progressive increase in the prevalence of common skeletal disorders with increasing age (a similar argument was subsequently presented in more detail by Mensforth and Lovejoy, 1985). In their reply, Bocquet-Appel and Masset (1983) challenged the evidence presented by Van Gerven and Armelagos and reasserted the conclusions of their earlier article.

Buikstra and Konigsberg (1985) also responded to the specific arguments in Bocquet-Appel and Masset's critique, and while Buikstra and Konigsberg acknowledged that systematic under-aging of older-adult skeletons was a widespread and persistent problem in palaeodemography they nonetheless demonstrated that meaningful comparisons could be made between the mortality profiles calculated from samples of archaeological skeletons. They explicitly rejected Bocqet-Appel and Masset's claim (1982: 329) that 'the information conveyed by the age indicators is so poor that the age distributions thus available can hardly reflect anything but random fluctuations and errors of method'.

Jackes (1985) demonstrated that age at death distributions calculated from pubic symphysis scores often showed unexpected peaks at particular ages, and that this was an artefact of the procedure for assigning to each skeleton the mean age associated with a particular symphysis score. Jackes recommended instead that ages should be assigned to skeletons according to probability distributions, so that skeletons with the same symphysis score would have assigned ages that were distributed normally around the mean age for that symphysis score. Jackes stated that her revised procedure for assigning ages at death would alleviate some of the problems highlighted by Bocqet-Appel and Masset (1982).

The eventual acceptance that there were serious problems with basing demographic inferences on traditional methods of age estimation led to the development of new methods based on Bayesian and maximum-likelihood techniques. These methods are described in more detail in Section 4.4.

4.1.3   Uniformitarian assumptions in palaeodemography

In order to use demographic information obtained from human skeletal material several assumptions about the nature of past biological and demographic processes have to be made and justified. The biological assumptions concern the assignment of sex and age at death to individual skeletons, matters which are described in detail in Sections 4.2 and 4.3 below. Morphological methods for estimating sex and age at death from the skeleton depend on the prior establishment, usually in modern reference series, of the relationship between skeletal morphology and biological sex or chronological age. The application of these methods to samples taken from past populations depends on an assumption that patterns of sexual dimorphism and rates of skeletal growth, maturation and degeneration were similar in the past and in the present day and were constant across different populations. Clearly, over the very wide span of human evolution from the time when human ancestors diverged from the ancestors of the African apes there have been substantial changes both in the nature and extent of human sexual dimorphism and in rates of skeletal maturation (see Section 5.2 below). Where appropriate data are available, these uniformitarian assumptions can be circumvented by developing new standards for the assignment of sex and age at death that are specific to the population under investigation.

Uniformitarian assumptions about past demographic processes are also required in some areas of palaeodemographic analysis. The construction of a life table from records of mortality depends on the assumption of population stability and either an absence of age-structured migration or at least a stable balance between emigration and immigration. Interpretation of life-table parameters derived from a skeletal sample also depends on assumptions about time-averaged rates of population growth during the period when the skeletal sample accumulated. Bayesian methods for the assignment of age at death (see Section 4.4 below) depend on the selection of appropriate age-specific prior probabilities of death, which in turn require uniformitarian inferences about past demographic parameters.

Finally the technique of pattern matching (Milner et al., 1989; Paine, 1989), in which the demographic structure of an archaeological sample is compared to model life-table mortality schedules, is based on the assumption that the age structure of the population represented in the archaeological assemblage must have originally resembled one of a family of model life tables. Meindl and Russell (1998: 390) have challenged this assumption, claiming that the widely-used Princeton model life tables are based on a restricted range of modern mortality experience in populations with artifically protracted longevity, and that the Princeton models are therefore inappropriate as comparata for the mortality schedules of past populations. This critique echoes similar statements made earlier by Lovejoy et al. (1977), and does not account for the fact that the Princeton model life tables provide a close match to historical and ethnographic data (see Chapter 3).

4.1.4   Bias in samples and in estimation

The term 'bias' is used here to refer to a systematic (i.e. consistent in direction) departure of a measured or estimated quantity from the true or expected value of that quantity (Orton, 2000: 23). A major potential source of bias in palaeodemographic data is the under-representation of the youngest age classes, which is a feature of some assemblages of human skeletal remains from archaeological contexts. The shortfall in numbers of children, particularly infants and young children, can occur even when large samples of skeletons are recovered from the cemeteries of communities in which deceased individuals of all ages are expected to have received normative funerary rites. Depending on the precise circumstances of burial at particular sites, the skeletal remains of infants and children may have a lower preservation potential (children's skeletons are smaller, their bones are less resistant to physical damage and bioturbation, and their graves are more easily disturbed or truncated) and a lower likelihood of recovery (children's skeletal remains are less easily recognised, they may have less elaborate graves, they may be overlooked when commingled with the remains of adults). The pattern of under-representation of infants in archaeological assemblages is not confined to human examples: archaeozoological samples of the skeletal remains of wild and domestic mammals may also show lower than expected numbers in the youngest age classes (Klein and Cruz-Uribe, 1984: 85).

Another bias in age-distributed demographic data has emerged from comparing adult mortality in archaeological samples with the mortality

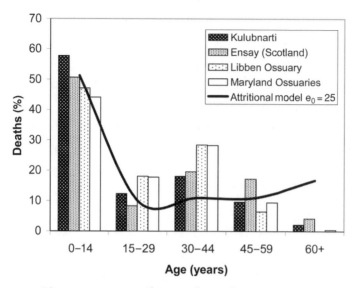

Figure 4.3 Age-specific mortality in four archaeological samples of human skeletal remains. Data sources are: Kulubnarti (Greene et al., 1986), Ensay (Miles, 1989), Libben (Lovejoy et al., 1977) and Maryland (Ubelaker, 1974).

observed in historically documented populations and with the patterns of mortality in model stable populations. Archaeological samples that have been aged using skeletal morphological indicators often show a peak of mortality in the young and middle adult years, usually in the interval between 30 and 45 years (Figure 4.3). This pattern, which is often accompanied by absent or very few individuals aged over 60 years, is seen in analyses of skeletal samples from all regions of the world, from prehistoric through to modern times, but this mortality distribution is not found in model life tables or in historical demographic data (Figure 4.4). The source of this peak of mid-adult mortality has been attributed to preservational bias favouring younger-adult skeletons (Walker et al., 1988) and to reduced longevity in past populations (Meindl et al., 1983; Meindl and Russell, 1998), but it may also reflect a generalised and systematic bias towards underestimating the age at death of older-adult skeletons (Weiss, 1973: 59; Boddington, 1987: 190).

Weiss (1972) documented a systematic and statistically significant bias in adult sex estimation in 43 published skeletal samples from diverse

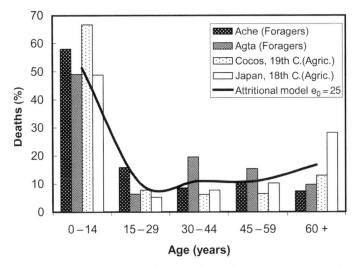

Figure 4.4 Age-specific mortality in hunter-gatherers and subsistence agriculturalists, compared to mortality in a model West Level 3 female life table with average life expectancy at birth (e_0) of 25 years. Hunter-gatherer data are from Hill and Hurtado, 1995, and Early and Headland, 1998; agriculturalist data are from Smith, 1960 and Janetta and Preston, 1991; model life-table data are from Coale and Demeny, 1983.

geographical regions and time periods. Most of the skeletal samples had an appreciable excess of adult skeletons assigned as males, and the overall sex ratio showed a 12% bias in favour of males when compared to the sex ratios recorded in living pre-industrial populations. The bias in favour of males was more extreme in older skeletons (those aged above 30 years) and may be attributable to a tendency, especially in earlier studies, for morphologically intermediate skeletons to have been erroneously classified as males (Weiss, 1972: 240). A similar bias in favour of adult males has been reported for Romano-British cemeteries (Waldron, 1994: 23). Reassessment of the sex attributions made by earlier researchers has the potential to reduce this bias. Ruff (1981) restudied a sample of 101 adult skeletons from Pecos Pueblo in which a previous study (Hooton, 1930) had assigned 61 (60.4%) as males. In Ruff's reanalysis only 51 (50.5%) of the skeletons were scored as male, a proportion that is closer to expected values.

Biological mortality bias refers to the situation where there are systematic differences between a sample of deaths from a population and the
surviving members from the same age groups of the living population.
It is often assumed that the principal causes of death in the past were
relatively undiscriminating and that most individuals in the population
had an approximately equal chance of dying in any given age interval.
Wood et al. (1992b) explored the consequences of individual variation in
frailty, whereby the risk of death at a given age is considerably greater in
some individuals (those designated as 'frail') than in others (those designated as 'robust'). According to this perspective, the individuals who die
in a particular age group, and thus who enter the burial record, may be
constitutionally different from those of the same age cohort who survive
and continue to be active members of the living population. If biological
mortality bias is substantial then this has important potential implications
both for demography and palaeopathology, depending on the extent to
which frail individuals might have different growth patterns or sustain
different frequencies of skeletal markers of disease. However, modelling
of the potential effects of mortality bias on growth rates calculated from
cross-sectional samples of children's skeletons suggests that the effects of
this potential source of bias are likely to be small (Saunders and Hoppa,
1993: 142–43).

4.2   ESTIMATION OF SEX

4.2.1   Human sex differences

Humans, like virtually all vertebrates and many other organisms, possess
two biological sexes. The social and cognitive recognition of the primary
human sex distinction is termed gender (Mays and Cox, 2000: 117). The
interplay between biological sex and social gender is complex and varies
between cultures, but for the purposes of biological anthropology a clear-
cut distinction is useful: *sex* refers to the biological genotype and its morphological expression as the phenotype, while *gender* refers to the social

registration and reinforcement of biological sex differences, often expressed most markedly in material culture and in social behaviour (Walker and Cook, 1998).

Much of the morphological difference between the sexes is genetically determined and is the result of two separate processes of natural selection. The sex-determining genes control the development of the primary sex organs which equip the individual for either the male or the female reproductive role. Because successful reproduction is the key to the survival of an individual's genes, these sex differences are under close control by stabilising selection. But the separate process of sexual selection also has an important influence on the visible or phenotypic differences between the sexes. To put it simply, some of the observable differences in morphology and behaviour between human males and human females are not adaptive in a mechanical sense, but are the result of one sex preferring certain aesthetically valued traits in their mating partner. Indirectly, the possession of these sexually selected traits may contribute to successful reproduction. The difference in physical form between male and female organisms is known as *sexual dimorphism* (Table 4.1). Externally the adult-human female body is clearly distinguished from the male by primary and secondary sexual characteristics. When we consider the human skeleton, although the differences between the sexes are less apparent, several factors can be identified as contributing to the biological differences between adult males and females.

4.2.2   *Morphological sex differences in pre-adolescent skeletons*
It is difficult to establish the sex of a juvenile human skeleton because the principal skeletal sex differences that characterise adult skeletons only emerge during and after puberty. A considerable amount of research has been applied to this question, and several authors have presented morphological traits and metrical procedures that are claimed to allow the diagnosis of sex from the skeletal remains of children (Boucher, 1957; Weaver, 1980; Hunt, 1990; Schutkowski, 1993; Molleson et al., 1998). Few of these

Table 4.1 *Factors contributing to differences between the skeletons of human adult males and females.*

Size	Adult males are on average larger than adult females, but the average size difference is not the same for all populations, and there is usually a substantial range of size overlap between the sexes. Volume and mass differences between the sexes are proportionately greater than the differences in linear dimensions, as a consequence of allometric scaling effects.
Robusticity	Males bones tend to be more robust, with larger joint surfaces and more prominent muscle attachments. The differences result partly from larger average volume and mass in males, but are also due to their greater muscle bulk and hormonally-mediated differential bone growth.
Reproduction	The morphology of the adult female hip bones and sacrum reflects adaptations for childbirth. As a consequence the female pelvis has a transversely expanded shape with a broader pelvic outlet, and diagnostic sex-specific features are present in the pubic region.
Cultural practices	The presence of culturally-determined sex differences in behaviour may provide additional information that may be useful in sexing skeletons. For example, sex differences in diet and nutrition, physical activity, interpersonal violence and disease susceptibility may all have skeletal consequences.

methods have been subjected to blind testing, and most have not controlled for age variation between the samples of each sex. Holcomb and Konigsberg (1995) measured the shape of the greater sciatic notch in 133 fetal ilia of known age and sex. They found a small, statistically significant difference in the shape of the notch between male and female fetuses, but there was considerable overlap in morphology between the sexes and only 60% of specimens could be classified to the correct sex using iliac shape.

Discriminant analysis has been used to investigate metrical differences in the crown dimensions of children's deciduous teeth (De Vito and Saunders,

1990), and discriminant functions for permanent teeth can also be applied to children aged above ~4 years. The crowns of the developing permanent teeth are present, though unerupted, in the child's jaw: this is the only part of the child's skeleton that will persist unchanged to adulthood. It is therefore possible to obtain detailed measurements of the teeth of the known-sex adult members of the skeletal population and then to use discriminant analysis to develop a mathematical function that distinguishes male and female permanent teeth. The resulting discriminant function can then be applied to the permanent tooth crowns in the juvenile specimens, with a claimed accuracy of above 90% (Rösing, 1983). However, it is a complex and time-consuming method that requires relatively large samples of reliably sexed adult skeletons, and is therefore not always readily applicable to archaeological samples.

4.2.3 Morphological sex differences in adult skeletons

The bony pelvis, including the hip bones and the sacrum, is the most reliable part of the adult skeleton for sex estimation because it is the only skeletal region which exhibits specific morphological adaptations to the different sexes' reproductive capacities. In the adult-female pelvis the postural and locomotor functions of the pelvis are modified by the requirement for the birth canal to allow the passage of a fully developed neonate. This is achieved by additional transverse growth of the pelvic bones which occurs around the time of puberty. This differential growth is manifest both in the overall shape of the pelvis, and in a series of specific morphological traits, each of which contributes to the overall adaptation.

After the pelvis, the skull (cranium and mandible) provides the next most reliable group of sex-specific morphological indicators. The principal sex-discriminating features of the human skull are related to overgrowth or hypertrophy of bone in males, and to the tendency for males to show greater development of musculature and articulations with more prominent muscle markings and larger joint surfaces. For most of the sex-diagnostic traits of the cranium, the presence of the trait indicates a male and its absence indicates a female. Skeletal hypertrophy is seen most clearly in the skull of the adult male in the supraorbital region, the nuchal region, the mastoid process, the attachment areas for the muscles of mastication and in the development of the mental trigone (chin) on the mandible. Recent research has indicated that these skeletal traits vary in their efficacy in sex discrimination (Rogers, 2005). When we move away from the pelvis and the skull, sex discrimination relies principally on the average size differences between the sexes, particularly in the sizes of the articular surfaces at the ends of the long bones. On average the muscle bulk and body weight of males is considerably greater than that of females, and muscle forces and static weight must be transmitted through the joint surfaces which as a consequence are on average larger in males than in females.

Skeletal features that are believed to be related to the birth process itself have been identified on the pelvis near the sacro-iliac joint (pre-auricular sulcus), on the postero-superior aspect of the pubis near the pubic symphysis and at the pubic tubercle (Stewart, 1970; Suchey et al., 1979; Bergfelder and Herrmann, 1980; Cox and Scott, 1992; Cox, 2000). In females parturition can produce cavitation or pitting at the margins of the pubic symphyseal surface, and similar changes have been reported around the sacro-iliac joint. Studies of the skeletons of women of known parity have established that there is a poor correlation between actual number of births and the extent of these skeletal changes (Cox, 2000), and while so-called 'parturition scars' are rarely found in nulliparous women (or in men), there are many multiparous women who do not show any visible skeletal changes (Suchey et al., 1979). Age changes at the pubic symphysis may modify and conceal earlier parturition features, and many women appear to be able to accommodate the stresses of childbirth without incurring lasting damage to the pelvic joints. It has been suggested that some of the pelvic changes previously interpreted as relating to parturition may instead reflect pelvic shape and biomechanical influences on the skeleton (Cox and Scott, 1992; Cox, 2000).

4.2.4 Accuracy of sex estimation

Male and female adult skeletal morphology varies across a continuum. There are always a few individuals whose skeletons are intermediate in form and it is impossible to sex these individuals accurately using morphological methods alone. In general, the accuracy of skeletal sexing increases as more parts of the skeleton are considered: with complete adult skeletons up to 100% accuracy in sexing has been claimed, provided that the range of sex variation in the population is already known (Krogman and İşcan, 1986: 259). The pelvis is the most reliable area for skeletal sexing. A blind test of the reliability of morphological sexing, applied to a mixed-race sample of adult pelvic bones, achieved 96% accuracy (Meindl et al., 1985b: 80). A similar level of accuracy has also been demonstrated using morphological traits of the pubic bone (Phenice, 1969; Sutherland and Suchey, 1991). The skull and the remainder of the postcranial skeleton provide less accuracy, but Meindl et al. (1985b) achieved 92% accuracy in a blind test using morphological criteria to assign sex to a mixed-race sample of adult skulls. It is likely that several of the above measures of accuracy are over optimistic as the sexing methods have usually been tested on populations whose variation is already familiar to the observer.

As with methods of adult-age estimation, the techniques for skeletal sexing have been developed using skeletons of known sex, but there are also indirect tests of the accuracy of the methods. For example, if it can reasonably be inferred that a cemetery contains approximately equal numbers of male and female adult skeletons, then we expect our skeletal sexing methods to classify about half the skeletons as male and half as female. Weiss (1972) demonstrated that this expectation is often not fulfilled, and that morphological methods for estimating sex from the skeleton have tended to produced a bias in favour of males.

4.2.5 Biomolecular methods of sex estimation

Methods for identifying the sex of skeletal remains using DNA have been reviewed by Brown (1998; 2000). The advantages of using DNA for sexing skeletal remains lie in the potential to estimate sex with equal reliability in juveniles and adults, and the theoretically low probability of misclassification as more than 99% of males and females have the standard sex chromosome complement of XY and XX respectively. Several protocols have been developed for sex identification that recognise sex-specific sequences in the amelogenin gene, which has different alleles on the X and Y chromosomes (Lassen et al., 1996; Stone et al., 1996; Götherstrom et al., 1997; Faerman et al., 1998). However, the utility of this approach for sex identification in ancient human remains is limited. The survival of DNA in ancient remains is highly variable and studies reporting amelogenin-based sexing of ancient remains show that on average only 60% of specimens tested were identified successfully (Brown, 2000: 465). In part this reflects the fact that amelogenin is a single copy gene which has a low probability of survival in ancient bone compared to mitochondrial DNA which is present in multiple copies in each cell.

4.3   ESTIMATION OF AGE AT DEATH

4.3.1   *Human skeletal development and ageing*

In common with other tissues of the body the skeleton grows in size and attains successive levels of maturity as the individual progresses through life from conception to the achievement of adulthood. Further age-related changes are observable in adult skeletal tissues as some parts of the skeleton continue to grow, remodel and degenerate throughout adult life. The timing and rate of developmental growth is genetically determined but is also influenced by maternal environment and by the health and nutritional status of the growing individual. Some physiological disturbances to growth cause temporary retardation of the rate of somatic growth which may be compensated by accelerated 'catch-up' growth once the adverse conditions have ameliorated. Growth rates are high prenatally and in the immediate postnatal period, and rates also increase briefly during adolescence (the 'adolescent growth spurt'). Rates of growth vary both within and between populations (Eveleth and Tanner, 1990), and this constrains attempts to draw a close correspondence between the extent of skeletal growth and the chronological age of the individual.

The term 'subadult' is used here to refer to all developmental stages before reaching skeletal maturity. The developing human passes through a succession of well-defined maturational stages. These are the *embryonic* stage, from conception to 8 weeks; the *fetal* stage, from 9 to 40 weeks gestational age; the *neonatal* stage, from birth to 1 month; *infancy*, from 2 to 11 months; *early childhood*, from 1 to 5 years, *later childhood* from 6 to 11 years, *adolescence* from 12 to 17 years, and *adulthood* from 18 years onwards.

Bones and teeth begin forming in the fetus well before birth. Ossification begins at eight weeks *in utero*, and the deciduous teeth begin calcifying at fifteen weeks. Most of the bones of the skeleton are initially formed as a cartilage model, in the middle of which appears the primary centre of ossification. Secondary centres of ossification appear at the ends of the bone, and are separated from the primary centre by intervening growth plates. These secondary centres subsequently become the bony epiphyses that support the articular surfaces (see Figure 4.5). Bone growth continues by the addition of new bone on surfaces facing the direction of bone growth, while resorption takes place on surfaces facing away from the growth direction. The crowns of the deciduous and the permanent teeth develop within the jaw, and the teeth subsequently develop roots as they erupt through the oral tissues into the mouth.

Towards the end of puberty most of the bones stop growing and the cartilagenous growth plates underneath the epiphyses are converted to bone. The epiphyses fuse to their respective diaphyses at different times but mainly from about 12 years onwards. Some growth centres in the skull and vertebral column fuse much earlier, while the medial end of the clavicle, the epiphyses of the vertebral bodies and the growth plates between the segments of the body of the sacrum do not fuse until the mid to late 20s. Most epiphyses fuse between 1 and 2 years earlier in girls than in boys, and fusion itself is a protracted process rather than a sudden event. With the cessation of somatic growth skeletal tissues continue to participate

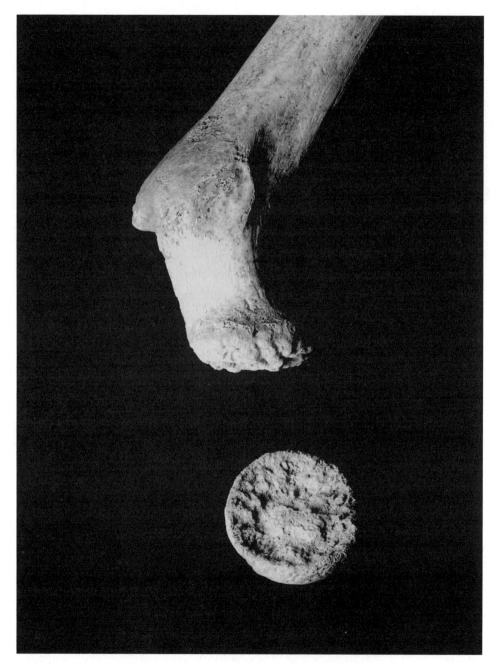

Figure 4.5 Unfused epiphysis at the proximal end of the femur in an individual aged about 8 years at death.

in processes of remodelling and degeneration which result in cumulative change to bones and teeth. These changes can be used as indicators of progression through stages of adult life.

4.3.2   Age estimation in fetuses and children

During fetal and early neonatal life the bones grow quickly, with about 20mm added to the length of long bone diaphyses in just 10 weeks, compared to an average of 20mm per *year* during the postnatal growth period. Thus in principle the age at death of a fetus can be estimated accurately from measurements of the size of its bones. There are several published studies of bone length in fetuses of known gestational age (Scheuer and Black, 2000a: 14) and data from these studies have been used to establish growth standards for the assessment of age at death in forensic and archaeological material (e.g. Scheuer et al., 1980; Kósa, 1989; Sherwood et al., 2000). These growth standards are influenced by the age structure of the reference series from which they are calculated, and revised standards based on Bayesian estimation methods are discussed below.

The timing of the initial appearance of primary and secondary ossification centres is well established from radiographic studies of living children, but these data are not particularly useful in archaeological age estimation. Unlike the developing tooth crowns (which may be retained in their crypts inside the jaw) ossification centres often do not survive burial and the epiphyses in young children's skeletons are infrequently recovered at excavation. The times at which the various ossification centres coalesce and the epiphyses fuse to the diaphyses have also been documented in modern populations, and these fusion events form the basis of maturational schedules that are more pertinent to the requirements of age estimation in subadult skeletons. It should be noted, however, that radiographic evidence for fusion of ossification centres may differ systematically from fusion assessed by visual inspection of bones. A comprehensive review of the timing of initial ossification and epiphyseal fusion in the human skeleton can be found in Scheuer and Black (2000b).

The deciduous teeth commence calcification between 13 and 20 weeks gestational age (Sunderland et al., 1987; Smith, 1991), but the crowns of these teeth do not complete formation until the postnatal period. Deciduous dental development proceeds faster in prenatal males than in females (Scheuer and Black, 2000b: 152). Developing deciduous teeth are observable in some archaeological fetal skeletons but they are often not recovered at excavation, especially if the delicate bones of the developing mandible and maxilla are damaged. The permanent teeth commence calcification at around the time of birth and their protracted development provides a continuous series of chronological markers throughout childhood and adolescence. In contrast to the prenatal formation of the deciduous dentition, the development of the permanent teeth tends to be more advanced in girls than in boys of the same age. Published standards for the chronology of human deciduous and permanent tooth formation, as with long bone diaphyseal length, are influenced by reference-series age structure, but in addition the different statistical methods used for assessing age of attainment of tooth formation stages contribute a further source of variation to the standard chronologies (Smith, 1991). Methods that are based on cumulative distribution functions provide the best basis for determining the age of attainment of particular dental development stages (Smith, 1991: 149).

The tooth crowns are formed within the jaw and then erupt through the gum into the mouth while the tooth roots grow downwards into the jaw. Stages of tooth crown and root development can be recognised either by visual inspection or from a radiograph of the jaw with the developing teeth inside it. Up to 14 discrete stages of tooth development can be recognised radiographically from the initial appearance of calcification of the tooth cusps through to closure of the root apex following eruption (Moorrees et al., 1963a, 1963b). Alternatively the height of the crown of the developing tooth can be measured and compared to standard growth curves calculated from known-age samples (Liversidge and Molleson, 1999; Liversidge et al., 1993). The resorption of the roots of the deciduous teeth prior to their exfoliation can also be used as a chronological marker in children aged between about 5 and 12 years (Moorrees et al., 1963a). As tooth development appears to be less influenced by dietary and other disturbances to growth than is the case for other tissues of the body, age estimates based on dental growth are considered more accurate and reliable than those based on bone growth (Smith, 1991: 143).

An additional source of data for age estimation in children can be found in dental microstructure. Teeth carry a record of their own development in the microscopic incremental structures in enamel, dentine and cementum. These structures are visible in microscopic thin sections and electron-microscopic images of developing tooth surfaces. The incremental markers include the Striae of Retzius – weekly growth increments in the enamel which are expressed on the outer surfaces of the tooth as perikymata – and enamel prism cross-striations, which represent daily variations in enamel secretion rates (Hillson, 1996). By counting the number of perikymata on the surface of a partially formed tooth, and adding about 26 weeks to account for the hidden increments that are buried in the occlusal enamel, plus a correction for the age at which enamel calcification begins, the age at death of a juvenile skeleton can be calculated (Bromage and Dean, 1985; Dean and Beynon, 1991; Dean et al., 1993; Huda and Bowman, 1995).

Several studies have indicated that skeletal growth rates calculated from observations of normal children in modern Western industrialised countries are higher than for children in past populations or for children in present-day communities which have poor nutrition and increased risk of disease (Humphrey, 2000). This finding has implications for the use of bone size as an indicator of age at death. Hoppa (1992) constructed growth profiles from long bone diaphyseal lengths in a series of archaeological populations, using dental development as an age marker for each skeleton. The resulting growth profiles showed consistently slower rates of long bone growth in the archaeological samples after 1 year of age when compared to the modern growth rates established in the Denver Growth Study (Maresh, 1955). A similar result was obtained by Humphrey (2000) who recorded femur diaphysis length from the skeletons of known-age children

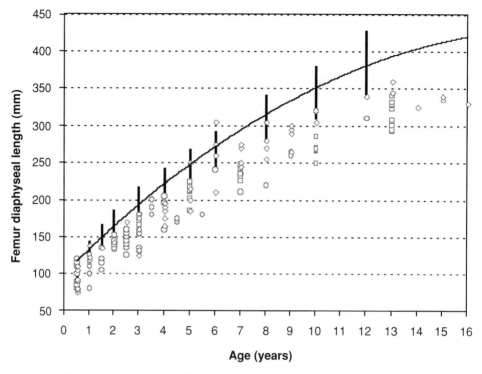

Figure 4.6 Growth profiles constructed from archaeological samples of skeletal remains, compared to the modern Denver growth standard (Maresh, 1955). The archaeological samples are prehistoric Europeans (square symbols: Piontek et al., 2001), Anglo-Saxons (diamond symbols: Hoppa, 1992) and 18th/19th century Londoners (circular symbols: Humphrey, 2000). Age at death in the archaeological samples was taken from mortuary documentation (18th/19th century skeletons) or was estimated from dental development (prehistoric and Anglo-Saxon skeletons). The solid line and vertical bars represent the trendline and +/− two standard deviations for the Denver growth standard.

buried in eighteenth- and nineteenth-century church crypts in London (see Figure 4.6). By the age of 15 months most of the London children were more than 2 standard deviations below the age-specific mean bone length established by the Denver Growth Study. However another nineteenth-century sample of children's skeletons studied by Saunders et al. (1993) showed no evidence of a deficit in growth rate compared to modern growth standards. These results support the conclusion that there are real differ-ences in growth rates among populations, and that the pattern of reduced growth observed in some skeletal samples is not simply a consequence of mortality bias (Saunders and Hoppa, 1993: 146).

4.3.3   *Age estimation in adults: macroscopic methods*

Overview

Age estimation from adult skeletal remains is one of the more difficult and error-prone procedures in biological anthropology. When the individual has reached adult size and growth ceases, age-related changes continue to occur in the bones and the teeth, though these changes do not proceed with the regularity and predictability of the developmental changes that occur during the subadult years. Most adult-ageing methods depend on measur-ing degenerative and reparative changes that reflect the cumulative effects of wear and tear on the skeleton, and the biological processes involved may be influenced by environmental factors such as diet, disease and physical activity.

Age-related changes in adult bones and teeth involve several aspects of gross morphology and microscopic structure. The final stages of skeletal maturation continue into the early years of adulthood, with some epiphy-ses remaining unfused into the third decade of life. Many of the joints with restricted mobility, including the cranial sutures, the fibrous joints of the vertebral column and some secondary cartilaginous joints such as the pubic symphysis, show age-related changes throughout adult life in which the bone surfaces adjacent to the joint tissues become remodelled or (in the case of cranial sutures) fused. Progressive demineralisation of long bones during adult life leads to expansion of the medullary cavity and thinning of the bone cortex and trabeculae: these changes are most easily visualised through radiography (Sorg et al., 1989). At the microscopic level age mark-ers are provided by the accumulation of osteons in cortical bone (Robling and Stout, 2000) and the development of root dentine transparency and accumulation of layers of cementum on the roots of the teeth (Whittaker, 2000).

Pubic symphysis ageing

A series of progressive age-related changes occur at the pubic symphysis, the fibrocartilaginous joint which connects the hip bones at the front of the pelvis (Figure 4.7). These changes have been investigated in several systematic research studies (Todd, 1920; McKern and Stewart, 1957; Nemeskéri et al., 1960; Meindl et al., 1985a; Brooks and Suchey, 1990) and they form the basis of what is considered to be one of the more reliable means of estimating age at death in adult skeletons (Suchey et al., 1986). In young adults the surface of the bone underlying the pubic symphysis has a distinctive appearance, with about 8 horizontal ridges and grooves crossing the surface from front to back. Thus the symphyseal surface in a young adult has a similar appearance to the bone surfaces that underlie the growth plate between an unfused epiphysis and its matching diaphysis. In older individuals the appearance of the pubic symphyseal surface is modified through the normal stresses acting on the joint. The transverse ridges become less well defined as the grooves become filled in with new bone. The front (ventral) and rear (dorsal) margins of the joint surface also become thickened, and the upper and lower margins of the face become delimited by the fusion of ossific nodules. Eventually these margins join to form a complete rim around the symphyseal face. In the oldest age categories the entire surface becomes pitted and porous and it develops an uneven appearance. (Figure 4.7).

Dental attrition

As soon as the permanent teeth have fully erupted into the mouth their occlusal surfaces begin to wear down, partly from abrasive particles in the diet but also from contact between the teeth in opposite jaws and from the non-dietary usage of teeth as tools. The pattern and rate of dental wear is influenced by cultural practices and by the incidence of dental

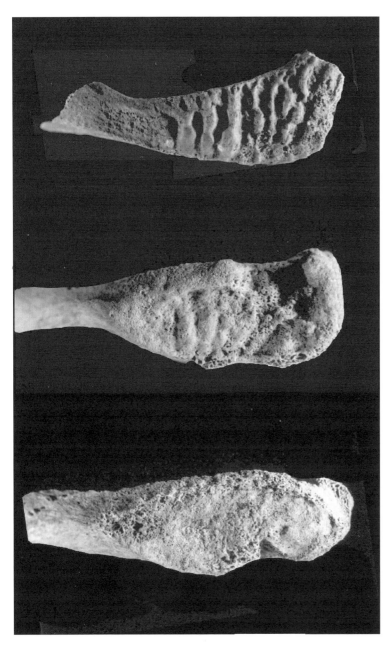

Figure 4.7 Age-related changes in the pubic symphysis. Top: ridged surface lacking defined margins, characteristic of adolescents; centre: loss of definition of ridges and development of defined margins, characteristic of younger adults; bottom: irregularities of symphyseal surface and margins characteristic of older adults.

disease, because the loss of teeth through decay, injury or gum disease may increase the loading, and hence the rate of wear, on the remaining healthy teeth. Although average rates of wear vary between populations, for a particular individual the rate of dental wear can be assessed by establishing the differential amount of wear along the molar tooth row (Miles, 1963, 2001). In an adult jaw, in which the permanent molars will have erupted at intervals of about 6 years, there will be a difference or gradient of wear between the first molar (greatest wear) and the third molar (least wear), as shown in Figure 4.8. The amount of wear can be recorded either by matching the teeth to a modal wear scheme or by measuring the area of dentine exposure (Richards and Miller, 1991) or the amount of reduction in crown height (Walker et al., 1991).

Other macroscopic ageing methods

Lovejoy et al. (1985) have described a system of adult-age estimation based around changes that occur on the auricular surface of the hip bone which forms the lateral surface of the sacro-iliac joint. The stages of their ageing scheme are characterised by changes in the transverse organisation, granularity, porosity and outline of the joint surface. Although the sequence of changes is not so readily apparent as in the pubic symphysis, one advantage of this method is that the auricular surface is often much better preserved than the pubic symphysis in archaeological skeletal remains. A revised version of this ageing method that utilises quantitative scoring of the component indicators has been published by Buckberry and Chamberlain (2002).

The sutures between the individual cranial bones are distinct in young adults, but gradually become obliterated in older individuals as the adjacent bones fuse together. This process has long served as a basis for age estimation, and the cranial vault bones are often well preserved in archaeological contexts. In the cranial suture closure scheme of Meindl and Lovejoy (1985) the degree of closure is recorded at five discrete locations on the superior part of the cranial vault and five locations on the lateral-anterior region

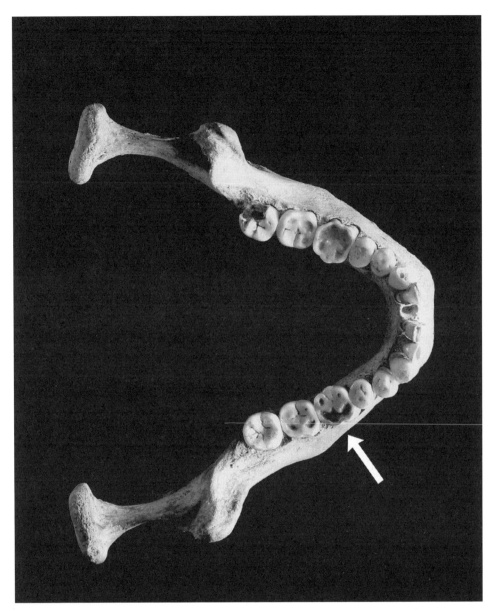

Figure 4.8 Pattern of wear on the occlusal surfaces of the lower teeth. A gradient of wear can be seen from the first molar (substantial exposure of dentine – arrowed), through the second molar (small areas of dentine exposure) to the third molar (wear confined to the enamel).

of the vault. Each location is given a score from 0 (open) to 4 (fully obliterated), and the scores are summed across the anatomical sites in each
of the two regions to give two composite scores, which are converted to
age estimates via a table of values of mean ages established from skeletons
with known age at death. Cranial sutures provide a relatively inaccurate
age estimation over a rather narrow interval, as the age distribution for
a given score is large, and individuals younger than 30 years usually have
open sutures, while in individuals over 50 years of age the cranial sutures
are mainly closed.

Finally, some pathological skeletal conditions such as Paget's disease of
bone and DISH are age progressive and are rarely seen in individuals under
about 40 years (Resnick, 2002). Degenerative arthritis and osteoporosis are
also more common in older adults, thus the presence of these conditions
can support an age estimate based on other evidence.

4.3.4   Age estimation in adults: microscopic methods

The search for reliable methods of estimating adult age at death has led to
the investigation of microscopic changes in bone and teeth that might occur
on a regular and progressive basis. Osteons are longitudinal vascular chan-
nels in compact bone that consist of a central Haversian canal surrounded
by concentric lamellae which are delimited on the outside by a reversal line.
They are generated by organised remodelling of bone, and the accumulation of osteons in human compact bone provides a means of measuring
the age of the bone that contains them. Osteon counting to estimate age at
death was pioneered by Ellis Kerley (1965). The method involves preparing
a ground thin section of bone suitable for viewing by transmitted-light
microscopy. The number of intact and fragmentary osteons are counted
within a defined field of view, and the age is then calibrated from a standard
curve that has been derived from a sample of individuals of known age at
death.

Osteon accumulation in bone does not, however, proceed uniformly
with increasing age of the individual. The actual physiological age of

unremodelled bone is nearly always less than the chronological age of the individual, and the discrepancy depends on which location in the skeleton is sampled. Also, the number of accumulated osteons eventually reaches an asymptote as newly created osteons remove all observable traces of earlier osteons. Various authors have published modified versions of Kerley's original method (reviewed in Robling and Stout, 2000).

Cementum growth is the basis of another microscopic method for estimating age at death in adult skeletons. Cementum is a thin bone-like tissue that forms a layer around the roots of the teeth, providing attachment for the periodontal ligament that anchors each tooth to its socket in the jaw. Cementum deposition commences as soon as the tooth has erupted, and cementum continues to accumulate throughout life. In animal and human populations which experience seasonal variations in diet cementum forms alternating light and dark bands that are arranged concentrically as annulations around the tooth root, in a manner analogous to the formation of tree rings (Lieberman, 1994). The dark bands of cementum are deposited in the reduced-growth season, which is usually the winter in temperate latitudes. The growth increments can be counted and added to the age of eruption of the tooth, so that the final age of the individual can be estimated.

The use of cementum in ageing human skeletal remains dates back to Gustafson (1950) who included overall cementum thickness (though not counts of individual cementum layers) as a criterion in his multifactorial dental-ageing method. The method has the potential to achieve very high accuracy when applied to freshly extracted teeth (Wittwer-Backofen et al., 2004), but there are difficulties in using the cementum annulation method to estimate age at death in archaeological human skeletal remains due to the thinness of the cementum layers (Hillson, 1996: 204) and their varying degrees of preservation.

Another microscopic ageing method, also originally developed by Gustafson, is that of root-dentine translucency. As ageing progresses the microscopic tubules within the dentine of the tooth root become infilled with secondary dentine. This process begins at the apex of the root and progressively involves the rest of the tooth root in a cervical direction. The tooth root is originally opaque because of refractive differences between the crystals of the dentine and organic material within the dentine tubules. When the tubules become mineralised the root gradually becomes transparent to transmitted light. Relatively high correlation coefficients have been reported between the extent of root translucency and chronological age in modern clinical material (Solheim, 1989; Drusini et al., 1991).

4.4   BAYESIAN AND MAXIMUM LIKELIHOOD APPROACHES TO AGE ESTIMATION

4.4.1   *General principles in estimating age from morphological indicators*
The relationship between chronological age at death and the state of a skeletal indicator is usually modelled and parameterised using a reference series comprised of a large number of skeletons, each of whose age and indicator state is known. Given knowledge of how chronological age and the morphological indicator state covary within a representative sample of a population, and by means of a uniformitarian assumption (that the relationship between age and indicator is constant across samples and populations) the age of any unknown or target skeleton can then be estimated provided that its skeletal indicator state can be observed.

The determination of age at death from the state of the skeletal indicator requires that the indicator state changes in some predictable fashion with the chronological age of the individual. The relationship between indicator state (I) and the individual's age (A) can be modelled by a continuous linear function, expressed algebraically as $I = f(A) + e$. According to this model the state of the indicator is determined by the individual's age A and by other factors, the latter being subsumed here under a random error term (e). If the function $f(A)$ relating I to A is known, then A can be predicted from I, though the accuracy of this prediction will depend on the magnitude of the error e, which in biological examples is often substantial and may increase with increasing age.

Traditional anthropological methods of age estimation have often used calculations of the central tendency of age for a particular indicator state in a reference series, or have used regressions of age on indicator state in the reference series (i.e. inverse regression), as a means of predicting the age of a target specimen. Both of these approaches suffer from the deficiency that the predicted age of the target specimen will be influenced by the age structure of the reference series (Bocquet-Appel and Masset, 1982; Konigsberg and Frankenberg, 1992; Konigsberg et al., 1997). In recent years alternative procedures have been developed for inferring age from indicator state that make use of Bayesian and maximum likelihood methods (Hoppa and Vaupel, 2002), and these will be outlined in the following sections.

4.4.2   Bayes' theorem and its application to age estimation

Konigsberg and Frankenberg (1992) pioneered the use of Bayesian statistical inference as a way to render age estimation independent of reference-series age structure. Bayes' theorem provides a logical formulation of the procedure by which current beliefs are revised in the light of new information (Buck et al., 1996). The theorem states that given a parameter (in this case age A) and some data (in this case the state of the morphological indicator I) that are held to influence the probability of the parameter, then the posterior probability of the parameter $[p(A|I)]$ is equal to its prior probability $[p(A)_{\text{prior}}]$ multiplied by the standardised likelihood of the data $[p(I \mid A)]$:

$$p(A \mid I) = \frac{p(I \mid A) \times p(A)_{\text{prior}}}{\int [p(I \mid A) \times p(A)_{\text{prior}}]}$$

Note that in this and subsequent equations, $p(x \mid y)$ designates the conditional probability of x, given y, and the denominator is equal to the integral across all possible ages of the expression in parentheses. For datasets in which the ages and indicator states are recorded as discrete categories, the integral becomes simply a sum across the designated age categories.

In plain words, the probability $[p(A|I)]$ of being a particular age A, given a particular state of the indicator I, is equal to the probability [p(I | A)] of possessing that indicator state, conditional on the individual being age A, divided by the overall probability of possessing the indicator state, multiplied by the prior probability [p(A)$_{prior}$] of being age A. Note also that this approach does not yield a single estimate of age for a given indicator state, but rather it generates a posterior probability density distribution across all possible ages (the prior probability of age is also expressed as a probability distribution across all possible ages).

Derivation of prior probabilities of age

In Bayesian age estimation the prior probability of age [p(A)$_{prior}$] serves as a weighting function that influences the calculation of the posterior probability of age, but unlike traditional regression-based approaches it is the investigator who selects an appropriate set of prior probabilities rather than allowing the age structure of the reference series to influence the age-estimation procedure. There are several alternatives in arriving at a decision on the most appropriate prior probability to use in any particular case.

One procedure is to assume a uniform prior probability across all age categories, a so-called 'uninformative prior' (Bocquet-Appel, 1986; Konigsberg and Frankenberg, 1992: 239). In this case Bayes' theorem gives:

$$p(A \mid I) = \frac{p(I \mid A)}{\int [p(I \mid A)]}$$

(Konigsberg and Frankenberg, 1992: 239)

Under the assumption of uniform prior probability of age, the probability of age given the state of the indicator [p(A|I)] is equal to the probability of the indicator given the age category, divided by the unweighted integral across all age categories of the conditional probabilities of the indicator given age.

The uniform prior can be used when no other information is available on which to judge the selection of a prior age distribution. However, in most natural populations there is an uneven distribution of individuals across age categories, and the age-specific probability of death also varies, and therefore the assumption of a uniform prior probability of age at death in the target sample is often unwarranted. As an alternative to using a uniform prior probability of age, fixed model age structures taken from model life tables, from historically documented age-at-death profiles or from hazard functions can be used as a source of prior probabilities. The simplest realistic age distributions to use in this context are the attritional mortality distribution, the catastrophic mortality distribution, and an intermediate profile consisting of a mixture of the attritional and catastrophic profiles.

Using a set of informative (i.e. determined, but non-uniform) priors, the probability of age given the state of an indicator $[p(A|I)]$ is:

$$p(A \mid I) = \frac{p(I \mid A) \times p(A)_{model}}{\int [p(I \mid A) \times p(A)_{model}]}$$

where the values of $p(A)_{model}$ are taken from the age structures or hazard functions and the values of $p(I|A)$ are, as usual, taken from the reference series of known-age and indicator status.

A third alternative to using uniform priors or model priors is to estimate the prior probabilities of age in the target sample from the distribution of target sample indicator states. Konigsberg and Frankenberg (1992) described a maximum likelihood estimation method for deriving the prior probabilities of age in this way, and the approach has since been formalised as part of the 'Rostock Manifesto' for age estimation in palaeodemography (Hoppa and Vaupel, 2002).

Prior probabilities of age derived from the target sample indicator states are used in the same way as the model age structures were in the equation above:

$$p(A \mid I) = \frac{p(I \mid A) \times p(A)_{target}}{\int [p(I \mid A) \times p(A)_{target}]}$$

where $p(I \mid A)$ is taken from the reference-series and $p(A)_{target}$ is obtained from the target sample indicator states by fitting an age distribution using maximum likelihood methods (see Table 4.2).

Table 4.2 *Options for the selection of prior probabilities of age in Bayesian age estimation.*

Prior probabilities	Derivation	Applications
Uniform	$p(A) =$ constant for all ages	Individual skeletal remains with no contextual information
Attritional	Model life-table mortality schedules/hazard models	Samples of normative burials from community cemeteries
Catastrophic	Model life-table living-population schedules	Homicides, mass disasters, human rights violations
Target Sample Estimation	MLE estimation for target sample age indicators	'Rostock Manifesto' age estimation

4.4.3   *Evaluative studies of Bayesian methods in age estimation*

Konigsberg and Frankenberg (1992) applied a form of Bayesian age-estimation, with maximum likelihood estimation of target sample age structure, to several morphological age indicators, including the McKern and Stewart pubic-symphysis ageing system, cementum-annulation counts in teeth and cranial-suture closure in the skulls of rhesus macaques. Each of their target samples was generated synthetically by taking a model age distribution and then assigning age-indicator states to the model age distribution according to the likelihoods of indicator given age in the appropriate reference series. Konigsberg and Frankenberg demonstrated that the age distributions for the target samples could be recovered accurately even in cases where the age distributions for the target sample and the reference series differed substantially.

Lucy et al. (1996) used data from a reference series of teeth from known age individuals in order to calculate posterior probabilities of age by Bayesian methods. Prior probabilities of age were taken from the reference-series age structure, and posterior probabilities of age were then calculated by combining the likelihoods of the separate age indicators. The

Table 4.3 *Distribution of femoral-head trabecular involution in a reference series of 422 adults of known age and in a target sample of 96 prehistoric skeletons from Loisy-en-Brie. Data are taken from Konigsberg and Frankenberg (2002), after Bocquet-Appel and Bacro (1997).*

| Age (years) | Femoral-head trabecular involution stages | | | | | |
	I	II	III	IV	V	VI
23–	8	19	30	7	1	0
30–	2	18	43	25	1	0
40–	0	6	29	27	5	1
50–	0	2	26	37	13	0
60–	0	0	9	28	9	1
70+	0	0	9	38	20	8
Loisy-en-Brie	2	8	31.5	40.5	12	2

accuracy of the results was established by comparing the known ages of the individuals in the reference series with the medians of the age distributions estimated for the same specimens using the Bayesian procedure. Inspection of the results presented in Lucy et al. (1996: 193) suggests that the distribution of age estimates derived by their Bayesian procedure replicates closely the age structure of the reference series, as might be expected since the prior probabilities of age were obtained directly from the age distribution of the reference series. Further examples of parametric Bayesian age estimation are described in Konigsberg et al. (1997), Konigsberg and Frankenberg (2002) and in the collection of papers from the Rostock workshops published in Hoppa and Vaupel (2002). Simpler, nonparametric Bayesian methods using contingency tables have been presented by Chamberlain (2000) and Gowland and Chamberlain (2002).

One problem that has emerged in the use of maximum likelihood methods for estimating target sample age distributions is that the estimations can converge on unrealistic age distributions if they are not constrained by a mortality model. Table 4.3 reproduces the distribution of femoral-head

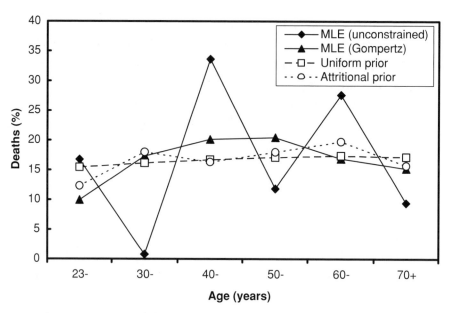

Figure 4.9 Estimated distribution of age at death for Loisy-en-Brie, using an unconstrained Maximum Likelihood Estimation (MLE) method (diamonds), a Gompertz hazard model MLE method (triangles) and the nonparametric Bayesian method of Chamberlain (2000) using uniform priors (circles) and attritional priors taken from Coale and Demeny 'West' female Level 2 model life tables (squares) priors. The unconstrained MLE method results in a highly irregular, multimodal mortality profile, whereas the other methods generate smooth mortality profiles.

trabecular involution in a reference series of 422 adults of known age at death and in a target sample of prehistoric skeletons from Loisy-en-Brie, France. The data are taken from Konigsberg and Frankenberg (2002), based on the dataset originally presented by Bocquet-Appel and Bacro (1997).

Konigsberg and Frankenberg (2002) calculated the age distribution in the Loisy-en-Brie target sample using two maximum likelihood estimation (MLE) methods: the first simply determined the proportions of individuals in discrete age categories that maximised the likelihood of obtaining the observed indicator states, while the second method fitted a two-parameter Gompertz mortality model to achieve the same objective. The results of these alternative methods are shown in Figure 4.9, alongside the age distributions obtained from the same data with the nonparametric method of Chamberlain (2000), using uniform and attritional prior probabilities of age. The unconstrained MLE method generates a highly irregular, multimodal mortality profile which is *a priori* unlikely to represent the true age structure of the prehistoric target sample. The best-fitting Gompertz hazard model MLE, and the nonparametric calculations using uniform and attritional priors, all generate relatively smooth mortality profiles which differ markedly from the results obtained using the unconstrained MLE.

4.4.4   *Alternative ways of modelling likelihoods: transition analysis and latent traits*

In Bayesian age estimation the likelihoods (i.e. the probabilities of possessing a particular indicator state conditional on age, or $p(I \mid A)$) are usually expressed either as a contingency table of discrete probabilities for each age/indicator category, or as a series of continuous probability functions against age for each indicator state. An alternative approach to determining these likelihoods is to model the timing of transitions between discrete adjacent indicator states, so that it is the age-specific probability of having completed the transition between one state and the following state that forms the basis of the likelihood: this approach is termed 'transition analysis' (Boldsen et al., 2002; Konigsberg and Herrmann, 2002). The approach assumes that changes between indicator states are unidirectional and that individuals only change between immediately adjacent indicator states at any given transition (Boldsen et al., 2002: 82), which are reasonable assumptions for most skeletal indicators. In transition analysis the transition probabilities are modelled using either logistic or probit regression, and the calculations can be adapted to consider multiple age indicators.

A 'latent-trait' approach has also been developed to account for the fact that when estimating age from multiple indicators it is strictly incorrect to assume that each indicator provides independent information about age. Indicators are inevitably intercorrelated, not solely through their collective dependence on age, but also because individuals vary in their rates of ageing (Holman et al., 2002). The assumption underlying latent-trait analysis is that each individual has their own, hidden (concealed, or 'latent') rate of ageing and because this factor, designated the 'latent trait', affects all age indicators simultaneously it is partially responsible for the intercorrelations among the age indicators. Although the latent trait is not directly observable, its effects can be modelled either by assuming that it has an effect on the average time between transitions in indicator states in an individual ('accelerated failure time model') or that it changes the individual's transition probabilities in a systematic way ('proportional hazard model').

4.4.5   Perinatal age estimation from long bone length

The diaphyseal lengths of the long bones are frequently used to estimate the age at death of perinatal (late-fetal and early-infant) skeletons, particularly in archaeological assemblages in which the developing tooth crowns are usually not sufficiently well preserved to allow age to be assessed. Traditionally, age estimation from fetal bone length has been carried out using regression equations obtained from inverse regressions of gestational age on bone length in known-age reference series. As long bone lengths are positively and approximately linearly correlated with age in perinatal skeletons these inverse regressions appear to give relatively precise age estimates with standard errors of around 2 to 3 weeks (Scheuer et al., 1980; Sherwood et al., 2000: 309). However, inverse regression methods are inappropriate when the intention is to obtain the age structure of a sample of perinatal skeletons, as the variation around the regression line is inevitably discarded when such estimates are compiled (see e.g. results presented in Owsley and Jantz, 1985, and in Mays, 1993).

An alternative method for estimating gestational age from skeletal long bone length using a nonparametric Bayesian method has been described by Gowland and Chamberlain (2002, 2003). Table 4.4 shows the distribution of femur length given age in a reference series of known-age fetal and perinatal skeletons (data are taken from Maresh and Deming, 1939; Maresh, 1955; Fazekas and Kósa, 1978; Scheuer et al., 1980, and Sherwood et al., 2000).

Table 4.4 *Diaphyseal length of femurs in known-age individuals. The cells contain the number of individuals in the reference series samples with a given age and bone length. Gestational ages are in weeks post-conception, lengths are in millimetres.*

Age	Femur diaphyseal length (mm)																
	10–	15–	20–	25–	30–	35–	40–	45–	50–	55–	60–	65–	70–	75–	80–	85–	90–
16	1	6	7	–	–	–	–	–	–	–	–	–	–	–	–	–	–
18	–	–	4	12	2	–	–	–	–	–	–	–	–	–	–	–	–
20	–	2	4	4	14	2	–	–	–	–	–	–	–	–	–	–	–
22	–	–	3	1	6	12	1	–	–	–	–	–	–	–	–	–	–
24	–	–	–	1	1	11	9	1	–	–	–	–	–	–	–	–	–
26	–	–	–	–	–	3	7	6	1	–	–	–	–	–	–	–	–
28	–	–	–	–	–	1	3	11	–	–	–	–	–	–	–	–	–
30	–	–	–	–	–	1	–	9	4	2	–	–	–	–	–	–	–
32	–	–	–	–	–	–	–	–	3	6	–	1	–	–	–	–	–
34	–	–	–	–	–	–	–	–	–	4	5	2	–	–	–	–	–
36	–	–	–	–	–	–	–	–	–	–	4	2	2	–	–	–	–
38	–	–	–	–	–	–	–	–	–	–	2	2	7	3	2	–	–
40	–	–	–	–	–	–	–	–	–	–	–	2	10	28	7	–	–
42	–	–	–	–	–	–	–	–	–	–	–	2	7	18	15	–	–
44	–	–	–	–	–	–	–	–	–	–	–	–	3	14	18	5	–
46	–	–	–	–	–	–	–	–	–	–	–	–	–	4	20	35	14
48	–	–	–	–	–	–	–	–	–	–	–	–	–	1	7	10	15

Table 4.5 *Posterior probabilities of gestational age given femur length, assuming uniform prior probabilities of age. Gestational ages are in weeks post-conception, lengths are in millimetres.*

	Femur diaphyseal length (mm)																
Age	10–	15–	20–	25–	30–	35–	40–	45–	50–	55–	60–	65–	70–	75–	80–	85–	90–
16	1.0	.85	.50	—	—	—	—	—	—	—	—	—	—	—	—	—	—
18	—	—	.22	.73	.12	—	—	—	—	—	—	—	—	—	—	—	—
20	—	.15	.15	.17	.56	.06	—	—	—	—	—	—	—	—	—	—	—
22	—	—	.13	.05	.27	.38	.04	—	—	—	—	—	—	—	—	—	—
24	—	—	—	.05	.05	.35	.37	.03	—	—	—	—	—	—	—	—	—
26	—	—	—	—	—	.13	.39	.21	.10	—	—	—	—	—	—	—	—
28	—	—	—	—	—	.05	.19	.43	—	—	—	—	—	—	—	—	—
30	—	—	—	—	—	.05	—	.33	.41	.11	—	—	—	—	—	—	—
32	—	—	—	—	—	—	—	—	.49	.55	—	.13	—	—	—	—	—
34	—	—	—	—	—	—	—	—	—	.33	.42	.24	—	—	—	—	—
36	—	—	—	—	—	—	—	—	—	—	.46	.33	.22	—	—	—	—
38	—	—	—	—	—	—	—	—	—	—	.12	.17	.38	.11	.08	—	—
40	—	—	—	—	—	—	—	—	—	—	—	.06	.19	.36	.10	—	—
42	—	—	—	—	—	—	—	—	—	—	—	.06	.15	.26	.23	—	—
44	—	—	—	—	—	—	—	—	—	—	—	—	.07	.21	.29	.14	—
46	—	—	—	—	—	—	—	—	—	—	—	—	—	.03	.17	.53	.30
48	—	—	—	—	—	—	—	—	—	—	—	—	—	.02	.14	.33	.70

Although Mays (2003: 1698) has criticised this reference dataset for its alleged high dispersion of femur length, this assertion is unwarranted as the average standard deviation of femur length controlling for age in the combined data from these studies is in fact less than 5mm (which is the size of the length categories employed in the analysis). Using these data the posterior probabilities of gestational age, given femur length, were calculated in a contingency table using the Bayesian procedure described in Section 4.4.2 above.

These posterior probabilities (Table 4.5) were then used to estimate age at death in a sample of 284 perinatal infant skeletons from Romano-British archaeological sites (Gowland and Chamberlain, 2002). Figure 4.10 shows that when compared to the inverse regression method, the Bayesian estimation method using uniform priors generated a broader distribution of ages at death with less evidence of the perinatal deaths being clustered sharply in the interval 38 to 40 gestational weeks. Gowland and Chamberlain (2003) present tables for estimating gestational age from the lengths of all major long bones, using either a uniform prior probability of age or a model prior probability distribution based on the age structure of a large sample of recorded perinatal deaths.

4.4.6   Age estimation and catastrophic mortality profiles

Attritional mortality can be considered the default mortality pattern for most populations under most circumstances, whereas catastrophic mortality in which the risk of death is high in all age categories is unusual, because a population subjected to repeated catastrophic episodes would rapidly decline to extinction. As discussed in Section 3.7 above, mortality in epidemics and in violent conflicts can generate catastrophic mortality profiles in which the age pattern of deaths mirrors the age structure of the living population. Catastrophic profiles have been recovered from skeletal assemblages from mass graves associated with outbreaks of bubonic plague (Margerison and Knüsel, 2002; Signoli et al., 2002; Dutour et al., 2003; Gowland and Chamberlain, 2005). Figure 4.11 shows the distribution

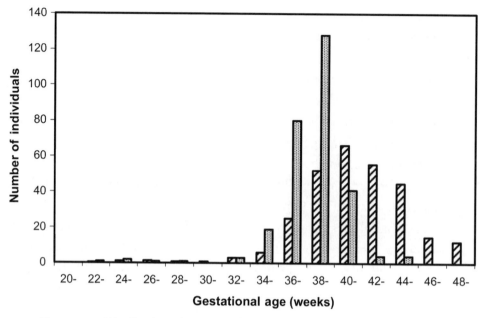

Figure 4.10   Distribution of gestational ages estimated from the diaphyseal lengths of femurs in 284 infant skeletons from Romano-British sites. Diagonal shading represents the distribution obtained from a Bayesian estimation method using uniform prior probabilities (see Gowland and Chamberlain, 2002 for details), the stippled shading represents the results obtained using a regression equation from Scheuer et al. (1980).

of age at death in 70 adult skeletons from the London Royal Mint cemetery which contained victims of the 'Black Death' plague of AD 1348–50. The ages have been estimated from the distribution of pubic-symphysis states using nonparametric Bayesian estimation, with catastrophic priors taken from the living-age profile of a stable model population with $e_0 =$ 30 (Gowland and Chamberlain, 2005). For comparison, also shown is the age distribution obtained from 27 skeletons from the Towton battlefield cemetery (Boylston et al., 2000), calculated from their pubic-symphysis indicator states in the same manner as for the Royal Mint site. Both samples show the high proportions of young-adult deaths characteristic of catastrophic mortality profiles, with the age at death distribution for the Royal Mint site agreeing well with the distribution of deaths in historically documented outbreaks of bubonic plague (see Figure 3.13). The Towton

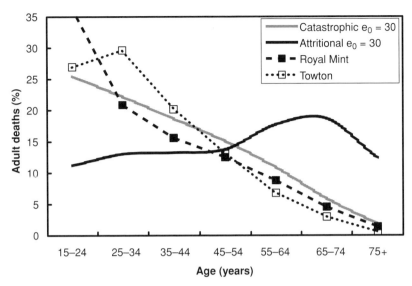

Figure 4.11 Distribution of adult ages at death for two catastrophic skeletal assemblages: the Royal Mint site cemetery (dashed line) and the Towton mass grave (dotted line). Age distributions were estimated from observations of the pubic symphysis using a nonparametric Bayesian estimation procedure described by Gowland and Chamberlain (2005). The distributions of ages of living individuals (catastrophic profile) and deaths (attritional profile) in a model population with average life expectancy at birth of 30 years ($e_0 = 30$) are also shown.

sample has been interpreted as a group of combatants, and nearly all of the skeletons exhibited fatal perimortem trauma, but the presence of a substantial proportion of older adults in the sample is more characteristic of non-combatant mortality (see Figure 3.14).

Boylston et al. (2000: 53) have suggested that combatants in medieval warfare may have been older than in modern conflicts, and further investigation of this possibility through analysis of other battlefield skeletal assemblages is desirable.

4.4.7 Prospects for the future

The Rostock workshops on palaeodemography, held in 1999 and 2000 at the Max Planck Institute for Demographic Research in Rostock, Germany, achieved a consensus on procedures for estimating age at death from skeletal remains and the 'Rostock Manifesto' advocated the application of Bayesian and maximum likelihood methods to problems of palaeodemographic estimation (Hoppa and Vaupel, 2002). It is likely that it will take a number of years for the recommendations of the Rostock Manifesto to be implemented as it requires all traditional age estimation techniques to be reappraised and there are still relatively few accessible skeletal collections of individuals of known-age at death.

4.5   ESTIMATION OF POPULATION NUMBERS FROM ARCHAEOLOGICAL DATA

4.5.1   House sizes and floor areas

Methods for estimating population size from the floor area of dwelling space have been reviewed by Hassan (1981) and by Kolb (1985). A widely cited study is by Naroll (1962), who analysed 18 globally distributed sedentary societies and proposed an approximate average ratio of 10m² of roofed space per person, a value that has since achieved such wide currency that it has been termed 'Naroll's Constant' (Brown, 1987). The estimates of space occupancy per person for individual settlements in Naroll's dataset varied between very wide extremes, but the notion that there may be some modal value for residential space use by villagers has been supported by similar, though generally lower, figures derived from several ethnographic studies. These include average values of 7–10m² of roofed area per person for Iranian rural village households (Le Blanc, 1971; Kramer, 1982), 6.5m² per person for lowland South American aboriginal villages (Curet, 1998), 6.1m² per person for Mesoamerican agricultural households (Kolb, 1985) and 5.3m² per person in New World multifamily dwellings (Casselberry, 1974). As might be expected, considerably smaller estimates of 2–4m² per person have been calculated for barrack room living space in military installations (Kardulias, 1992). In applying these kinds of formulae to archaeological evidence it is important to distinguish habitation space from storage and livestock-housing space, and to take into account the proportion of buildings or rooms that were occupied at any given time. Stratigraphic information about the relative ages of houses is essential as a settlement may be occupied for a longer time period than the use-life of any of its constituent dwellings.

An alternative approach to estimating population numbers from settlement data is simply to multiply the number of identified households by an estimate of average household size (Schacht, 1981). As outlined in Section 3.2.3 above, ethnographic estimates of household size in agricultural communities converge on a narrow range of values, and by assuming a reasonable central value for the numbers of individuals per household (e.g. a median value of 5) some of the difficulties associated with accurate measurements of dwelling space can be mitigated.

4.5.2   Settlement sizes

In archaeological field investigations it is often difficult or impossible to determine the area of dwelling space, but the overall spatial extent of a settlement can usually be discerned in a straightforward manner from the spatial distribution of cultural material. The estimation of population size from settlement area is not straightforward as there appears to be an allometric relationship between population and settlement size, with the allometric exponent varying for different classes of settlement (Wiessner, 1974). Wiessner proposed the formula:

$$\text{Area} = \text{constant} \times (\text{population})^{b}$$

where the exponent takes the values $b = 2$ for open camps, $b = 1$ for enclosed or defended villages and $b = {}^{2}/_{3}$ for urban communities.

For open settlements the exponent of 2 indicates that settlement area increases as the square of population size: according to Wiessner (1974) this is because dwellings in open camps tend to be organised circumferentially around a central area, so that doubling the number of dwellings doubles the diameter of the village and increases the settlement area by a factor of four. In enclosed villages the areal density is expected to remain constant and settlement area then increases in direct proportion to the size of the population. In urban communities population density tends to increase with increasing population size, leading to an exponent of less than one.

The hypothesis that the settlement area of hunter-gatherer camps increases in proportion to the square of population size has been corroborated by an extensive comparative study of Australian aboriginal settlements which showed that maximum residential density in these hunter-gatherer communities decreased markedly as the size of the community increased (Fletcher, 1990). For village-, town- and city-scale settlements, unfortunately, there is no single constant that can be employed to transform settlement area into population size, as there appear to be wide inter-regional variations in the spatial density of human settlement (Kramer, 1982: 163). Typical modal densities derived from ethnographic data are around 30 persons/ha for highland agricultural villages in Mexico (De Roche, 1983); 100 to 150 persons/ha for nucleated Iranian villages (Kramer, 1982; Sumner, 1989); 130 persons/ha for pre-industrial urban centres (Storey, 1997) and 160 persons/ha for lowland South American aboriginal villages (Curet, 1998). Much higher estimated densities, ranging from about 250 to 1200 persons per hectare, have been derived from analyses of housing floor plans in some ancient cities (Postgate, 1994; Storey, 1997). A regular relationship between the area of Roman military camps and the size of the forces that occupied them has been proposed by Richardson (2000), and the calculated density of 127 persons/ha for these camps is close to the value derived above for non-industrial settlements.

4.5.3   Site catchments and resource utilisation

In site catchment analysis the spatial extent of an area utilised by a community is delineated and characterised in terms of its economic potential (Vita-Finzi and Higgs, 1970; Dennell, 1980). By determining the amount and nature of resources available to the occupants of a site, and by assuming self-sufficiency and isolation from adjacent communities, an estimate of site carrying capacity (maximum sustainable-population size) can be arrived at. The approach is perhaps better suited to modelling the use of natural resources by hunter-gatherer communities, who fit the criteria of isolation and self-sufficiency better than do most pastoral or agricultural communities (Dennell, 1980: 7–8), but a detailed example of the modelling of carrying capacity in prehistoric agricultural communities of Eastern Arizona has been presented by Zubrow (1975). Some other examples of the use of site catchment analysis in the investigation of demographic hypotheses are cited by Roper (1979: 134).

Quantitative measures of the production and consumption of resources, including amounts of food residues, quantities of building materials, artefact counts and volumes of storage pits, can also be used as proxies for population size (Hassan, 1981; Schact, 1981). As with estimates of population size from settlement evidence, the analysis of resource utilisation can be useful for determining long-term rates of population growth, which is an essential prerequisite for the accurate application of stable population models in palaeodemography. However, even when it can be established that population numbers are proportional to the amounts of material remains, it is not easy to convert material evidence of resource usage into actual population numbers, and this approach is therefore better suited to the analysis of change through time of relative rather than absolute population size. Schiffer (1976: 59) formally proposed a 'discard equation' that allows the size of a community to be inferred from the volume of discarded artefacts, but this requires knowledge of artefact use-life as well as the quantity of undiscarded artefacts in use per person at any given time during the period of site occupation (Gallivan, 2002).

Ashton and Lewis (2002) used estimates of the rate of stone artefact accumulation in river terrace gravels in the Middle Thames Valley, England, as a proxy for human population density in the Lower and Middle Palaeolithic. By mapping the areas of the gravel deposits and the historical extent of quarrying and urban development they were able to control for variations in preservation and artefact collection intensity, and their results showed a marked decline in human activity (expressed as artefacts per unit area per year) between Oxygen Isotope Stage 10 (350,000 years ago) and the start of Oxygen Isotope Stage 5 (140,000 years ago).

Marsden and West (1992) used a range of proxies for the scale of human activity in order to monitor changes in population size in Roman

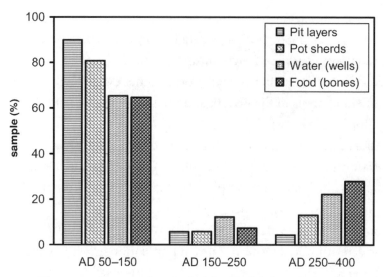

Figure 4.12 Proxy archaeological data indicating relative changes in
population size in Roman London between AD 50 and AD 400 (data taken
from Marsden and West, 1992). The numbers of dated layers in rubbish pits,
dated ceramic sherds, numbers of wells and total weights of animal bones
from dated contexts all indicate a decline in human activity after 150 AD.

London from AD 50 to AD 400 (Figure 4.12). Assuming equal probabilities of discovery and recording of remains from different time periods,
they assessed the number of excavated rubbish pits, the number of dat-
able ceramic types ('spot dates'), the number of wells (as an indicator
of demand for water supply) and the weight of animal bones from three
successive time periods within the period of interest. Across all classes of
resource there was evidence for a decline in human activity after AD 150,
interpreted as a reduction in the size of the urban population after that
date. Marsden and West provided some control over the possibility of differential survival of material from different time periods by also assessing
residual Roman pottery recovered from much later depositional contexts:
the chronological distribution of residual pottery sherds confirmed that the
volume of discard was higher in the earlier Roman than in the later Roman
periods.

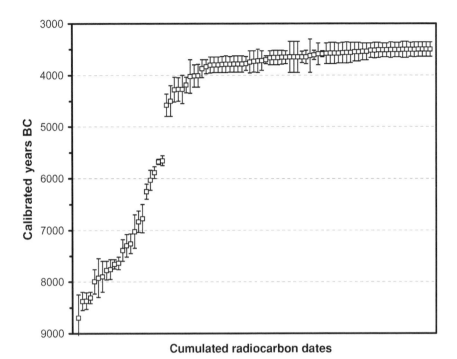

Figure 4.13 Distribution of ^{14}C dates obtained on human bone from
Mesolithic and early Neolithic archaeological sites in Britain between 9000
and 3500 calibrated years BC. The data points are calibrated dates on single
skeletons plus and minus two standard errors (the data are taken from
Blockley, 2005). The frequency of dates declines after 6500 BC, coinciding with
the isolation of Britain from continental Europe by rising sea levels, and there
is a gap in the distribution of dates between 5600 and 4600 BC. The transition
from foraging to farming in the early Neolithic occurs in Britain around 4000
BC and is accompanied by a marked increase in the frequency of dates,
reflecting the much greater number of excavated Neolithic burial sites
compared to those of Mesolithic foragers.

4.5.4 Monitoring population size from radiocarbon dating distributions

Radiocarbon (^{14}C) determinations are used frequently by archaeologists
to establish the dates of stratigraphic deposits and to obtain direct dates
on artefacts and animal and human remains. In many regions of the world
there exist extensive datasets of ^{14}C dates and these provide a new resource
for modelling past population processes (Figure 4.13). Subject to certain

important assumptions, the frequencies of dates on cultural material and deposits can serve as a proxy for human activity (Rick, 1987), and discontinuities in ^{14}C distributions can be interpreted as reflecting changes through time in the distributions and densities of human populations. The accumulation of large databases of radiocarbon determinations, together with the increased precision and smaller sample requirements of accelerator mass spectrometry (AMS) dating, has widened the opportunity to utilise ^{14}C data in palaeodemographic analysis.

This approach has been used to investigate the contraction and extinction of the last Neanderthal population in Europe (Pettitt, 1999; Bocquet-Appel and Demars, 2000), the re-colonisation of Europe by humans after the last glacial maximum (Housley et al., 1997; Gamble et al., 2004; Fort et al., 2004), the initial human colonisation of the Americas (Anderson and Faught, 2000) and mid-Holocene demographic extinction and population replacement on the southeastern Pampas of Argentina (Barrientos and Perez, 2005). One interesting finding that has emerged from the study of Pleistocene colonisation events in Europe based on ^{14}C distributions is that the rate of advance of Palaeolithic hunters was relatively rapid and comparable with rates established for the later spread of Neolithic agriculture in the same continent (Housley et al., 1997; Fort et al., 2004).

Evolutionary and genetic palaeodemography

5.1 AGE AND SEX STRUCTURE IN ANIMAL POPULATIONS

5.1.1 *Natural animal populations*

Demographic profiles and life tables have been obtained for many animal species, using data obtained either from the age structure of stable and stationary animal populations or from recorded ages at death of representative samples of animal mortality. Many vertebrate species resemble humans in possessing a two-component age-specific attritional mortality pattern, with a juvenile phase where initially high mortality rates decline rapidly as the animal matures and a post-juvenile phase where mortality rates either stabilise or increase slowly but progressively with age (Deevey, 1947; Caughley, 1966: 916, see also Figure 5.1).

In most mammals the sex ratio at birth averages close to unity, though in some species there may be considerable variance in the sex ratio of offspring, especially in polygynous animals (Trivers and Willard, 1973). Mortality rates can also differ substantially between the sexes, with male animals often experiencing higher age-specific mortality as a result of reproductive competition and exclusion of subordinate males from access to resources. As a result the adult sex ratio in wild-animal populations is frequently biased towards females (Collier and White, 1976).

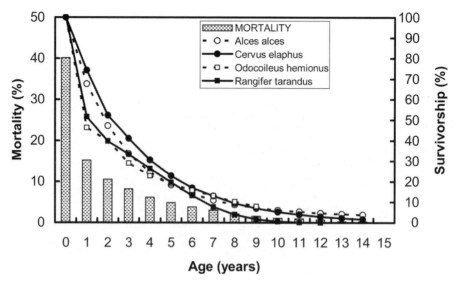

Figure 5.1   Survivorship curves (right-hand axis) and average mortality (left-hand axis) for natural cervid populations. Data are from Boer, 1988 (*Alces alces*, moose, females only); Lyman, 1987 (*Cervus elaphus*, red deer/wapiti/elk, average of males and females); Taber and Dasmann, 1957 (*Odocoileus hemionus*, black-tailed deer/mule deer, average of males and females) and Leader-Williams, 1988 (*Rangifer tarandus*, reindeer/caribou, average of males and females). The mortality profile is essentially unimodal with the peak of the distribution in the first year of life, and with little evidence of senescence as shown by a lack of increased mortality in the oldest age categories.

5.1.2   Demography of non-human primates

Humans and non-human primates exhibit the general mammalian demographic pattern of high infant mortality, followed by decreasing mortality in the juvenile years and increasing age-specific mortality rates in later adulthood (Dunbar, 1987; Gage, 1998). Among wild primate populations male age-specific mortality often greatly exceeds that of females, as in many species the males are more likely to emigrate from their natal group and are therefore exposed to a higher risk of predation during periods of relative isolation during the period of transition between groups. Adult-male primates are also more likely to experience fatal trauma as a result of intragroup conflict, for example during competition for reproductive access to females. Mortality rates tend to be lower in captive groups of primates than in wild populations of the same species (Gage, 1998).

Rates of physical and behavioural development and maturation vary markedly between the major taxonomic groups within primates, as shown by comparative studies of skeletal growth (Smith, 1989; Smith et al., 1994; Watts, 1990) and by the documentation in captive and wild primates of life-history variables such as gestation length, age at weaning, age of sexual maturity and longevity (Harvey et al., 1987). As a broad generalisation, maturation times are approximately doubled in great apes compared to Old-World monkeys, and are increased again by a factor of 1.5 between great apes and modern humans. For example, mothers' age at first birth is typically 4 to 6 years in cercopithecine monkeys, 12 years in the chimpanzee *Pan troglodytes*, and around 18 years in modern humans (Harvey et al., 1987: 184–185). As expected on theoretical grounds (Cole, 1954), variations in life-history characteristics and developmental timing have an appreciable effect on rates of mortality and fertility in primate populations.

Figure 5.2 shows survivorship curves derived from published model life tables calculated for cercopithecine monkeys (sexes combined), *Pan troglodytes* females and modern *Homo sapiens* females. The cercopithecine survivorship curve summarises the mortality pattern observed in eight large populations of *Macaca* and *Papio*, one of which was a wild population while the others were either provisioned or fully captive groups (Gage and Dyke, 1988, 1993). Gage and Dyke fitted a three-component (five-parameter) Siler mortality model to each of the cercopithecine datasets, and the means of the parameter values were then used to generate a set of age-specific mortality rates from which an instantaneous life-table model was constructed. The average life expectancy at birth (e_0) for this life table is 15.8 years. The *Pan troglodytes* model life table was calculated by similar methods using data from three major captive-breeding colonies (Dyke et al., 1995). The average life expectancy at birth for the captive chimpanzee populations is 29 years, a value that is much larger than average female life expectancy in wild chimpanzee populations (Hill et al., 2001) but is close to the average female life expectancy for wild orang-utans (Wich et al., 2004).

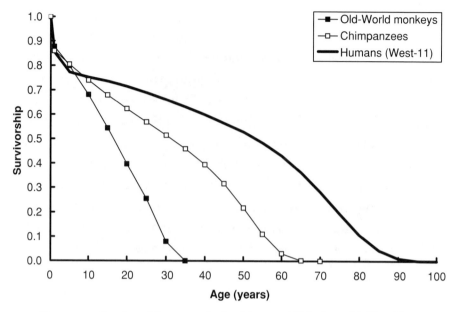

Figure 5.2   Survivorship curves derived from published model life tables calculated for cercopithecine monkeys (sexes combined), *Pan troglodytes* females and modern *Homo sapiens* females. Data are taken from Gage and Dyke (1988, 1993); Dyke et al. (1995) and Coale and Demeny (1983).

The *Homo sapiens* survivorship curve is taken from the Level 11 'West' model life table for females, in which average life expectancy at birth is 45 years (Coale and Demeny, 1983). This model life table has a level of mortality that is intermediate within the modern human range of variation, and it was chosen because it represents a population with average life expectancy approximately three times that of cercopithecines and 1.5 times greater than chimpanzees.

These separate survivorship curves can be transformed from a strictly chronological scale to a common developmental scale by converting the ages of the non-human primates to their biological equivalent in human years. The cercopithecine age scales were therefore multiplied by 3, and those of *Pan troglodytes* by 1.5, to achieve comparability with the human data (Figure 5.3). When compared in this fashion it can be seen that when differences in rates of maturation and longevity are controlled for, the

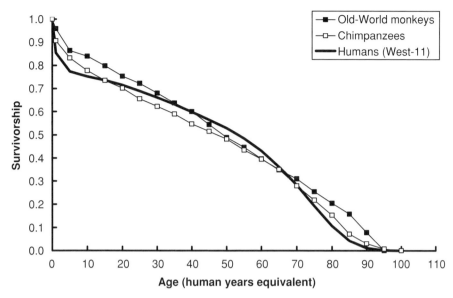

Figure 5.3 Survivorship curves for cercopithecine monkeys, *Pan troglodytes* females and modern *Homo sapiens* females, compared to a common developmental scale (data sources as in Figure 5.2).

mortality experience of cercopithecines and chimpanzees is broadly comparable with that of a human population experiencing intermediate levels of mortality. The non-human primate survivorship curves appear slightly 'flatter' (i.e. less inflected) than the human curve, suggesting that age-specific mortality rates in the non-human primates may be relatively lower at very young and very old ages compared to the pattern in the 'West' model human population.

5.2   DEMOGRAPHY OF FOSSIL HOMINIDS

5.2.1   *Maturation times and longevity in fossil hominids*
The human fossil record extends back 6 million years to a time around the cladogenetic event when the evolutionary lineages leading to living African apes (gorillas, chimpanzees and bonobos) divided from the lineage leading to modern *Homo sapiens*. Human palaeontologists now recognise

about fifteen fossil species within the human evolutionary lineage (Collard, 2003), and these are referred to here collectively by the term 'hominids', an expression that is being replaced in some quarters by the term 'hominins' in recognition of the fact that ancestral human species cluster taxonomically at the tribal rather than the family level. Hominids are characterised by a suite of unique morphological, physiological and behavioural adaptations that include bipedal posture and locomotion, encephalisation, enhanced manual dexterity and changes in life-history variables.

Despite previous suggestions that the relatively rapid growth rates demonstrated by anthropoids might also characterise fossil hominid species (Weidenreich, 1939), the first studies of the demography of fossil hominids assumed that rates of maturation in fossil hominids resembled those of modern *Homo sapiens* (McKinley, 1971; Mann, 1975). Since that time considerable evidence has accumulated in favour of the hypothesis that both tooth crown-formation times and tooth-eruption times were accelerated in fossil hominids when compared to modern *Homo sapiens* (Beynon and Dean, 1988; Smith and Tompkins, 1995; Dean et al., 2001; Ramirez Rozzi and Bermúdez de Castro, 2004). Chronological data for anterior dental-crown formation, based on counts of perikymata, and data for the eruption of the first permanent molar in four hominid species are shown in Table 5.1. These results show that fossil species of hominids matured in about two thirds of the time taken for modern humans to reach maturity, a developmental pattern that is closer to that observed in great apes such as the chimpanzee. If demographic parameters such as longevity and age-specific survivorship closely track rates of maturation in primates, then developmental schedules potentially provide a useful source of demographic data for extinct hominid species.

There has been some speculation concerning the selective advantages of delayed maturation in humans. Evolutionary theory predicts that individuals usually benefit from reproducing with a minimum of delay, so that under normal circumstances there should be selective pressure *against* delayed maturation. Suggested explanations for delayed maturation fall

Table 5.1 *Average duration (in years) of the formation of the permanent upper central incisor I^1 and the chronological age of gingival emergence of the permanent lower first molar M$_1$ in modern* Homo sapiens *and fossil hominid species. Data are taken from Beynon and Dean (1988), Stringer et al. (1990), and Dean et al. (2001).*

Species	I^1 crown formation	M$_1$ emergence
Homo sapiens	4.7	6.1
Homo neanderthalensis	3.1	–
Homo ergaster	2.9	4.0
Australopithecus	3.5	3.5
Paranthropus	2.5	3.3

into two categories: first, if early reproduction is penalised (either through higher infant mortality, or through early maturation compromising the parent's future survival and fertility) then there will be benefits to delaying the onset of maturation and the initiation of reproduction (Stearns, 1992; Gage, 1998). An alternative explanation is that there can be advantages to maturing slowly if the resulting increase in body size (or perhaps in the enhancement of social skills) provide increases in total fertility rate that more than compensate for reduced survival of individuals to age of first reproduction (Charnov, 1993; Hill and Kaplan, 1999).

Estimation of longevity in fossil hominids is rendered difficult by the problem of assessing adult age at death in extinct species. This problem has been addressed by Caspari and Lee (2004) who examined the ratio of older to younger adults in dental samples of fossil hominids representing australopithecines, early *Homo*, Neanderthals and early Upper Palaeolithic *Homo sapiens*. The authors assessed age at death by seriation of occlusal dental wear and they standardised the interspecific differences in timing of maturation and rates of ageing by using double the estimated age of eruption of the third permanent molar as the demarcation point between younger- and older-adult age categories. Caspari and Lee found that the proportion of older adults in their samples increased steadily from 10%

Table 5.2 *Numbers and proportions of old adults in mortality samples of australopithecines, early* Homo, *Neanderthals, and early Upper Palaeolithic* Homo sapiens *(Caspari and Lee, 2004), with comparable data from a West Level 1 model life table (Coale and Demeny (1983) and a wild chimpanzee life table (Hill et al., 2001). Fossil hominid data are numbers of individuals, life-table data are proportions of total deaths in population. Old adults are defined as individuals whose age is more than double the age at which skeletal maturity is achieved: following Caspari and Lee (2004) this is calculated as 15 years in modern humans and 12 years in chimpanzees.*

	Old adults	Young adults	Proportion of old adults (%)
Australopithecines	37	316	10
Early *Homo*	42	166	20
Neanderthals	37	96	28
Homo sapiens (EUP)	50	24	68
Homo sapiens (West 1)	30	10	75
Chimpanzees	25	16	61

in *Australopithecus* to 28% in *Homo neanderthalensis*, but there was an additional dramatic increase in the early Upper Palaeolithic when the proportion of older adults in the sample reached 68%, a value consistent with model life-table estimates for attritional deaths in high-mortality present-day human populations (Table 5.2).

5.2.2 *Demography of* Australopithecus *and early* Homo

Inferring population structure from palaeontological samples of skeletal remains is particularly fraught with difficulty, because the distribution of ages at death in a palaeontological assemblage not only reflects the age structure and age-specific mortality in the living population, but may also be unduly influenced by taphonomic and recovery biases. Taphonomic biases are those relating to the deposition and preservation of skeletal remains in the fossil record (including mortuary practices), while recovery bias includes human factors influencing the probability of detection and recovery of the remains. If taphonomic and recovery biases are important and significant confounding factors, then we might expect different depositional contexts to result in different apparent age structures in the hominid fossil record.

Early studies of the demography of the South African australopithecines noted that average estimated age at death was significantly lower in the 'robust' australopithecines *Paranthropus robustus* than in the 'gracile' australopithecines *Australopithecus africanus* (McKinley, 1971; Mann, 1975). Mann (1975: 71) discussed the competing explanations for the age difference between the taxa, and he discounted real underlying differences in survivorship in favour of taphonomic factors, including differences between the hominid sites in the quality of fossil preservation and the evidence for carnivore accumulation of fossils at Swartkrans, the principal source of robust australopithecine fossils.

In order to investigate taphonomic and recovery bias the numbers of hominid cranial and dental remains from some of the more productive hominid sites have been tabulated in terms of their proportions of adults and subadults. The age categories are defined approximately as in Trinkaus (1995), with the adult category corresponding to individuals with completed skeletal development (aged 18 years or more on a modern human developmental scale) and subadults including all individuals aged less than 18 years (Table 5.3).

The interesting feature of these distributions is that the samples recovered by surface collection at Hadar and Koobi Fora show a clear predominance of adults, whereas the material from excavated sites (including the East African site of Olduvai Gorge, and the remaining samples, which are all derived from cave excavations) generally have much higher ratios of immatures to adults, with the exception of the Sterkfontein *Australopithecus africanus* sample in which only 28% of indviduals are subadult. Thus the difference between the South African 'robust' and 'gracile' australopithecine age distributions, highlighted by the analyses of McKinley (1971) and Mann (1975), can probably be attributed to the underrepresentation of immature individuals in the 'gracile' australopithecine sample.

Table 5.3 *Proportions of subadults (defined as individuals with incomplete skeletal or dental development) in samples of fossil hominids. Sources of data – Koobi Fora: Wood, 1991; Hadar: Johanson et al., 1982; Kimbel et al., 1982; White and Johanson, 1982; Kimbel et al., 1994; Sterkfontein: Mann, 1975; Brain, 1981; Lockwood and Tobias, 2002; Swartkrans: Mann, 1975; Brain, 1981; Grine, 1993; Zhoukoudian: Weidenreich, 1939; Neanderthals: Trinkaus, 1995; Olduvai Gorge: Tobias, 1991; Atapuerca: Bermúdez de Castro et al., 2004.*

Site and species	Subadults	Adults	Subadults(%)
Surface collected sites			
Koobi Fora (*Homo*)	7	28	20
Koobi Fora (*Paranthropus boisei*)	10	29	26
Hadar (*Australopithecus afarensis*)	17	41	29
Excavated sites			
Sterkfontein (*Australopithecus africanus*)	22	56	28
Swartkrans (*Paranthropus robustus*)	79	80	50
Zhoukoudian (*Homo erectus*)	15	23	39
Neanderthals (*Homo neanderthalensis*)	106	100	52
Olduvai Gorge (*Homo habilis*)	13	6	68
Atapuerca (*Homo heidelbergensis*)	19	9	68

Although there are different ways of interpreting these data (in particular, the agents of accumulation of the hominid fossils are poorly known, and may vary between the fossil sites), the clearest distinction is between those sites investigated by surface collection as compared to those where the fossils were recovered by controlled excavation. Although different species are involved, it is improbable that *Paranthropus* would have had a markedly different age distribution between Koobi Fora and Swartkrans, and thus we can infer that the immature individuals are likely to have been depleted in the Koobi Fora sample. For the sake of argument, we can assume that a high proportion of subadults to adults represents the 'true' mortality distribution for these species, and that any marked deviation from a high proportion of subadults may indicate the influence of taphonomic bias.

Table 5.4 *Distributions of age at death in* Homo heidelbergensis *(Bermúdez de Castro et al., 2004) and* Homo neanderthalensis *(Trinkaus, 1995).*

Category (range in years)	Homo heidelbergensis		Homo neanderthalensis	
	N	%	N	%
Neonate (<1)	0	0	10	4
Child (1–4)	1	4	29	14
Juvenile (5–9)	0	0	30	15
Adolescent (10–19)	18	64	37	18
young adult (20–39)	6	21	80	39
old adult (40+)	3*	11	20	10

* includes those individuals listed as aged 35+ in Bermúdez de Castro et al. (2004)

5.2.3   Demography of Homo heidelbergensis *and* Homo neanderthalensis
The Middle Pleistocene site of Sima de los Huesos in the Sierra de Atapuerca (Burgos, Spain) has yielded an exceptionally large and well-preserved sample of hominid remains which are all assigned to the species *Homo heidelbergensis*. The Atapuerca-SH sample has been studied repeatedly from a demographic perspective (Bermúdez de Castro and Díez, 1995; Bermúdez de Castro and Nicolás, 1997; Bocquet-Appel and Arsuaga, 1999; Bermúdez de Castro et al., 2004). In the most recent of these analyses the mandibular, maxillary and dental remains from Atapuerca-SH were assigned to 28 separate individuals, and the ages at death of the fossils were estimated using modern human standards of age estimation (Bermúdez de Castro et al., 2004). The Atapuerca-SH sample is dominated by the remains of adolescents (aged 10–19 years, in terms of modern human skeletal development) and young adults (20–39 years), and there are few individuals assigned to the oldest-adult age category (Table 5.4, Figure 5.4). It is also notable that there is just one child under the age of 10 years in the Atapuerca-SH sample, in contrast to the age distribution in a pooled sample of *Homo neanderthalensis* where about one third of the sample are less than 10 years old (Trinkaus, 1995).

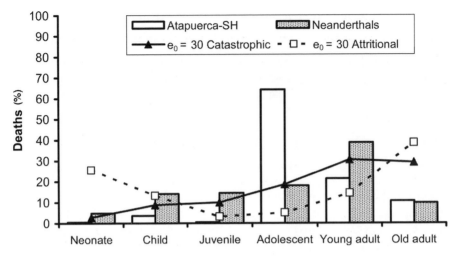

Figure 5.4   Age distributions in samples of *Homo heidelbergensis* and *Homo neanderthalensis* compared to the distributions of ages at death in catastrophic and attritional mortality profiles for modern humans. Data are taken from Bermúdez de Castro et al. (2004), Trinkaus (1995) and Coale and Demeny (1983).

The very high proportion of adolescents (64%) in the Atapuerca-SH sample exceeds the numbers expected even in catastrophic patterns of mortality, but it resembles the age distribution found in the collection of *Homo neanderthalensis* fossils from the site of Krapina, where 43% of the sample of 23 individuals were allocated to the adolescent age category (Trinkaus, 1995: 126). High proportions of adolescents have also been observed in other hominid samples, such as European Middle Pleistocene sites (Bermúdez de Castro et al., 2004) and at Olduvai Gorge (Tobias, 1991), so the pattern may not be unique to the Atapuerca assemblage. Bermúdez de Castro and Nicolás (1997) argued that the Atapuerca-SH age at death data should not be interpreted as either a natural attritional or a catastrophic mortality profile, because very high fertility rates would be required in order to sustain population numbers in the face of high mortality levels amongst pre-reproductive age individuals. Bocquet-Appel and Arsuaga (1999) observed that the age profile at Atapuerca resembles a catastrophic profile with the very young and very old individuals removed.

In consequence they suggest that the Atapuerca sample may have included primarily the more mobile members of a hominid community who were seeking to escape from a regional environmental crisis, and under this scenario the remains of the very young and the elderly from the hominid community might be expected to be located at a distance from the known Sima de los Huesos fossil site.

Trinkaus (1995) collated data on age at death for a sample of 206 Neanderthals (*Homo neanderthalensis*) from 77 sites in Europe and Asia. Age estimation was carried out using modern human standards of skeletal development and, for adult individuals, a combination of bone histological ageing, joint-surface metamorphosis and the Miles method for estimating age from dental wear. When compared to historically documented modern human attritional mortality profiles the Neanderthal sample shows underrepresentation of young children and old adults, and an excess of deaths in the adolescent and young-adult age categories (Table 5.4, Figure 5.4). Weighting of the data, so that each site makes an equal contribution to the total, had only a marginal effect in reducing the high level of adolescent mortality. Trinkaus invoked catastrophic mortality as a partial explanation of the high level of young-adult mortality in the Neanderthal dataset, and he explained the dearth of old-adult deaths as reflecting exclusion of this age category from the rock shelter and cave sites where the majority of Neanderthal remains have been recovered.

The predominance of young adults in the samples of *Homo heidelbergensis* and *Homo neanderthalensis* is quite unlike the pattern of attritional mortality in documented modern human populations and in chimpanzees, where it is usual for 40% or more of the adults to survive into the old-adult age category. The *Homo neanderthalensis* age profile provides a reasonably good match to a modern human catastrophic mortality profile, especially if we allow for some systematic underestimation of adult age at death in the hominid samples (Figure 5.4). Both Trinkaus (1995) and Bermúdez de Castro et al. (2004) argued that the techniques that they used for estimating age at death do not substantially underestimate the ages of adult individuals, but, as we have seen earlier, the traditional anthropological ageing methods do not generate realistic adult-age distributions for human populations and they generally give systematic underestimates of age when applied to older adult individuals.

A further difficulty with these datasets is that the subadult ages have been estimated by applying modern human standards of skeletal development, but as shown in Section 5.2.1 above it is probable that all fossil hominid species had accelerated dental maturation compared to modern humans. Allowing for this difference in dental maturation would have the effect of reducing all subadult chronological age estimates by approximately one third, although the relative distribution of individuals across developmental categories would remain the same.

5.3   HUMAN GENETIC PALAEODEMOGRAPHY

5.3.1   Genetic studies of present-day populations

With continuing advances in molecular biological methods there are increasing opportunities to investigate the demographic histories of populations through genetic analysis. In studies of present-day populations the geographical variations in the frequency of classical genetic markers (mainly variants in the structural genes encoded by nuclear DNA) have been used to reconstruct large-scale prehistoric population movements (Sokal et al., 1991; Cavalli-Sforza et al., 1994). Also useful in this regard are haploid genetic loci, including the maternally inherited mitochondrial DNA and the male-specific non-recombining parts of the Y chromosome (Donnelly and Tavaré, 1995; Harpending et al., 1993). These parts of the genome can be used to define distinct genetic lineages, with the divergence between the lineages being proportional to the time since the lineages shared a most recent common genetic ancestor. This allows the investigator to reconstruct the phylogenetic history of a group of related populations, and the divergence between populations may correspond to major demographic events such as large-scale migrations and colonisations (Goldstein and Chikhi, 2002).

Periods of rapid population expansion also leave a distinctive genetic signature, for example in the distribution of pairwise differences between the DNA sequences of individuals in a population and in the geometric patterns of lineage relationships (Harpending et al., 1998; Rogers, 1995; Richards et al., 1996; Forster, 2004). In a population that has undergone a substantial expansion of numbers through intrinsic growth (i.e. through fertility exceeding mortality) most of the genetic mutations in the population will have occurred post-expansion, in separate genetic lineages, and each mutation will thus be present in just one or two copies in the population. A pairwise comparison between the DNA sequences of individuals will show the effects of this in a narrow distribution of differences, and a phylogeny of genetic lineages will exhibit a 'starlike' topology in which the lineages radiate from a common ancestral sequence (Harpending et al., 1993; Rogers, 1995). In a population that is stationary or has increased only at a slow rate the proportion of shared ancestral mutations will be greater and the spread of pairwise sequence differences will be broader and often multimodal.

Comparisons of diversity in mitochondrial DNA and Y-chromosome DNA in the same populations have revealed a difference in the average transgenerational migration rate of the sexes, with the females having a history of much higher migration rates than males (Seielstad et al., 1998). This finding, which has been demonstrated separately among both African and European modern population samples, has been linked to the historical predominance of patrilocality among human populations, especially since the adoption of agriculture when communities became more settled and some lineages established their tenure on land through male-line inheritance. In patrilocal societies the women, rather than the men, migrate transgenerationally and, given equivalent effective population sizes, the sex-specific between-population genetic diversity is reduced in females relative to the diversity in the males of the same population.

Studies of genetic variation in the Y chromosome have revealed the male genetic contribution made by immigration from continental Europe into the British Isles during the early medieval period. These studies show close genetic affinities between the present-day populations of central England and northwest Holland, Germany and Denmark, consistent with large-scale immigration into England during the last 2,000 years (Weale et al., 2002). More detailed Y-chromosome studies suggest that the Danish and German migrants primarily settled in central and northern England and mainland Scotland, rather than in the regions of southern England that are traditionally viewed as the Anglo-Saxon heartland (Capelli et al., 2003).

5.3.2   *Genetic studies of ancient populations*

Studies of ancient DNA extracted from archaeological human remains have the potential to corroborate or refute hypotheses about population history, but the difficulty and expense of ancient-DNA analysis ensures that most published projects have had relatively small sample sizes, limiting the extent to which inferences can be made concerning ancient population genetics. Some of the most important ancient DNA results have been obtained from the skeletal remains of the extinct hominid species *Homo neanderthalensis.* Following the initial report of the recovery of mitochondrial DNA from the type specimen of *Homo neanderthalensis* from Feldhofer Cave, Germany (Krings et al., 1997), additional mtDNA sequences have been obtained from Neanderthal fossils from sites in Russia (Ovchinnikov et al., 2000), Croatia (Krings et al., 2000; Serre et al., 2004), Belgium (Serre et al., 2004), France (Serre et al., 2004; Beauval et al., 2005) and Spain (Laluela-Fox et al., 2005). All of the Neanderthal mtDNA sequences recovered in these analyses were different from mtDNA types present in living human populations, and comparisons of the mtDNA sequences suggest that the *Homo sapiens* and *Homo neanderthalensis* genetic lineages diverged between 365,000 and 853,000 years ago (Ovchinnikov et al., 2000).

An alternative source of genetic information about past populations is provided by morphometric analyses of skeletal remains, although the size, shape and structure of bones and teeth is only partly determined by the genome. A widely used measure of genetic diversity is F_{ST}, the proportion of total genetic variance that is attributable to differences between separate population groups. F_{ST} increases with increasing time since the initial divergence between the population groups, and increases faster when effective population sizes are small, but is decreased in proportion to the rate of migration between the groups because migration has the effect of reducing between-group genetic variance. F_{ST} is usually calculated directly from gene-frequency data (Reynolds et al., 1983; Cavalli-Sforza et al., 1994) but good proxies to F_{ST} can also be derived from craniometric data (Relethford, 1994) and from the frequencies of discrete skeletal morphological traits that have high heritabilities (Tyrrell and Chamberlain, 1998).

6

Demography and disease

6.1 DISEASE IN ARCHAEOLOGICAL POPULATIONS

6.1.1 Concepts and evidence of disease

Disease, illness and sickness

A contemporary dictionary definition of disease is *a disorder or want of health in mind or body: an ailment: cause of pain* (Schwarz et al., 1990). This broad but succinct definition summarises the widely held modern Western view that there is both a biological dimension to disease – the underlying organic disorder that perturbs the normal or optimal functioning of the individual – and a social or psychological dimension – the recognition and expression of the disorder as a discomforting or socially disvalued condition. From the theoretical perspective of medical anthropology, the term 'disease' is usually applied strictly to the biomedical abnormality or pathology, while 'illness' and 'sickness' are variably used to designate the individual consciousness and social recognition of the presence of an underlying disease condition (Young, 1982; McElroy and Townsend, 1996). These distinctions are important in understanding the occurrence and spread of diseases in populations, because individual and social responses to disease play a part in determining the overall frequencies of disease in communities and in the manner in which a society manages the burden of disease amongst its members.

In biomedical research that is directed primarily towards the understanding, control and treatment of ill-health, diseases are usually distinguished and classified according to their causative agents. These agents
include genetic abnormalities, parasitic and opportunistic infections
by microbial and invertebrate organisms, failures in physiological and
metabolic functions and external environmental agents including nutrition, climate and physical injury or trauma (Underwood, 2004). In historical and archaeological studies of ancient diseases these classifications
are often supplemented by considering specific organ systems that are
affected by disease, such as the synovial joints in the case of degenerative joint disease, and the teeth and surrounding structures in the case
of dental disease. As the soft tissues of the body are rarely preserved in
archaeological contexts, those diseases which leave a macroscopic, microscopic or chemical signature in the bones and the teeth have been the main
focus of palaeopathological research (Ortner and Putschar, 1985; Roberts
and Manchester, 1995; Aufderheide and Rodríguez Martín, 1998; Schultz,
2001). Increasingly researchers are turning to the methods of biomolecular
archaeology in order to detect disease organisms that only affect the soft
tissues of the body and therefore may not be evident from studies of human
skeletal remains.

Epidemiological concepts
Epidemiologists utilise two principal measures of disease frequency: *incidence*, which quantifies the rate of appearance of new cases of disease in a
population during a specified period of time, and *prevalence*, which measures the proportion of individuals in a population possessing the disease
at a given moment of time (Waldron, 1994). The applicability of these
alternative measures depends on the duration of the disease process. For
acute diseases of short duration, that terminate either in the death or the
recovery of the individual, measures of incidence are most appropriate,
whereas for chronic and irreversible disease conditions the prevalence of
the disease is the more suitable measure of disease frequency. In the study

of non-fatal infectious diseases which are transmitted amongst members of a population, further distinctions are made between the frequencies of susceptible, infected and immune (i.e. recovered infected) individuals, as the relative proportions of these numbers are key determinants of the patterns of disease transmission in the population (Anderson and May, 1991). Epidemiological data are usually stratified by age, and often by sex, because susceptibilities to both chronic and acute diseases are often strongly affected by these parameters (Coggon et al., 2003: 17).

Sources of evidence for diseases in past populations
Evidence relating to the occurrence and frequency of diseases in past populations includes descriptive historical materials such as texts, inscriptions and artistic representations; abnormalities observed in human skeletal remains and preserved soft tissues; biomolecular evidence in the form of host and pathogen genetic material, as well as biomolecules generated in immune responses; perturbations to demographic structures due to disease-related mortality; and artefactual evidence for medical and surgical treatment. Some of these sources of evidence point only to the physical presence of a disorder in an individual, and we often have no way of knowing how or even whether the disorder was perceived as an illness or recognised as an instance of sickness by the individual or by their community. Social perceptions of disease are complex and changeable, as was seen in the case of leprosy in the past and is true of present-day conditions such as physical disability, HIV infection and mental disease. Documents, iconography and evidence of treatment provide some indication of the social perception of disease in the past, while inferences can also be made about the way in which socioeconomic circumstances and living conditions, including hygiene, access to health care, wealth, diet, interpersonal violence and so on may have contributed to the incidence of disease in a population.

While macroscopic and microscopic studies of human skeletal remains provide a principal source of data about ancient-human disease, genetic evidence for the origins and history of disease obtained from ancient tissue samples is an increasingly important additional source of information (Zink et al., 2002). As the genomes of present-day humans and pathogens are catalogued and explored in ever greater detail, many genes that determine or influence disease expression in humans are being identified, and patterns of evolution and diversification of pathogens are being reconstructed. In some cases coalescent theory can be used to estimate the date of origin and timing of expansion of particular species and strains of pathogen (e.g. Brosch et al., 2002).

6.1.2   Infectious and epidemic diseases

Skeletal evidence

Palaeopathologists classify bone infections into specific infections, in which a particular disease organism causes a specific and therefore diagnostic response in the bone, and non-specific infections which produce generalised signs of inflammatory reaction to infection such as periostitis (inflammation of the periosteal membrane on the external cortical surface of the bone) and osteomyelitis (subcortical bone infection). In periostitis, inflammation of the periosteum leads to a form of hyperostosis with a characteristic thin porous layer of woven bone being deposited on the periosteal surface of the cortex of the affected skeletal element. After the infection has disappeared this periosteal deposit may become remodelled and eventually indiscernible as it becomes integrated with the bone cortex. In osteomyelitis, pus-forming bacteria invade the medullary cavity, causing destruction and cavitation of the surrounding bone which responds by forming a thick deposit of irregular new bone around the site of infection (see Figure 6.1). Often the infection is drained by a small hole or sinus that connects the inside of the bone to the surrounding soft tissues. When infectious pathogenic organisms are introduced into bone they are often persistent, especially if foreign material is present, as may occur after a penetrating injury or a compound fracture (Underwood, 2004: 713).

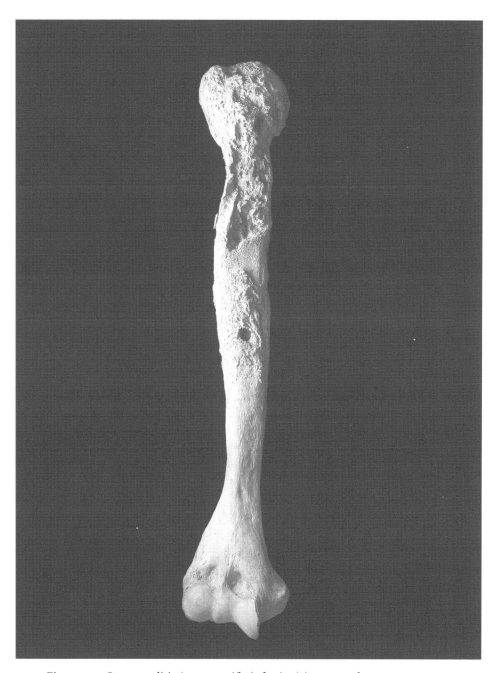

Figure 6.1 Osteomyelitis (non-specific infection) in an arm bone.

A small number of infectious diseases produce specific changes in the external appearance of bones, and these conditions therefore can be diagnosed with reasonable accuracy in archaeological skeletons (Aufderheide and Rodríguez Martín, 1998). Such diseases include leprosy, tuberculosis, and some of the treponemal diseases (including venereal syphilis). In leprosy the organism *Mycobacterium leprae* can cause diagnostic skeletal changes in the bones of the face as a direct result of bacterially induced bone resorption and in the bones of the hands and feet as a secondary consequence of bacterial invasion of the peripheral nervous system, which causes loss of sensation in these vulnerable extremities.

Tuberculosis in humans is usually caused by either *Mycobacterium tuberculosis*, derived from inhalation of infected aerosolised droplets expelled by other infected humans, or by *Mycobacterium bovis*, derived from the ingestion of infected meat or milk or by inhalation of droplets from animals. Tuberculosis infection causes osteomyelitic changes at characteristic skeletal sites in a small proportion of infected individuals. These lesions are found most frequently in the spine, hips or knees, with involvement of the vertebral bodies eventually leading to collapse and kyphosis of the spine in a condition called Pott's disease. Pulmonary tuberculosis may also cause periostitis on the visceral surfaces of the ribs, although the mechanism for this inflammatory response is unclear. Infection by *Treponema pallidum* causes the disease conditions known as venereal syphilis, bejel (endemic syphilis) and yaws. Primary skeletal sites for venereal syphilis are the cranial vault and face, especially the frontal and nasal areas, and the long bone diaphyses. Cranial lesions are typically star-shaped and erosive ('caries sicca') with aggressive periosteal reaction and bone remodelling around the margins of the lesions.

Biomolecular evidence

Significant new evidence for the evolution of infectious organisms and for their occurrence in ancient-human remains has been provided by the analysis of biomolecules that are specific to particular species and strains of pathogen. These methods are particularly useful in palaeopathological analysis because they potentially enable disease to be detected when no skeletal changes are visible (either because the disease does not affect bone, or because the individual's immune response prevented the infection from causing skeletal changes, or because the individual died before bone changes occurred). Biomolecular methods also allow the evolutionary history of an infective agent to be tracked through time, either by sequencing ancient DNA or by phylogenetic analysis of extant disease strains.

The *Mycobacterium tuberculosis* complex of organisms includes nearly identical strains of bacilli that infect humans (*M. tuberculosis*, *M. africanum* and *M. canettii*), primates (*M. simiae*), rodents (*M. microti*) and a broad range of animals including domesticated cattle (*M. bovis*). *M. tuberculosis* was thought to have evolved from *M. bovis* following the origins of cattle domestication, a hypothesis supported by the low frequency of *M. tuberculosis* in skeletal remains from pre-agricultural populations (Aufderheide and Rodríguez Martín, 1998) and by the fact that the host spectrum for modern *M. bovis* is much broader than that of *M. tuberculosis*. This highly plausible animal-to-human transmission hypothesis has been refuted by analysis of variable genomic regions in DNA from worldwide samples of human and animal *M. tuberculosis* complex strains (Brosch et al., 2002). These studies have shown that the strains of *Mycobacterium* typically infecting humans retain ancestral genetic sequences, whereas the *M. microti* and *M. bovis* strains that are found in animal hosts represent later-derived descendants of the *M. tuberculosis* complex.

Mycobacterial DNA appears to survive well in ancient remains, and the existence of short diagnostic DNA marker sequences, such as the IS6110 repetitive element, has allowed the identification of the presence of *M. tuberculosis* and *M. africanus* in the skeletons and dried soft tissues of individuals up to 5,400 years old (Crubézy et al., 1998; Konomi et al., 2002; Zink et al., 2004). *M. tuberculosis* can also be detected in ancient remains using mycolic acid biomarkers (Gernaey et al., 2001). Other microbial pathogens claimed to have been detected in skeletal remains using biomolecular methods include bubonic plague (Drancourt et al., 1998), Corynebacterium infection (Zink et al., 2001), Chagas disease (Guhl et al., 1999), leprosy (Rafi et al., 1994), malaria (Taylor et al., 1997) and venereal syphilis (Kolman et al., 1999).

The importance of these new approaches to the diagnosis of ancient infectious disease lies in their potential to detect a much greater proportion of infected cases, including individuals who died before they developed diagnostic lesions in their skeletons. However, these results must be interpreted with caution as many reports of the successful detection of ancient pathogens using ancient DNA fail to satisfy stringent authentification criteria including replication of results in independent laboratories, tests of biochemical preservation in the tissue samples and quantification of original amounts of target DNA template (Cooper and Poinar, 2000). For example, the discovery of *Yersinia pestis* DNA in archaeological skeletons reported by Drancourt et al. (1998) has not been corroborated, despite exhaustive attempts by two independent laboratories to replicate their results (Thomas et al., 2004), likewise *Treponema pallidum*, the organism responsible for venereal syphilis, has been shown not to survive in syphilitic skeletal remains from archaeological sites only a few hundred years old (Bouwman and Brown, 2005).

Demographic evidence

Although all human populations are potentially vulnerable to bone infections, increases in the prevalence of infections have been noted in various world regions following a transition from foraging to farming subsistence practices (Table 6.1, see Larsen, 1997: 85–87). This pattern of change is believed to have been caused by the increased opportunities for transmission of infectious disease in the higher-density populations and sedentary communities associated with agricultural food production.

Epidemics of infectious diseases that are associated with high case fatality have the potential to generate assemblages of human skeletons with catastrophic mortality profiles (see Chapter 4 above) as well as contributing

Table 6.1 *Changes in prevalence of selected health conditions at the transition from foraging to farming in seven world regions. The symbols +, − and o indicate increased, decreased and unchanged prevalences respectively. −/+ indicates that there is conflicting evidence from different studies within a given world region. Data are taken primarily from Larsen (1997).*

	North America	Central America	South America	Europe	West and South Asia	East Asia	North Africa
Dental caries	+		+	+	+	+	+
Dental enamel hypoplasia	+	−	+		+	−	
Anaemia*	−/+			+	+		+
Infections of bone	+	+	+	+		+	o
Degenerative joint disease	−/+			−	−		
Growth retardation	−/+	−/+	o	+	+		+

*cribra orbitalia and porotic hyperostosis

to longer-term declines in population numbers. In early modern Britain several lethal infections including bubonic plague, cholera, smallpox and typhus had mortality rates of between 20% and 80% of infected cases (Roberts and Cox, 2003) and these diseases together with other infections were in part responsible for a series of mortality crises and temporary, localised episodes of population decline during this period (Scott and Duncan, 1998). Additional mortality effects of infectious disease can be discerned in the seasonal patterns of deaths observed especially in large urbanised communities. Records of the month of death obtained from tombstone inscriptions in Imperial Rome showed a single marked peak of mortality occuring in late summer and early autumn (Figure 6.2), a time of year when infectious diseases affecting the respiratory and digestive systems (Shaw, 1996) as well as malaria (Scheidel, 1996) had their greatest impact on the population.

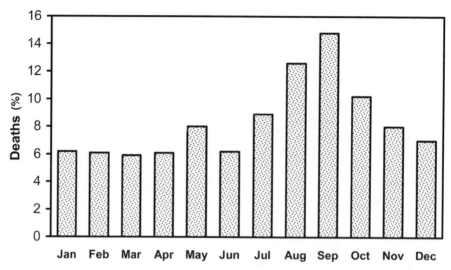

Figure 6.2   Season of mortality in Rome, based on 2125 Christian tombstone inscriptions dating from the third to the sixth century AD. The data are taken from Scheidel, 1996, Figure 4.1, after Nordberg, 1963.

Much larger effects of the introduction of infectious disease on population numbers have been proposed in the case of the catastrophic decline in numbers of Native Americans following contact with European settlers from the sixteenth to nineteenth centuries (Verano and Ubelaker, 1992). Although the pre-contact size of the aboriginal population of North America has been a topic of persistent debate (Daniels, 1992; Ubelaker, 1992) and the exclusive role of communicable disease in post-contact population decline has been questioned (e.g. Thornton, 1997), there is broad agreement that epidemics of infectious disease introduced by European immigrants caused devastating morbidity and loss of life amongst non-immune native populations.

6.1.3   Metabolic, nutritional and deficiency diseases

Skeletal evidence
Nutritional deficiency diseases have been a particular focus of interest among archaeologists as these diseases may reflect both dietary practices

and differential social access to particular types of foods (Stuart-Macadam, 1989). The maintenance of normal bone structure depends on adequate nutrition and on the presence of essential vitamins in the diet. Two principal hormones, somatotrophin or growth hormone produced by the pituitary gland and thyroxin produced by the thyroid are essential for normal bone growth: severe deficiency of either of these hormones results in a stunting of growth or dwarfism. Another essential requirement for bone growth is Vitamin D, and a deficiency of this vitamin is seen in poorly nourished individuals who are not exposed to sunlight, such as occurred in children in industrial cities in Britain in the nineteenth and early twentieth centuries. Chronic vitamin-D deficiency gives rise to rickets in children and osteomalacia in adults (Ortner and Mays, 1998). Vitamin C (ascorbic acid) is an essential dietary component that is plentiful in fresh, raw foods but is rapidly depleted and destroyed by storage and cooking. A chronic deficiency of vitamin C gives rise to scurvy, which can cause observable skeletal changes including periodontitis and periostitis from subperiosteal haemorrhage (Janssens et al., 1993; Ortner and Ericksen, 1997; Ortner et al., 1999; Ortner et al., 2001). Scurvy is associated with famine, but also used to occur in individuals such as sailors who did not consume fresh fruit or vegetables for extended periods of time. Vitamin-C deficiency persists as a clinical condition in modern societies, amongst especially older individuals who do not consume a balanced diet that includes fresh fruit and vegetables.

Anaemia is the condition of damaged or depleted erythrocytes (red blood cells), which have the essential function of transporting oxygen to the living tissues of the body. Anaemia can result from a variety of causes, including genetic defects in haemoglobin production, dietary iron deficiency, deficiency of vitamin B12, and blood loss from trauma, menstruation or internal parasite load. The body's main response to chronic anaemia is to attempt to increase the number of circulating red blood cells by activating the erythropoietic cells which are found in the red marrow inside the ribs, sternum, vertebrae, skull, pelvic girdle and the long bone metaphyses. In children, the increase in the amount of red marrow leads to an expansion of the marrow-containing spongy bone at the expense of the overlying cortex and in the skull this can manifest itself as porotic hyperostosis of the cranial vault and cribra orbitalia, the distinctive porosity found in the roofs of the orbital cavities (see Figure 6.3; also Stuart-Macadam and Kent, 1992). An increase in anaemia may have occurred in populations adopting agriculture, as sedentism may lead to increases in the burden of intestinal parasites, especially in children.

Osteoporosis is a condition of abnormal loss of bone mineral, caused either by metabolic imbalance of bone resorption and formation ('primary osteoporosis') or as a result of specific nutritional or pathological causes ('secondary osteoporosis'). Loss of bone mineral is a natural concomitant of the ageing process, and the term osteoporosis is reserved for conditions where the depletion is sufficiently advanced to render the sufferer liable to bone fracture. Trabecular bone has higher rates of turnover and is therefore more liable to manifest osteoporosis-related fracture, particularly in load-bearing areas such as the proximal femur, distal radius and the vertebral bodies. Mineral loss can be quantified by measurement of bone mineral density or by microscopic study of the morphology of bone trabeculae (Brickley, 2000).

Dental evidence

Teeth provide evidence of diet both through the patterns of wear on the occlusal surfaces and through the dental pathology that arises from particular dietary practices (Hillson, 2000). The principal pathological conditions of the teeth that have been linked to diet are dental caries, periodontal disease and abscesses, and the consequent ante-mortem tooth loss which is detectable through remodelling of the dental alveoli.

Dental caries is a condition in which bacterial fermentation of dietary carbohydrates, especially sugars, on the surface of the teeth produces acids that cause localised demineralisation and cavitation of the enamel and underlying dentine. The disease progresses and accelerates as these cavities trap food particles allowing a larger population of cariogenic bacteria to

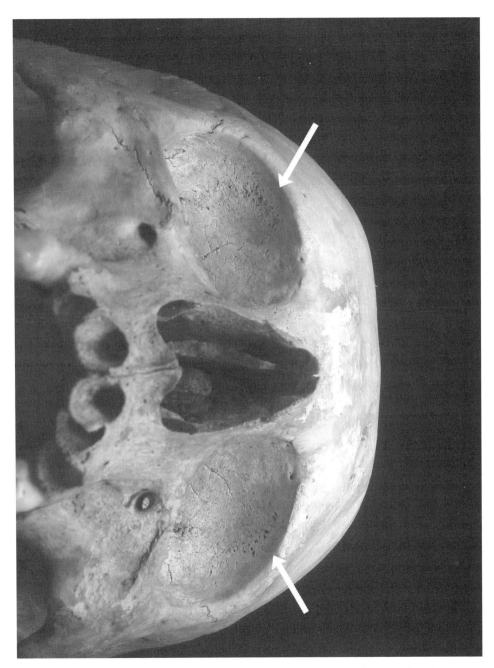

Figure 6.3 *Cribra orbitalia*, manifest as pitting (arrowed) in the bone forming the roofs of the orbital cavities.

develop: eventually the crown of the tooth is destroyed. The prevalence of dental caries is directly associated with the amount of soft and sticky carbohydrates in the diet, and the condition is usually uncommon in pre-agricultural communities (Larsen et al., 1991). Periodontal disease is recognised archaeologically by progressive resorption of the margins of the tooth sockets exposing the roots of the teeth. This alveolar resorption has been linked to chronic gum disease (gingivitis) and to the accumulation of bacteria-containing plaque on the teeth, although non-dietary factors including oral hygiene may contribute to its development (Hildebolt and Molnar, 1991).

Dental calculus, or tartar, is a mineralised deposit that accumulates on the non-occlusal surfaces of the teeth above the gum line. It is usually white, yellow or light brown in colour and consists of the calcified remnants of food debris and bacterial plaque. Dental calculus is more common in individuals who consume a high protein/low carbohydrate diet, but its prevalence is also influenced by dental-hygiene practices (Lieverse, 1999). Finally enamel hypoplasia appears as transverse lines and pits on the non-occlusal enamel surface and is the result of a temporary stress-related disturbance to enamel growth during the period when the tooth crown was calcified. Dietary deficiencies and episodes of illness during childhood are known to produce these enamel defects, and their presence has been used to infer conditions of life in past populations (Goodman and Rose, 1991).

Chemical and biomolecular evidence
All living organisms ultimately derive their constituent chemical elements from the environment, but the position or 'trophic level' of each organism in the food web determines the proximate source of its diet and hence the extent to which it incorporates the metabolic products of other organisms. The lighter elements such as carbon, nitrogen and oxygen have stable isotopes that behave sufficiently differently during chemical reactions to allow them to be used as dietary tracers. Stable-isotope ratios in the atmosphere and the oceans are relatively constant, but growing and respiring organisms

are discriminatory in their uptake, metabolism and excretion of these light stable isotopes, and this allows the identification of the sources of different foods and the trophic levels occupied by past populations. The atmosphere contains a small proportion of the stable isotope of nitrogen ^{15}N, which increases in concentration in animal tissues at successively higher trophic levels providing a means of estimating the contributions of different food sources in human diets. For example, nursing infants obtain their proteins from their mother's milk, and the isotopic fractionation that occurs when these proteins are incorporated into the infant's skeleton provides a means of determining the timing and duration of weaning (see Figure 6.4, also Katzenberg et al., 1996). The proportion of a stable isotope of carbon, ^{13}C, in the diet is influenced by the biomes from which the dietary constituents are obtained (e.g. terrestrial versus marine) and by the photosynthetic metabolic pathways utilised by different plants. The analysis of the stable-isotope composition of collagen in bones and teeth has made a substantial contribution to knowledge of prehistoric human diet and to understanding of the timing and extent of past dietary transitions (Katzenberg, 2000; Sealy, 2001).

6.1.4   Neoplastic and congenital diseases

Skeletal evidence
Neoplastic conditions detectable in skeletal remains include primary bone tumours, which originate from disorders of bone-cell activity, and secondary tumours (metastases) which spread from neoplastic growths that originate in non-bone tissues. Primary bone tumours are further subdivided into the relatively common benign conditions, such as osteoma and osteochondroma, in which the growth is localised to the tissue of origin, and the rarer malignant or invasive conditions, such as osteosarcoma and multiple myeloma. Secondary bone tumours can either cause bone resorption (osteolytic lesions) or bone deposition (osteoblastic lesions), or a combination of both processes. In addition, some soft-tissue tumours

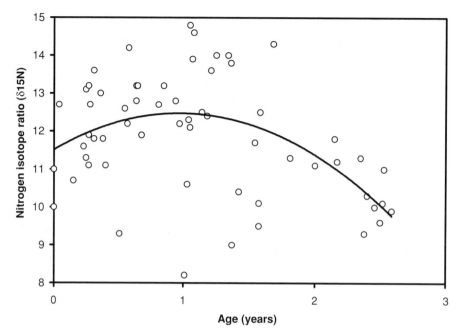

Figure 6.4   Nitrogen isotope ratios in infant skeletons from a 19th-century population in Canada (data taken from Herring et al., 1998: Table 3). The $\delta15N$ values reach a maximum in infants aged around 1 year. In older individuals the values decline towards adult levels as bone incorporates amino acids derived from the post-weaning diet. The curve is a quadratic trendline fitted through the data ($r^2 = 0.24$, $p < 0.001$).

that grow next to bone, for example meningiomas, can induce a response in the adjacent skeletal tissues.

Evidence for tumours or neoplastic disease is relatively rare in the archae-ological record, although such cases may be under-reported (Anderson, 2000: 217). The most common instances of neoplastic disease in human skeletal material are ivory ('button') osteoma (Eshed et al., 2002) and osteo-chondroma, a benign bone tumour which arises usually in adolescents dur-ing the period of maximal bone growth. In present-day populations the most common clinical bone cancers are secondary or metastatic tumours that develop from a primary tumour located elsewhere in the body, but these tend to occur in older adults and frequencies in skeletal assemblages will therefore depend on the age structure of the sample.

Table 6.2 *Modern frequencies of congenital diseases (per thousand live births) that are diagnosable from skeletal remains. Data from Anderson (2000), Roberts and Cox (2003) and Underwood (2004). Note that the frequency of Down's Syndrome may have been lower in the past because of its dependency on maternal age.*

Disease	Frequency
Spina bifida aperta or cystica (in both stillbirths and live births)	2.5
Congenital dislocation of the hip	1.0
Cleft palate	0.8
Down's syndrome	0.7
Hydrocephaly	0.4
Achondroplasia	0.1
Osteogenesis imperfecta	0.025

Congenital or genetically determined abnormalities affecting the skeleton occur at low incidence among present-day populations (Table 6.2), and this accounts for the infrequency with which they tend to be encountered in the archaeological record (Brothwell, 1967). For example, achondroplasia is a rare condition in which the limb bones are severely shortened leading to dwarfism while the skull develops normally. Although achondroplasia only occurs today in about 1 in 25,000 live births, a surprising number of achondroplastic dwarfs have been identified among excavated skeletal remains, and there is supporting documentary and artistic evidence that these people were valued and enjoyed wealth and status in some past societies (Brothwell, 1967: 432; Dasen, 1988). A similar association of short stature and high social status has been recognised in the case of an Upper-Palaeolithic acromesomelic dwarf from Italy (Frayer et al., 1987).

Biomolecular evidence

In principle, genetically determined abnormalities could be detected through the analysis of DNA extracted from ancient skeletal remains, but in practice efforts to achieve this have been hampered by the fact that most heritable abnormalities result from mutations in functionally coding nuclear DNA, which exists only as single copies within the nucleus of each cell and is inherently difficult to study with ancient-DNA methods. Pusch et al. (2004) attempted to amplify and sequence lengths of DNA from short statured skeletons believed to have suffered from achondroplasia, dating from between 1,000 and 5,000 years ago. The sequence targeted was a 164-bp stretch of the fibroblast growth factor receptor 3 gene (FGFR3), which has a single base transition in individuals affected by achondroplasia. The diagnostic mutation was identified in DNA from two out of four positive ancient cases that were tested, but unfortunately the achondroplasia mutation was also detected in ancient-DNA sequences obtained from several healthy control individuals. Pusch et al. (2004) attributed this anomalous result to artificial sequence alterations generated by their PCR method when testing damaged ancient DNA.

Other reported successes in the biomolecular identification of congenital disease include the detection of the mutation in the β–globin gene responsible for sickle cell anaemia in DNA extracted from bone in a recent autopsy case (Faerman et al., 2000) and the use of in-situ hybridisation to detect chromosomal abnormalities in a 250-year-old stored human-tissue sample (Hummel et al., 1999). These results are encouraging, but it remains to be demonstrated that genetic mutations can be successfully identified in DNA obtained from archaeological material.

6.1.5   Trauma and homicide

Skeletal evidence
Trauma refers to an acute physical injury or wounding of living tissues. When hard tissues are stressed beyond their breaking point they will fracture, and the shape of the fracture surface provides information about the strength and direction of the applied force. In addition to acute forceful injury, bone can also fracture from repeated low levels of physical stress, or from moderate stress to a pre-existing weakness such as a region of

osteoporotic bone. Trauma may also cause dislocation of the joints, and if these injuries are left untreated they eventually cause changes to the articular surfaces of the bone. Bone responds to trauma with a natural repair mechanism. Bone fragments are initially bound together by fibrous tissue, then the smaller bone fragments are removed by cell-mediated resorption and new bone mineral is deposited around the fibrous tissue to form a bony callus enclosing the site of the fracture. The callus reaches its greatest size a few months after the initial injury, and the callus is then subjected to remodelling until the original strength and rigidity of the bone is restored.

Successful union of fractures depends on the bone fragments being immobilised, otherwise movement between the fragments will delay or prevent the healing process. Well-healed fractures show a continuous, smooth join between the broken ends of the bone, but in archaeological material there is frequently some shortening and deformity as a result of poor alignment between long bone fragments. Fractures may have short- and long-term complications. Fractures sites may communicate with the surface of the skin, allowing entry of bacteria and infection of the fracture site. Healed fractures that result in shortening and bone deformity may lead to abnormal stresses being placed on the adjacent joints, which in turn may result in degenerative joint disease.

Although the nature of the applied force can often be determined from the geometry of the fracture surface, it is not always possible to distinguish accidental from intentional injury in the analysis of bone fractures. There is considerable variation amongst cultures in the nature of interpersonal conflict, but injuries to the cranium such as fractures of the nasal bones are considered more likely to be caused by interpersonal violence (Walker, 1997). Mid-shaft fractures of the ulna and radius are widely interpreted as 'parrying' injuries sustained in defending the body against a deliberate blow from a weapon but these can also occur as a consequence of accidental trauma (Jurmain, 1999: 218). Linear incisions from sharp-edged weapons, penetrating injuries from projectiles and massive blunt-force trauma are characteristic of injuries sustained in violent interpersonal conflict (Larsen, 1997).

Demographic evidence for conflict and homicide

Recent publications have testified to an increasing recognition of the social importance of violent conflicts in prehistory (Martin and Frayer, 1997; Carman and Harding, 1999; Gilchrist, 2003; Parker Pearson and Thorpe, 2005). Archaeological evidence for collective violence is diverse but problematic in its interpretation, with contentious issues arising from the difficulty of distinguishing between symbolic and physical functions of artefacts interpreted as weapons, and in determining the extent and nature of any interpersonal violence that may have taken place. Material-cultural evidence for violent conflict includes weaponry and armour, defensive fortifications and iconographic representations of battle, while biological anthropology can supply evidence from the patterns of physical trauma visible on human skeletal remains.

Victims of traumatic violence are often assumed to be combatants, but this assumption has rarely been scrutinised, and only recently has there been any attempt to examine palaeodemographic evidence for prehistoric conflict (Bishop and Knüsel, 2005). The latter authors examined demographic data from prehistoric skeletal assemblages with high frequencies of perimortem violent trauma, previously interpeted as victims of warfare. They used a modified juvenility index (the ratio of deaths aged 7 to 16 years to the deaths aged 17 years and above in a given sample) and the proportion of females amongst the adult deaths as estimators of the demographic composition of their samples (Table 6.3). For the European prehistoric sites, the age and sex profiles are more consistent with attacks on non-combatant communities, rather than combatant mortality, as shown by the substantial proportions of juveniles and female adults in most of the samples (Maiden Castle is the only site analysed that did not have any subadult skeletal material). The estimated 95% confidence intervals for the juvenility index in contemporary non-combatant populations ranged from 0.35 to 0.71, and the confidence intervals for the expected proportion of adult females ranged from 26% to 61% (Bishop and Knüsel, 2005), values that encompass most of the prehistoric samples included in the study. The results of their analysis show that attacks on demographically

Table 6.3 *Proportions of juveniles and of adult females in skeletal assemblages from European prehistoric conflict sites. Data are from Bishop and Knüsel (2005) and Bouville (1980).*

Site	Location	Date	Number of individuals	Juvenility index $(d_{7-16} \div d_{17+})$	Adult sex ratio (% females)
Cadbury	Britain	Iron Age	92	0.39	33
Danebury	Britain	Iron Age	102	0.73	31
Maiden Castle	Britain	Iron Age	32	0.00	31
Roaix	France	Chalcolithic	71	0.47	n/a
Schletz	Austria	Neolithic	67	0.20	33
Talheim	Germany	Neolithic	34	0.28	44
Ofnet	Germany	Mesolithic	83	0.77	62

representative groups of non-combatants could account for the mortality profiles in these mass-mortality assemblages.

Infanticide

Infanticide is the deliberate killing or fatal neglect of a live-born child within a defined time interval following birth, typically during the first year of life. Infanticide may be carried out for a variety of reasons, including control of fertility, elimination of sickly or physically disabled offspring, manipulation of family sex ratios, ritual sacrifice or social pathology (Dickeman, 1975; Scrimshaw, 1984). The fact that infanticide was and is widespread and often socially sanctioned amongst human communities has led to proposals that the killing of infants by their care-givers may be an adaptive behaviour under certain conditions. Such circumstances include (i) when there is uncertainty about the genetic relatedness between the care-giver and the dependent offspring, (ii) when the likelihood is low that the offspring will survive to reproductive maturity, and (iii) when the responsible care-giver has better, alternative uses for the investment that the dependent offspring will require to survive to maturity (Daly and Wilson, 1984: 488–89). Ethnographic studies of foraging and subsistence farming communities show that younger children, female children, twins and children who have lost one or both parents are often at greater risk of being killed by members of their own community (Daly and Wilson, 1984; Hill and Hurtado, 1995).

Archaeological identification of infanticide has been primarily through identifying the demographic signature of perinatal mortality and through recognising the non-normative contexts of the burials of supposed infanticide victims. Analyses of the distributions of age at death estimates for perinatal skeletons from Roman settlement sites have shown clustering of deaths at around the time of birth, a pattern that it is suggested is consistent with infanticide (Smith and Kahila, 1992; Mays, 1993). Gowland and Chamberlain (2002; 2003) have challenged this interpretation on the basis that regression-based age estimation methods generate artifically narrow age distributions, although Mays (2003) has questioned the validity of the Bayesian approach to infant-age estimation from skeletal measurements.

6.2   SOCIAL AND DEMOGRAPHIC IMPACTS OF DISEASE

6.2.1   Demographic responses to disease

Diseases with a fatal outcome obviously contribute to overall mortality and place constraints on potential rates of population growth. In addition, severe mortality crises precipitated by outbreaks of virulent epidemic disease such as bubonic plague can have a lasting impact on population dynamics, especially in populations in which both the birth rate and population size are related to available resources in a density-dependent fashion. Scott et al. (1996) and Scott and Duncan (1998) have described how an episode of plague in the small English town of Penrith in 1597–98, which killed an estimated 40% of the population, set in train a long-wavelength oscillation in the birth and death rates that persisted for up to 200 years. The cycle length of this oscillation, 44 years, was driven by a density-dependent response in birth rate, death rate and migration following the plague outbreak. After the precipitating mortality crisis, the population of Penrith was slowly restored by a combination of rising birth rate and immigration from neighbouring communities (itself an important contributor to increased fertility) until the size of the population had risen to a level where increased mortality from communicable disease and poor nutrition, combined with emigration, led to a compensating fall in population numbers. The Penrith population cycle repeated itself every 44 years until the density-dependent limits on population size were removed towards the end of the eighteenth century by improvements in agricultural production and in transport (Scott and Duncan, 1998: 140). A similar long-wavelength oscillation in birth and death rates occurred in London following the Great Plague of 1665 (Scott and Duncan, 1998: 187).

The phenomenon of localised inward migration to sustain population numbers in response to high levels of disease-related mortality was a feature of post-medieval urban centres in Europe (Tilly, 1978: 65–66). This replacement migration was driven by the increased employment opportunities and enhanced wages created by labour shortages in the towns and cities. Reduction in disease-related mortality, either indirectly through improvements to nutrition or directly through advances in hygiene, preventive medicine and treatment, was also one of the factors that brought about the demographic transition in European populations during the eighteenth and nineteenth centuries (Kirk, 1996: 368).

Fertility rates are also influenced by disease, especially sexually transmitted diseases that can induce sub-fertility or sterility, and an elevated incidence of infectious sterility has been proposed as an explanation of low fertility rates in some foraging communities (Harpending, 1994).

6.2.2   Social responses to disease

Treatment

Direct evidence for the treatment of disease is hard to detect from skeletal remains, but effective herbal remedies for painful disorders and the treatment of fractures using splints and bandages to immobilise the broken bones were probably used in many communities (Roberts, 2000a), as were tooth extraction and other remedies for dental disease (Milner and Larsen, 1991). Healing after amputation through a long bone can be recognised by development of a bony callus at the site of amputation followed by closure of the exposed medullary cavity (Mays, 1996), although this need not constitute treatment because amputation could equally be performed as a judicial punishment rather than as a therapeutic measure, or could result from accidental trauma. Similarly trepanation, in which a piece of the skull vault is removed surgically, may in some instances have been undertaken to alleviate conditions such as persistent pain or for epilepsy, but equally could have been conducted for ritual reasons. Many hundreds of instances of trepanation have been found from sites around the world (Arnott et al., 2003), and in most archaeological examples the surrounding bone shows evidence of healing, indicating that the patient or subject survived for at least several months after the procedure had been carried out (Aufderheide and Rodríguez Martín, 1998).

Isolation

Isolation of potential or actual disease carriers by temporary or permanent exclusion from the community has long been an institutional response to diseases that were thought to be contagious (McNeil, 1979: 160). Cities in later medieval and early modern Europe, especially the major ports on the coast of the Mediterranean Sea, enforced quarantine regulations in order to isolate travellers arriving from countries where outbreaks of plague had occurred.

Isolation was also enforced in cases of leprosy, an endemic disease that increased in prevalence in Europe from the eleventh to the thirteenth centuries AD (Roberts, 1986). Leprosy was recognised by medieval physicians to be a communicable disease, and there is historical and archaeological evidence that the disease was successfully diagnosed at least in severe cases. This period of increasing prevalence of leprosy witnessed the foundation of leprosy hospitals and the introduction of legal measures to restrict contacts between leprosy sufferers and the rest of society. The subsequent decline of the disease in later medieval Europe probably owes less to the efficacy of the isolation policy and more to the rise of urbanisation and the increasing prevalence of tuberculosis, which may have conferred some cross-immunity to leprosy and displaced the disease through a process of competitive exclusion (Lietman et al., 1997).

Evidence for compassion

Archaeological evidence for the long-term survival of individuals with disabling physical impairments is relatively uncommon, and this has led to claims that, when found, skeletons which exhibit signs of long-standing severe physical impairment provide evidence for compassion in past societies. Dettwyler (1991: 380–81) cautions against simplistic assumptions about and interpretations of the survival of individuals with impairments, pointing out that whether an impairment constitutes a disability or a handicap in the sense of rendering the sufferer non-productive is a social question, rather than a biological one. Roberts (2000b) suggests that societies can respond in several ways to disability, ranging from support and care through neutrality to neglect and ostracism, and with a corresponding range of status being accorded to the affected individual. Furthermore, humans (like other animals) are adept at coping with and adapting to disability (Keenleyside, 2003), so we cannot assume the existence of disability solely on the basis of skeletal changes. The variety of psychological and social responses to disease and disability are perhaps as important as the evidence for physical impairment in considering the impact of disability in the past.

7

Concluding remarks

7.1 THE RELEVANCE OF DEMOGRAPHY FOR ARCHAEOLOGY

Archaeology seeks to achieve an understanding of humankind through the study of the material remains of past cultures. In most circumstances these cultural remains are incomplete, and are often rather unrepresentative of the people and societies that generated them, therefore an important role of demographic studies within archaeology is to help place constraints on the kinds of populations that could have existed in the past and to evaluate the nature of the demographic processes that contributed to patterning in the archaeological record. A comprehensive and well-tested body of theory exists in anthropological and historical demography, so archaeologists do not need to depend on adventitious circumstances of preservation and recovery in order to achieve meaningful reconstructions of past population structures and processes. Although human societies are extraordinarily diverse, the demographic structure of any viable (i.e. self-sustaining, or demographically stable) population can be located within a limited range of possible variation. The application of this uniformitarian principle can be of great benefit to palaeodemography, firstly as a reality check when appraising the results of palaeodemographic analyses, and secondly as a source of prior probabilities for Bayesian and maximum likelihood estimation of population characteristics and parameters.

A wide range of important archaeological questions can be approached and addressed through palaeodemographic methods – these include the impact of environmental change on human populations; the nature of populational responses to changes in subsistence technology; the extent to which population expansion, migration and colonisation accompanied cultural change; the interaction between population structure and communicable disease; the balance of attritional and catastrophic mortality in past populations; the level of mortality attributable to warfare, infanticide and other forms of interpersonal violence; and the role of population processes in social conflict and cultural collapse. The prospects of significant progress in investigating these questions are enhanced by the availability of new analytical methods that are being developed in biomolecular and environmental archaeology, as well as by increasingly sophisticated reconstructions of past human activity patterns based on analyses of resource usage and the history of landscape occupation.

As well as these practical applications of demographic methods to archaeological questions, the theoretical perspectives provided by demographic models of past populations can be particularly illuminating. Demographic studies can help repopulate the past with individuals whose presence is suspected yet the material evidence for their existence is lacking. For example, children have a low visibility in the archaeological record, not only because children are under-represented in mortality samples (see Section 4.1.4 above) but also because the discovery of material cultural residues attributable to children is rare, except in the restricted context of mortuary deposits. Yet simple demographic modelling, based on the high infant and childhood mortality rates that characterised pre-modern populations, indicates that children probably constituted a third or more of past living populations (and that an equivalent proportion of the population's total person-years were lived in childhood). The presence of a large cohort of economically dependent children in a population also implies the existence of sufficient adult care-givers to ensure their survival. Howell (1982) and others have noted that some palaeodemographic reconstructions of attritional cemetery samples posit excessive young-adult deaths that would have resulted in high rates of orphancy amongst the children, limited overlap between successive generations and a virtual absence

of grandparents, conditions that are unprecedented in historically documented populations and that are incompatible with long-term population
survival.

7.2   HOW MEANINGFUL ARE THE RESULTS OF
PALAEODEMOGRAPHIC ANALYSIS?

The challenge to palaeodemography issued by Bocquet-Appel and Masset
in 1982 has led to nearly a quarter of a century of reappraisal of the bases on
which population structure and dynamics are inferred from archaeological
evidence. Much of the debate has focused on the reconstruction of mortality profiles from samples of human skeletal remains and the extent to which
these mortality patterns diverge from demographic norms. It is now widely
accepted that in addition to the vagaries of taphonomic factors affecting
sample composition, systematic biases occur in palaeodemographic data
and that these stem, in part, from the uncritical application of traditional
anthropological methods for estimating age and sex from skeletal remains.
These methodological biases have been addressed both from a statistical
standpoint (particularly through the development of new anthropological
methods that take account of the variation both in the reference series and
in the target series of skeletons) and from a theoretical perspective that
highlights the uniformitarian nature of population processes and seeks to
avoid creating past population structures that have no analogues in the
historical or ethnographic records. The new approaches to palaeodemography that are emerging from this protracted period of introspection and
revision, as exemplified by the contributions to the Rostock workshops on
palaeodemography (Hoppa and Vaupel, 2002), are more explicit in their
aims and methods and they encourage a guarded optimism for the future
of the discipline.

Substantial progress is being made in the application of palaeodemographic methods in the interpretation of mass-mortality assemblages of
human skeletal remains. Recent research on this topic has investigated
the demographic signatures of outbreaks of fatal diseases such as bubonic

plague, as well as delineating the age and sex profiles of victims of armed conflict and infanticide. Further work is in progress on detecting the demographic impacts of ancient natural disasters including earthquakes and volcanic eruptions. These examples of applied palaeodemography make use of the fact that the demographic processes under investigation are well understood from an anthropological and historical demographic perspective, with reliable comparative data being available from epidemiological and ethnographic studies of present-day and recent historical populations. Further studies of high-mortality population samples need to be undertaken – for example, slavery is thought to have played an important social and economic role in prehistory as well as in classical times, yet there has been little detailed investigation (and no palaeodemographic analysis) of slavery in pre-Roman populations (Parker Pearson and Thorpe, 2005).

In addition to studies of skeletal samples, new approaches to the analysis of proxy data such as artefact usage and radiometric date distributions are extending the reach of palaeodemography back into very early time periods for which the quantity of surviving human remains is limited and the scope for reconstructing mortality patterns from human skeletal remains is correspondingly restricted. For example, Ashton and Lewis (2001) have used artefact densities to track population decline in the Thames Valley in the Late Middle Pleistocene, despite the lack of other evidence (such as skeletal remains or occupation sites) for the hominids that were present in Britain at that time. By extending the time range of palaeodemographic evidence in this way there is the potential to discover correlations between major climatic transitions and continental-scale human population movements.

7.3   HOW DIFFERENT WERE POPULATIONS IN THE PAST?

The application of uniformitarian principles in palaeodemography requires the validation of certain assumptions about the nature of past populations. There is good historical and ethnographic evidence that, despite wide variations in levels of mortality and fertility, there are some life-history parameters that are relatively constant amongst human populations, for example longevity and the age of female reproductive senescence. Rates of skeletal maturation in children show some variation amongst human populations (as evidenced by studies of long bone growth, which reveal slower rates of growth in some past populations) but the timing of stages of dental development appears to be relatively invariant, at least within the species *Homo sapiens*. The issue of recent changes in longevity is more controversial, and there are a number of instances where palaeodemographic evidence has been interpreted as supporting the hypothesis for short lifespans prior to the modern era. However, the historical and ethnographic evidence agrees with life-history theory in suggesting that longevity is a property that scales in proportion with other life-history variables and is therefore likely to be relatively invariant across populations of *Homo sapiens*.

Both fertility and generation length show some systematic differences between ethnographically recorded foragers and subsistence farmers, with foragers generally having a lower potential for rapid population growth. Nonetheless it is clear that under favourable circumstances foragers could sustain continuous and rapid population expansion, as must have been the case in the continental-scale colonisation of northwestern Europe and the Americas by Pleistocene foragers towards the end of the last Ice Age. The calculated rates of geographic expansion in Pleistocene hunter-gatherer colonisation events are comparable to those that occurred at the origins of agriculture in Europe, and this lends some support to the notion that *Homo sapiens* can be characterised as an 'r-selected' colonising species that is adapted to rapid recovery and expansion from extreme population crashes (Hill and Hurtado, 1995: 470). The ability to exploit the opportunities for geographical expansion provided by climatic change and by advances in subsistence technology may be a general property of human populations, and therefore it may be misleading to regard hunter-gatherers as being typically adapted to stationary (zero-growth) population conditions at or near the carrying capacity of their habitat.

The basic bimodal pattern of attritional mortality, in which the oldest and youngest individuals are at greater risk of death, can be reconstructed for some past populations. Comparative studies of populations practising foraging and subsistence agriculture suggest that infectious disease and trauma were amongst the principal causes of death in the past, and in most populations between one third and one half of attritional deaths would have occurred in individuals under 15 years of age. The potential for catastrophic mortality events was also ever present through the mechanisms of epidemic disease, natural disasters and violent inter-group conflict. Catastrophic mortality may be under-recognised in the archaeological record as the social disruption that accompanies natural and human-induced catastrophes is often inimical to the organised burial of the victims (a fact that has been illustrated quite starkly by the many thousands of missing presumed dead as a result of the Indian Ocean tsunami of December 2004).

It is possible that catastrophic mortality may form an important constraint on long-term rates of human population growth, and studies of human genetic diversity have confirmed that some populations have passed through genetic 'bottlenecks' caused by drastic reductions in population size. Simple modelling suggests that if human populations have an average short- to medium-term potential for growth in numbers of 1% per annum, yet long-term population growth averages close to zero, then episodes of catastrophic mortality amounting to a loss of half of the living population every 70 years would be required to keep numbers in check. In this hypothetical situation catastrophic mortality would represent 25% of total deaths, with attritional mortality making up the remaining 75% of deaths. If short-term growth rates were of the order of 2% per annum then the catastrophic mortality required to limit long-term growth would amount to 50% of total mortality.

These simple calculations suggest that catastrophic mortality may play a greater role in population history than previously suspected, and further research into the identification and quantification of episodes of catastrophic death and their impact on past populations is highly desirable. Intriguingly, the available samples of skeletal remains of *Homo habilis*, *Homo heidelbergensis* and *Homo neanderthalensis* show an excess of adolescent and young-adult deaths, which would be expected if these samples represent catastrophic rather than attritional mortality (see Section 5.2.3 above). The same pattern of excess young-adult deaths has been identified by Caspari and Lee (2004) in samples of *Australopithecus* and fossil species of *Homo*, but the latter authors interpret their findings as evidence for reduced longevity prior to the evolution of modern *Homo sapiens*. However, this excess of young-adult mortality is not characteristic of attritional mortality in wild-primate populations, so neither should it be expected amongst early hominids. Rather than hypothesising reduced natural longevity, it is more likely that these age-at-death profiles indicate a substantial contribution of catastrophic mortality to the hominid fossil record. The pattern of excess young-adult mortality is exactly what would be expected if predation by large carnivores were a major contributor to the hominid fossil record. Large carnivores that hunt by stalking or by ambush techniques select their prey in proportion to encounter rates, and thus these predators generate mortality profiles that reflect the age structure of the living-prey population (Stiner, 1991: 160–61). In the case of later species of *Homo*, instances of predation by large carnivores were probably less frequent, but intra-specific violence would be expected to generate a similar mortality profile to that resulting from carnivore predation. It may be the case that attritional mortality profiles only become visible in the hominid fossil record with the advent of normative burial practice during the Middle Palaeolithic.

7.4   DEMOGRAPHIC PROCESSES AND CULTURAL CHANGE

Despite the theorisation of population growth as a potent agent of social transformations, the links between demographic parameters, subsistence levels and cultural change in prehistory and in early historical times are not clear cut. For instance, while there is strong evidence for higher fertility amongst agriculturalists compared to foraging communities, it is not apparent whether this elevated fertility is linked to the shift from high mobility to greater sedentism, or the increasing availability and quality of food sources (especially foods suitable for sustaining infants after early weaning), or the potential for agriculturalist children to make an earlier contribution to the household economy, or indeed a combination of all three factors.

Perhaps the most straightforward kind of hypothesis to test concerning demographic/cultural interaction is the proposal that major cultural transitions were associated with large-scale migrations or colonisations, as opposed to being achieved through cultural diffusion or indigenous cultural innovation (Shennan, 2000, 2002). In addressing this type of hypothesis several categories of evidence can be examined, including the determination of population affinities from genetic or morphological studies of human remains, the detection of migrants through their isotopic signatures, and the investigation of rates of spread of colonising populations by detailed analysis of archaeological dating evidence. Although such studies are still limited in scope, the results obtained so far suggest that relatively high rates of migration, rapid processes of colonisation and substantive genetic turnover may have accompanied the major cultural transitions in northwest European prehistory.

Another populational phenomenon that has attracted the attention of palaeodemographers is 'cultural collapse' followed by subsequent recovery or non-recovery of population numbers in specific geographical regions or urban centres. Modelling of recovery times for historically documented urban populations following conflict-induced or natural disaster-induced population loss indicates that in most instances intrinsic population growth is greatly augmented by immigration from adjacent regions, and recovery of population size therefore occurs in a much shorter timespan than would be predicted from simple exponential growth (Me-Bar and Valdez, 2004). Where intrinsic growth rates are low, and there are reduced opportunities for in-migration, the likelihood of non-recovery following population decline is much greater. This latter situation may have occurred in the medieval Norse settlements of Greenland, an island which was initially colonised by Europeans in AD 986 but was completed depopulated of colonists by AD 1500. In Greenland it appears that the combined effects of climatic change, economic decline, disease and out-migration may have reduced the Norse population below a sustainable level, and with little incentive to resettlement the population finally entered a two-hundred-year period of terminal decline (Lynnerup, 1998). Although this represents a small-scale example of cultural collapse (the Norse population of Greenland never exceeded a few thousand living individuals) the same kind of factors may also have operated on much larger communities at a regional scale, for example in the collapse of the Mesoamerican Mayan civilisation around AD 800.

The relationship between the frequency of disease and cultural history is a fertile field for research, and advances in the standardisation of diagnostic criteria in palaeopathology, coupled with the presentation of disease frequency data in a form that allows comparisons between time periods and across cultures (e.g. Roberts and Cox, 2003), provide better opportunities for testing hypotheses of disease/culture interactions and co-evolution. Many diseases that afflict human populations in the present day have great antiquity, but infectious disease organisms also show evolutionary adaptability in their capacity to cross between host species, develop resistance to treatments and respond to the new opportunities for infection that are provided by changes in human cultural behaviour. Opportunities for migration and colonisation are intimately connected with patterns of disease, as shown by migration into depopulated regions following major episodes of epidemic mortality, and by the 'virgin soil' epidemics that devastated native American populations during the European colonisation of the New World.

7.5   CHALLENGES FOR THE FUTURE

In addition to ongoing efforts to solve long-standing methodological problems, there are many opportunities to exploit new sources of palaeodemographic data in order to obtain quantitative estimates of the parameters of past populations. The advent of new analytical approaches that utilise chemical and biomolecular evidence has provided insights into the histories and affinities of past populations, and allows the possibility of measuring the extent and pace of migration on a local or regional scale. Biomolecular methods can also be applied in the detection of the organisms responsible for outbreaks of epidemic disease and in conjunction with coalescent theory provide a means of establishing the evolutionary history of diseases that affect human populations. The widespread availability and increasing precision of radiocarbon dates, especially those that are obtained directly on human remains or on securely stratified archaeological materials, has provided an additional impetus to the reconstruction of population numbers using proxy measures of human activity, with the result that long-term population processes and correlations between demographic and environmental variables can potentially be explored.

One of the most important challenges facing palaeodemography is to understand the pattern of evolution of modern human life-history traits and to discern the impact of these traits on demographic structure and dynamics in the different hominid species that are known from the fossil record. We have a reasonably good understanding of the demography of our closest living relatives amongst the primates, but there is relatively little known of human demographic history over the six or seven million years since the human lineage diverged from the lineage of the African apes. The evidence from dental and skeletal development indicates that earlier maturation prevailed in fossil hominid species, as is also the case for our closest primate relatives, but there are competing explanations for the emergence of the delayed maturation that is a unique characteristic of the species *Homo sapiens.* There are also major questions to be answered concerning the nature of interactions between sympatric hominid species, in particular whether demographic factors were important in the extinction of previously successful hominid lineages such as the robust australopithecines and our closest fossil relative, *Homo neanderthalensis.*

Hoppa and Vaupel (2002: 3–4) point out that in order to improve methods for palaeodemographic estimation there is a need for researchers to gain access to more and better-documented collections of reference skeletons with known life-history attributes. Although this is a requirement that might conflict with ethical concerns about the long-term storage and curation of human skeletal remains, it is important for biological anthropologists to be able to record skeletal attributes in as wide a range of samples as possible current skeletal reference collections are mainly from populations of north European origin, while populations from other parts of the world are under-represented in the collections currently available. As part of the effort to validate the uniformitarian assumptions that underpin palaeodemography it is desirable to study rates of maturation and senescence in a wide range of modern human populations. These tasks are amongst many that are likely to provide productive lines of enquiry for future generations of palaeodemographers.

REFERENCES

Acsádi, G. and Nemeskéri, J. 1970. *History of Human Life Span and Mortality.* Budapest: Akadémiai Kiadó.

Adams, W. Y., Van Gerven, D. P. and Levy, R. S. 1978. The retreat from migrationism. *Annual Review of Anthropology* 7: 483–532.

Alterman, H. 1969. *Counting People: the Census in History.* New York: Harcourt, Brace and World.

Ammerman, A. J. and Cavalli-Sforza, L. L. 1973. A population model for the diffusion of early farming in Europe. In Renfrew, C. (ed.) *The Explanation of Culture Change.* London: Duckworth, pp. 343–357.

Amundsen, D. W. and Diers, C. J. 1970. The age of menopause in classical Greece and Rome. *Human Biology* 42: 79–86.

1973. The age of menopause in medieval Europe. *Human Biology* 45: 605–612.

Anderson, D. G. and Faught, M. K. 2000. Paleoindian artefact distributions: evidence and implications. *Antiquity* 74: 507–513.

Anderson, D. G. and Gillam, J. C. 2000. Paleoindian colonization of the Americas: implications from an examination of physiography, demography and artefact distribution. *American Antiquity* 65: 43–66.

Anderson, R. M. and May, R. M. 1991. *Infectious Diseases of Humans.* Oxford: Oxford University Press.

Anderson, T. 2000. Congenital conditions and neoplastic disease in British palaeopathology. In Cox, M. and Mays, S. (eds.) *Human Osteology in Archaeology and Forensic Science.* London: Greenwich Medical Media, pp. 199–226.

Angel, J. L. 1969. The bases of paleodemography. *American Journal of Physical Anthropology* 30: 427–438.

Anthony, D. W. 1990. Migration in archaeology: the baby and the bathwater. *American Anthropologist* 92: 895–914.

Ariès, P. 1962. *Centuries of Childhood: A Social History of Family Life.* New York: Vintage Books.

Armenian, H. K., Melkonian, A., Noji, E. K. and Hovanesian, A. P. 1997. Deaths and injuries due to the earthquake in Armenia: a cohort approach. *International Journal of Epidemiology* 26: 806–813.

Arnott, R., Finger, S. and Smith, C. U. M. (eds.) 2003. *Trepanation: History, Discovery and Theory.* Lisee: Swets and Zeitlinger.

Ashton, N. and Lewis, S. 2002. Deserted Britain: declining populations in the British Late Middle Pleistocene. *Antiquity* 76: 388–396.

Aufderheide, A. C. and Rodríguez Martín, C. 1998. *The Cambridge Encyclopedia of Human Palaeopathology.* Cambridge: Cambridge University Press.

Bagnall, R. S. and Frier, B. W. 1994. *The Demography of Roman Egypt.* Cambridge: Cambridge University Press.

Ball, W. 1996. The first census. *Geographical Magazine*, January: 16–18.

Barrientos, G. and Perez, S. I. 2005. Was there a population replacement during the Late mid-Holocene in the southeastern Pampas of Argentina? Archaeological evidence and palaeoecological bias. *Quaternary International* 132: 95–105.

Beauval, C., Maureille, B., Lacrampe-Cuyaubère, F. et al. 2005. A late Neandertal femur from Les Rochers-de-Villeneuve, France. *Proceedings of the National Academy of Sciences of the USA* 102: 7085–7090.

Benedictow, O. J. 1987. Morbidity in historical plague epidemics. *Population Studies* 41: 401–431.

Bentley, G. R., Jasienska, G. and Goldberg, T. 1993. Is the fertility of agriculturalists higher than that of nonagriculturalists? *Current Anthropology* 34: 778–785.

Bergfelder, T. and Herrmann, B. 1980. Estimating fertility on the basis of birth traumatic changes in the pubic bone. *Journal of Human Evolution* 9: 611–613.

Bermúdez de Castro, J. M. and Díez, J. C. 1995. Middle Pleistocene mortality pattern and fertility: the case of the Atapuerca hominids (Sima de los Huesos, Burgos, Spain). *Revista Espanola de Paleontologia* 10: 259–272.

Bermúdez de Castro, J. M. and Nicolás, E. 1997. Palaeodemography of the Atapuerca-SH Middle Pleistocene hominid sample. *Journal of Human Evolution* 33: 333–355.

Bermúdez de Castro, J. M., Martinón-Torres, M., Lozano, M., Sarmiento, S. and Muela, A. 2004. Palaeodemography of the Atapuerca-SH hominin sample: a revision and new approaches to the palaeodemography of the European Middle Pleistocene population. *Journal of Anthropological Research* 60: 5–26.

Beynon, A. D. and Dean, M. C. 1988. Distinct dental development patterns in early fossil hominids. *Nature* 335: 509–514.

Binford, L. R. 1968. Post-Pleistocene adaptations. In Binford, S. R. and Binford, L. R. (eds.) *New Perspectives in Archeology*. Chicago: Aldine, pp. 313–341.

Binford, L. R. and Chasko, W. J. 1976. Nunamiut demographic history: a provocative case. In Zubrow, E. B. W. (ed.) *Demographic Anthropology, Quantitative Approaches*. Albuquerque: University of New Mexico Press, pp. 63–143.

Bishop, N. A. and Knüsel, C. J. 2005. A palaeodemographic investigation of warfare in prehistory. In Parker Pearson, M. and Thorpe, I. J. N. (eds.) *Warfare, Violence and Slavery in Prehistory*. British Archaeological Reports, International Series, 1374: 201–216.

Blockley, S. M. 2005. Two hiatuses in human bone radiocarbon dates in Britain (17000 to 5000 cal BP). *Antiquity* 79: 505–513.

Blurton Jones, N. G., Smith, L. C., O'Connell, J. F., Hawkes, K. and Kamuzora, C. L. 1992. Demography of the Hadza, an increasing and high density population of savanna foragers. *American Journal of Physical Anthropology* 89: 159–181.

Blurton Jones, N. G., Hawkes, K. and O'Connell, J. F. 2002. Antiquity of postreproductive life: are there modern impacts on hunter-gatherer postreproductive life spans? *American Journal of Human Biology* 14: 184–205.

Bocquet-Appel, J-P. 1986. Once upon a time: paleodemography. *Mitteil. Berlin Gesell. Anthropol. Ethnol. Urges.* 7: 127–133.

Bocquet-Appel, J-P. and Arsuaga, J-L. 1999. Age distributions of hominid samples at Atapuerca (SH) and Krapina could indicate accumulation by catastrophe. *Journal of Archaeological Science* 26: 327–338.

Bocquet-Appel, J-P. and Bacro, J. N. 1997. Brief communication: estimates of some demographic parameters in a Neolithic rock-cut chamber (approximately 2000 BC) using iterative techniques for ageing and demographic estimators. *American Journal of Physical Anthropology* 102: 569–575.

Bocquet-Appel, J.-P. and Demars, P. Y. 2000. Neanderthal contraction and modern human colonization of Europe. *Antiquity* 74: 544–552.

Bocquet-Appel, J.-P. and Masset, C. 1982. Farewell to paleodemography. *Journal of Human Evolution* 11: 321–333.

1983. Paleodemography: resurrection or ghost? *Journal of Human Evolution* 14: 107–111.

Boddington, A. 1987. From bones to population: the problem of numbers. In Boddington, A., Garland, A. N. and Janaway, R. C. (eds.) *Death Decay and Reconstruction: Approaches to Archaeology and Forensic Science.* Manchester: Manchester University Press, pp. 179–197.

Boer, A. H. 1988. Mortality rates of moose in New Brunswick: a life table analysis. *Journal of Wildlife Management* 52: 21–25.

Boldsen, J. L., Milner, G. R., Konigsberg, L. W. and Wood, J. W. 2002. Transition analysis: a new method for estimating age from skeletons. In Hoppa, R. D. and Vaupel, J. W. (eds.) *Paleodemography. Age Distributions from Skeletal Samples.* Cambridge: Cambridge University Press, pp. 73–106.

Boserup, E. 1965. *The Conditions of Agricultural Growth.* Chicago: Aldine.

Boucher, B. J. 1957. Sex differences in the foetal pelvis. *American Journal of Physical Anthropology* 15: 581–600.

Bourgeois-Pichat, J. 1965. The general development of the population of France since the eighteenth century. In Glass, D. V. and Eversley, D. E. C. (eds.) *Population in History.* London: Arnold, pp. 474–506.

Bouville, C. 1980. L'hypogée chalcolithique de Roaix apport a l'étude de la démographie en Provence. *Bulletin et Mémoire de la Societé d'Anthropologie de Paris* 7: 85–89.

Bouwman, A. S. and Brown, T. A. 2005. The limits of biomolecular palaeopathology: ancient DNA cannot be used to study venereal syphilis. *Journal of Archaeological Science* 32: 703–713.

Boylston, A., Holst, M. and Coughlan, J. 2000. Physical anthropology. In Fiorato, V., Boylston, A. and Knüsel, C. (eds.) *Blood Red Roses. The Archaeology of a Mass Grave from the Battle of Towton AD 1461.* Oxford: Oxbow Books, pp. 45–59.

Brain, C. K. 1981. *The Hunters or the Hunted. An Introduction to African Cave Taphonomy*. Chicago: University of Chicago Press.

Brickley, M. 2000. The diagnosis of metabolic disease in archaeological bone. In Cox, M. and Mays, S. (eds.) *Human Osteology in Archaeology and Forensic Science*. London: Greenwich Medical Media, pp. 183–198.

Bromage, T. G. and Dean, M. C. 1985. Re-evaluation of the age at death of immature fossil hominids. *Nature* 317: 525–527.

Bronson, B. 1975. The earliest farming: demography as cause and consequence. In Polgar, S. (ed.) *Population, Ecology and Social Evolution*. The Hague: Mouton, pp. 53–78.

Brooks, S. and Suchey, J. M. 1990. Skeletal age determination based on the os pubis: a comparison of the Acsádi-Nemeskéri and Suchey-Brooks methods. *Human Evolution* 5: 227–238.

Brosch, R., Gordon, S. V., Marmiesse, M. et al. 2002. A new evolutionary scenario for the *Mycobacterium tuberculosis* complex. *Proceedings of the National Academy of Sciences of the USA* 99: 3684–3689.

Brothwell, D. 1967. Major congenital anomalies of the skeleton: evidence from earlier populations. In Brothwell, D. and Sandison, A. T. (eds.) *Diseases in Antiquity*. Springfield: Thomas, pp. 423–443.

Brown, B. M. 1987. Population estimation from floor area: a re-study of 'Naroll's Constant'. *Behavior Science Research* 21: 1–49.

Brown, K. A. 1998. Gender and sex – what can ancient DNA tell us? *Ancient Biomolecules* 2: 3–15.

2000. Ancient DNA applications in human osteoarchaeology: achievements, problems and potential. In Cox, M. and Mays, S. (eds.) *Human Osteology in Archaeology and Forensic Science*. London: Greenwich Medical Media, pp. 455–473.

Brunborg, H., Lyngstad, T. H. and Urdal, H. 2003. Accounting for genocide: how many were killed in Srebrenica? *European Journal of Population* 19: 229–248.

Buck, C. E., Cavanagh, W. G. and Litton, C. D. 1996. *Bayesian Approach to Interpreting Archaeological Data*. Chichester: Wiley.

Buckberry, J. L. and Chamberlain, A. T. 2002. Age estimation from the auricular surface of the ilium: a revised method. *American Journal of Physical Anthropology* 119: 231–239.

Buikstra, J. E. and Konigsberg, L. W. 1985. Paleodemography: critiques and controversies. *American Anthropologist* 87: 316–333.

Burmeister, S. 2000. Archaeology and migration. Approaches to an archaeological proof of migration. *Current Anthropology* 41: 539–567.

Canny, N. (ed.) 1994. *Europeans on the Move. Studies on European Migration, 1500–1800.* Oxford: Clarendon Press.

Capelli, C., Redhead, N., Abernethy, J. K. et al. 2003. A Y chromosome census of the British Isles. *Current Biology* 13: 979–984.

Carman, J. and Harding, A. (eds.) 1999. *Ancient Warfare: Archaeological Perspectives.* Stroud: Sutton.

Carneiro, R. L. 1970. A theory of the origin of the state. *Science* 169: 733–738.

Caspari, R. and Lee, S-H. 2004. Older age becomes common late in human evolution. *Proceedings of the National Academy of Sciences of the USA* 101: 10895–10900.

Casselberry, S. E. 1974. Further refinement of formulae for determining population from floor area. *World Archaeology* 6: 117–122.

Caughley, G. 1966. Mortality patterns in mammals. *Ecology* 47: 906–918.

Cavalli-Sforza, L. L., Menozzi, P. and Piazza, A. 1994. *The History and Geography of Human Genes.* Princeton: Princeton University Press.

Chamberlain, A. T. 2000. Problems and prospects in palaeodemography. In Cox, M. and Mays, S. (eds.) *Human Osteology in Archaeology and Forensic Science.* London: Greenwich Medical Media, pp. 101–115.

Chan, C-C., Lin, Y-P., Chen, H-H., Chang, T-Y., Cheng, T-J. and Chen, L-S. 2003. A population-based study on the immediate and prolonged effects of the 1999 Taiwan earthquake on mortality. *Annals of Epidemiology* 13: 502–508.

Charnov, E. L. 1993. *Life History Invariants.* Oxford: Oxford University Press.

Childe, V. G. 1936. *Man Makes Himself.* London: Watts.

Coale, A. J. 1957. How the age distribution of a human population is determined. *Cold Spring Harbor Symposia on Quantitative Biology* 22: 83–88.

Coale, A. J. and Demeny, P. 1983. *Regional Model Life Tables and Stable Populations.* 2nd edition. Princeton: Princeton University Press.

Coale, A. J. and Trussell, T. J. 1974. Model fertility schedules: variations in the age structure of childbearing in human populations. *Population Index* 40: 185–258.

Coale, A. J. and Watkins, S. C. 1986. *The Decline of Fertility in Europe*. Princeton.

Coggon, D., Rose, G. and Barker, D. J. P. 2003. *Epidemiology for the Uninitiated*. London: BMJ Books.

Cohen, M. N. 1977. *The Food Crisis in Prehistory: Overpopulation and the Origin of Agriculture*. New Haven: Yale University Press.

Cole, L. C. 1954. The population consequences of life history phenomena. *Quarterly Review of Biology* 29: 103–137.

Collard, M. 2003. Grades and transitions in human evolution. *Proceedings of the British Academy* 106: 6–100.

Collier, S. and White, J. P. 1976. Get them young? Age and sex inferences of animal domestication in archaeology. *American Antiquity* 41: 96–102.

Cooper, A and Poinar, H. N. 2000. Ancient DNA: do it right or not at all. *Science* 289: 1139.

Cox, M. 2000. Assessment of parturition. In Cox, M. and Mays, S. (eds.) *Human Osteology in Archaeology and Forensic Science*. London: Greenwich Medical Media, pp. 131–142.

Cox, M. and Scott, A. 1992. Evaluation of the obstetric significance of some pelvic characters in an 18th Century British sample of known parity status. *American Journal of Physical Anthropology* 89: 431–440.

Crawford, S. 1999. *Childhood in Anglo-Saxon England*. Stroud: Sutton.

Crosby, A. W. 1976. Virgin soil epidemics as a factor in the aboriginal depopulation in America. *William and Mary Quarterly* 33: 289–299.

Crubézy, E., Ludes, B., Poveda, J-D., Clayton, J., Crouau-Roy, B. and Montagnon, D. 1998. Identification of *Mycobacterium* DNA in an Egyptian Pott's disease of 5400 years old. *Comptes Rendu d' Academie des Sciences, Paris. Life Sciences* 321: 941–951.

Curet, L. A. 1998. New formulae for estimating prehistoric populations for lowland South America and the Caribbean. *Antiquity* 72: 359–375.

Daly, M. and Wilson, M. 1984. A sociobiological analysis of human infanticide. In Haufstater, G. and Hrdy, S. B. (eds.) *Infanticide: Comparative and Evolutionary Perspectives*. New York: Aldine, pp. 487–502.

Daniels, J. D. 1992. The Indian population of North America in 1492. *William and Mary Quarterly* 49: 298–320.

Dasen, V. 1988. Dwarfism in Egypt and Classical Antiquity: iconography and medical history. *Medical History* 32: 253–276.

Daugherty, H. G. and Kammeyer, K. C. W. 1995. *An Introduction to Population,* 2nd edition. New York: The Guilford Press.

Dean, M. C. and Beynon, A. D. 1991. Histological reconstruction of crown formation times and initial root formation times in a modern human child. *American Journal of Physical Anthropology* 86: 215–228.

Dean, M. C., Beynon, A. D., Thackeray, J. F. and Whittaker, D. K. 1993. A longitudinal study of tooth growth in a single individual based on long and short period incremental markings in dentine and enamel. *International Journal of Osteoarchaeology* 3: 249–264.

Dean, [M.]C., Leakey, M. G., Reid, D., Schrenk, F., Schwartz, G. T., Stringer, C. and Walker, A. 2001. Growth processes in teeth distinguish modern humans from *Homo erectus* and earlier hominins. *Nature* 414: 628–631.

Deevey, E. S. 1947. Life tables for natural populations of animals. *The Quarterly Review of Biology* 22: 283–314.

Dennell, R. 1980. The use, abuse and potential of site catchment analysis. In Findlow, F. J. and Ericson, J. E. (eds.) *Catchment Analysis. Essays on Prehistoric Resource Space.* Los Angeles: Department of Anthropology, University of California, pp. 1–20.

De Roche, C. D. 1983. Population estimates from settlement area and number of residences. *Journal of Field Archaeology* 10: 187–192.

Dettwyler, K. A. 1991. Can paleopathology provide evidence for 'compassion'? *American Journal of Physical Anthropology* 84: 375–384.

De Vito, C. and Saunders, S. R. 1990. A discriminant function analysis of deciduous teeth to determine sex. *Journal of Forensic Sciences* 35: 845–858.

De Waal, A. 1989. Famine mortality: a case study of Darfur, Sudan 1984–5. *Population Studies* 43: 5–24.

Dickeman, M. 1975. Demographic consequences of infanticide in man. *Annual Review of Ecology and Systematics* 6: 107–137.

Donnelly, P. and Tavaré, S. 1995. Coalescents and genealogical structure under neutrality. *Annual Review of Genetics* 29: 401–421.

Drake, M. 1969. *Population and Society in Norway, 1735–1865.* Cambridge: Cambridge University Press.

Drancourt, M., Aboudharam, G., Signoli, M. and Dutour, O. 1998. Detection of 400-year-old *Yersinia pestis* DNA in human dental pulp: an approach to the diagnosis of ancient septicemia. *Proceedings of the National Academy of Sciences of the USA* 95: 12637–12640.

Drusini, A., Calliari, I. and Volpe, A. 1991. Root dentine transparency: age determination of human teeth using computerized densitometric analysis. *American Journal of Physical Anthropology* 85: 25–30.

Dumond, D. E. 1965. Population growth and cultural change. *Southwestern Journal of Anthropology* 21: 302–324.

Dunbar, R. I. M. 1987. Demography and reproduction. In Smuts, B. B., Cheney, D. L., Seyfarth, R. M. et al. (eds.) *Primate Societies*. Chicago: University of Chicago Press, pp. 240–249.

Dutour, O., Ardagna, Y., Maczel, M. and Signoli, M. 2003. Epidemiology of infectious diseases in the past. In Greenblatt, C. and Spigelman, M. (eds.) *Emerging Pathogens: the Archaeology, Ecology and Evolution of Infectious Disease*. Oxford: Oxford University Press, pp. 151–165.

Dyke, B., Gage, T. B., Alford, P. L., Swenson, B. and Williams-Blangero, S. 1995. Model life tables for captive chimpanzees. *American Journal of Primatology* 37: 25–37.

Early, J. D. and Headland, T. N. 1998. *Population Dynamics of a Philippine Rain Forest People. The San Ildefonso Agta*. Gainesville: University of Florida Press.

Eaton, J. W. and Mayer, A. J. 1953. The social biology of very high fertility among the Hutterites: the demography of a unique population. *Human Biology* 25: 206–264.

Ehrlich, P. R. 1968. *The Population Bomb*. New York: Ballantine Books.

Ell, S. R. 1989. Three days in October of 1630: detailed examination of mortality during an early modern plague epidemic in Venice. *Reviews of the Infectious Diseases* 11: 128–139.

Eshed, V., Latimer, B., Greenwald, C. M. et al. 2002. Button osteoma: its etiology and pathophysiology. *American Journal of Physical Anthropology* 118: 217–230.

Eveleth, P. B. and Tanner, J. M. 1990. *Worldwide Variation in Human Growth*. 2nd edition. Cambridge: Cambridge University Press.

Faerman, M., Bar-Gal, G. K., Filon, D. et al. 1998. Determining the sex of infanticide victims from the late Roman era through ancient DNA analysis. *Journal of Archaeological Science* 25: 861–865.

Faerman, M., Nebel, A., Filon, D., Thomas, M. G., Bradman, N., Ragsdale, B. D., Schultz, M. and Oppenheim, A. 2000. From a dry bone to a genetic portrait: a case study of sickle cell anemia. *American Journal of Physical Anthropology* 111: 153–163.

Fazekas, I. G. and Kósa, F. 1978. *Forensic Fetal Osteology*. Budapest: Akadémiai Kiadó.

Fletcher, R. 1990. Residential densities, group sizes and social stress in Australian aboriginal settlements. In Meehan, B. and White, N. (eds.) *Hunter-Gatherer Demography*. Oceania Monographs 39. Sydney: University of Sydney, pp. 81–95.

Forster, P. 2004. Ice ages and the mitochondrial DNA chronology of human dispersals: a review. *Philosophical Transactions of the Royal Society of London B* 359: 255–264.

Fort, J., Pujol, T. and Cavalli-Sforza, L. L. 2004. Palaeolithic populations and waves of advance. *Cambridge Archaeological Journal* 14: 53–61.

Frayer, D. W., Horton, W. A., Macchiarelli, R. and Mussi, M. 1987. Dwarfism in an adolescent from the Italian late Upper Palaeolithic. *Nature* 330: 60–62.

Gage, T. B. 1989. Bio-mathematical approaches to the study of human variation in mortality. *Yearbook of Physical Anthropology* 32: 185–214.

1990. Variation and classification of human age patterns of mortality: analysis using competing hazards models. *Human Biology* 62: 589–617.

1998. The comparative demography of primates: with some comments on the evolution of life histories. *Annual Review of Anthropology* 27: 197–221.

Gage, T. B. and Dyke, B. 1988. Model life tables for the larger Old World monkeys. *American Journal of Primatology* 16: 305–320.

1993. Model life tables for the larger Old World monkeys: a revision. *American Journal of Primatology* 29: 287–290.

Gage, T. B., Dyke, B. and Riviere, P. G. 1984. Estimating mortality from two censuses: an application to the Trio of Surinam. *Human Biology* 56: 489–501.

Gallivan, M. D. 2002. Measuring sedentariness and settlement population: accumulations research in the Middle Atlantic region. *American Antiquity* 67: 535–557.

Gamble, C., Davies, W., Pettitt, P. and Richards, M. 2004. Climate change and evolving human diversity in Europe during the last glacial. *Philosophical Transactions of the Royal Society B* 359: 243–254.

Gernaey, A. M., Minnikin, D. E., Copley, M. S., Dixon, R. A., Middleton, J. C. and Roberts, C. A. 2001. Mycolic acids and ancient DNA confirm an osteological diagnosis of tuberculosis. *Tuberculosis* 81: 259–265.

Gilchrist, R. (ed.) 2003. The Social Commemoration of Warfare. *World Archaeology* 35(1).

Goldstein, D. B. and Chikhi, L. 2002. Human migrations and population structure: what we know and why it matters. *Annual Review of Genomics and Human Genetics* 3: 129–152.

Goldstein, M. S. 1953. Some vital statistics based on skeletal material. *Human Biology* 25: 3–12.

Goodman, A. H. and Rose, J. C. 1991. Dental enamel hypoplasias as indicators of nutritional status. In Kelley, M. A. and Larsen, C. S. (eds.) *Advances in Dental Anthropology*. New York: Wiley-Liss, pp. 279–293.

Götherstrom, A., Lidén, K., Ahlström, T., Källersjö, M. and Brown, T. A. 1997. Osteology, DNA and sex identification: morphological and molecular sex identifications of five Neolithic individuals from Ajvide, Gotland. *International Journal of Osteoarchaeology* 7: 71–81.

Gowland, R. L. and Chamberlain, A. T. 2002. A Bayesian approach to ageing perinatal skeletal material from archaeological sites: implications for infanticide in Roman Britain. *Journal of Archaeological Science* 29: 677–685.

2003. A new method for estimating gestational age from skeletal long bone length. In Robson Brown, K. A. (ed.) *Archaeological Sciences 1999*. Oxford, British Archaeological Reports, British Series 1111: 42–58.

2005. Detecting plague: palaeodemographic characterisation of a catastrophic death assemblage. *Antiquity* 79: 146–157.

Grayson, D. K. 1990. Donner party deaths: a demographic assessment. *Journal of Anthropological Research* 46: 223–242.

1996. Human mortality in a natural disaster: the Willie Handcart Company. *Journal of Anthropological Research* 52: 185–205.

Greene, D. L., Van Gerven, D. P. and Armelagos, G. J. 1986. Life and death in ancient populations: bones of contention in paleodemography. *Human Evolution* 1: 193–207.

Grine, F. E. 1993. Description and preliminary analysis of new hominid craniodental fossils from the Swartkrans Formation. In Brain, C. K. (ed.)

Swartkrans: a Cave's Chronicle of Early Man. Pretoria: Transvaal Museum, pp. 75–116.

Grupe, G., Price, T. D., Schröter, P., Söllner, F., Johnson, C. M. and Beard, B. L. 1997. Mobility of Bell Beaker people revealed by strontium isotope ratios of tooth and bone: a study of southern Bavarian skeletal remains. *Applied Geochemistry* 12: 517–525.

Guha-Sapir, D. and van Panhuis, W. G. 2003. The importance of conflict-related mortality in civilian populations. *The Lancet* 361: 2126–2128.

Guhl, F., Jaramillo, C., Vallejo, G. A., Yockteng, R., Cárdenas-Arroyo, F., Fornaciari, G., Arriaza, B. and Aufderheide, A. C. 1999. Isolation of *Trypanosoma cruzi* DNA in 4,000-year-old mummified human tissue from Northern Chile. *American Journal of Physical Anthropology* 108: 401–407.

Gustafson, G. 1950. Age determinations on teeth. *Journal of the American Dental Association* 41: 45–54.

Harlow, M. and Laurence, R. 2002. *Growing Up and Growing Old in Ancient Rome.* London: Routledge.

Harpending, H. 1994. Infertility and forager demography. *American Journal of Physical Anthropology* 93: 385–390.

Harpending, H. C., Sherry, S. T., Rogers, A. R. and Stoneking, M. 1993. The genetic structure of ancient human populations. *Current Anthropology* 34: 483–496.

Harpending, H. C., Batzer, M. A., Gurven, M., Jorde, L. B., Rogers, A. R. and Sherry, S. T. 1998. Genetic traces of ancient demography. *Proceedings of the National Academy of Sciences USA* 1998; 95: 1961–1967.

Harrison, G. A. 1995. *The Human Biology of the English Village.* Oxford: Oxford University Press.

Harvey, P., Martin, R. D. and Clutton-Brock, T. H. 1987. Life histories in comparative perspective. In Smuts, B. B., Cheney, D. L., Seyfarth, R. M. et al. (eds.) *Primate Societies.* Chicago: University of Chicago Press, pp. 181–196.

Hassan, F. A. 1973. On mechanisms of population growth during the Neolithic. *Current Anthropology* 14: 535–540.

1978. Demographic archaeology. In Schiffer, M. B. (ed.) *Advances in Archaeological Method and Theory* Vol. I. New York: Academic, pp. 49–103.

1981. *Demographic Archaeology.* New York: Academic.

Hawkes, K., O'Connell, J. F. and Blurton Jones, N. G. 1997. Hadza women's time allocation, offspring provisioning, and the evolution of long postmenopausal life spans. *Current Anthropology* 38: 551–577.

Hazlewood, L. and Steele, J. 2004. Spatial dynamics of human dispersals. Constraints on modelling and archaeological validation. *Journal of Archaeological Science* 31: 669–679.

Headland, T. N. 1989. Population decline in a Philippine Negrito hunter-gatherer society. *American Journal of Human Biology* 1: 59–72.

Helgason, A., Sigurdardóttir, S., Nicholson, J., Sykes, B., Hill, E. W., Bradley, D. G., Bosnes, V., Gulcher, J. R., Ward, R. and Stefánsson, K. 2000. Estimating Scandinavian and Gaelic ancestry in the male settlers of Iceland. *American Journal of Human Genetics* 67: 697–717.

Henry, L. 1959. L'âge du décès d'après les inscriptions funéraires. *Population* 14: 327–329.

Herold, M. W. 2002. US bombing and Afghan civilian deaths: the official neglect of 'unworthy' bodies. *International Journal of Urban and Regional Research* 26: 626–634.

Herring, D. A., Saunders, S. R. and Katzenberg, M. A. 1998. Investigating the weaning process in past populations. *American Journal of Physical Anthropology* 105: 425–439.

Hewlett, B. S. 1991. Demography and childcare in preindustrial societies. *Journal of Anthropological Research* 47: 1–37.

Hildebolt, C. F. and Molnar, S. 1991. Measurement and description of periodontal disease in anthropological studies. In Kelley, M. A. and Larsen, C. S. (eds.) *Advances in Dental Anthropology* New York: Wiley-Liss, pp. 225–240.

Hill, K., Boesch, C., Goodall, J., Pusey, A., Williams, J., and Wrangham, R. 2001. Mortality rates among wild chimpanzees. *Journal of Human Evolution* 40: 437–450.

Hill, K. and Hurtado, A. M. 1995. *Ache Life History. The Ecology and Demography of a Foraging People.* New York: Aldine de Gruyter.

Hill, K. and Kaplan, H. 1999. Life history traits in humans: theory and empirical study. *Annual Review of Anthropology* 28: 397–430.

Hillson, S. 1996. *Dental Anthropology.* Cambridge: Cambridge University Press.

2000. Dental pathology. In Katzenberg, M. A. and Saunders, S. R. (eds.) *Biological Anthropology of the Human Skeleton*. New York: Wiley-Liss, pp. 249–286.

Holcomb, S. M. C. and Konigsberg, L. W. 1995. Statistical study of sexual dimorphism in the human fetal sciatic notch. *American Journal of Physical Anthropology* 97: 113–125.

Hollingsworth, M. F. and Hollingsworth, T. H. 1971. Plague mortality rates by age and sex in the Parish of St. Botolph's Without Bishopgate, London, 1603. *Population Studies* 25: 131–146.

Hollingsworth, T. H. 1969. *Historical Demography*. London: Hodder and Stoughton.

Holman, D. J., Wood, J. W. and O'Connor, K. A. 2002. Estimating age-at-death distributions from skeletal samples: multivariate latent-trait approach. In Hoppa, R. D. and Vaupel, J. W. (eds.) *Paleodemography. Age Distributions from Skeletal Samples*. Cambridge: Cambridge University Press, pp. 193–221.

Hooton, E. A. 1930. *The Indians of Pecos Pueblo. A Study of their Skeletal Remains*. New Haven: Yale University Press.

Hopkins, K. 1966. On the probable age structure of the Roman population. *Population Studies* 20: 245–264.

Hoppa, R. D. 1992. Evaluating human skeletal growth: an Anglo-Saxon cxample. *International Journal of Osteoarchaeology* 2: 275–288.

Hoppa, R. D. and Vaupel, J. W. (eds.) 2002. *Paleodemography. Age Distributions from Skeletal Samples*. Cambridge: Cambridge University Press.

Housley, R. A., Gamble, C. S., Street, M. and Pettitt, P. B. 1997. Radiocarbon evidence for the Lateglacial human recolonisation of Northern Europe. *Proceedings of the Prehistoric Society* 63: 25–54.

Howell, N. 1979. *Demography of the Dobe !Kung*. New York: Academic Press.
1982. Village composition implied by a paleodemographic life table: the Libben site. *American Journal of Physical Anthropology* 59: 263–270.

Howells, W. W. 1960. Estimating population numbers through archaeological and skeletal remains. In Heizer, R. F. and Cook, S. F. (eds.) *The Application of Quantitative Methods in Archaeology*. Chicago: Quadrangle, pp. 158–185.

Huda, T. F. J. and Bowman, J. E. 1995. Age determination from dental microstructure in juveniles. *American Journal of Physical Anthropology* 97: 135–150.

Hummel, S., Herrmann, B., Rameckers, J., Müller, D., Sperling, K., Neitzel, H. and Tönnies, H. 1999. Proving the authenticity of ancient DNA by comparative genomic hybridization. *Naturwissenschaften* 86: 500–503.

Humphrey, L. 2000. Growth studies of past populations: an overview and an example. In Cox, M. and Mays, S. (eds.) *Human Osteology in Archaeology and Forensic Science.* London: Greenwich Medical Media, pp. 23–38.

Hunt, D. R. 1990. Sex determination in the subadult ilia: an indirect test of Weaver's nonmetric sexing method. *Journal of Forensic Sciences* 35: 881–885.

Iraq Body Count. 2004. Available at www.iraqbodycount.net/bodycount.htm

Jackes, M. K. 1985. Pubic symphysis age distributions. *American Journal of Physical Anthropology* 68: 281–299.

Janetta, A. B. and Preston, S. H. 1991. Two centuries of mortality change in central Japan: the evidence from a temple death register. *Population Studies* 45: 417–436.

Janssens, P. A., Marcsik, A., de Meyere, C. and de Roy, G. 1993. Qualitative and quantitative aspects of scurvy in ancient bones. *Journal of Paleopathology* 5: 25–36.

Jantz, R. L. and Owsley, D. W. 2001. Variation among early North American crania. *American Journal of Physical Anthropology* 114: 146–155.

Johanson, D. C., White, T. D. and Coppens, Y. 1982. Dental remains from the Hadar Formation, Ethiopia: 1974–1977 collections. *American Journal of Physical Anthropology* 57: 545–603.

John, A. M. 1988. Plantation slave mortality in Trinidad. *Population Studies* 42: 161–182.

Jones, H. 1990. *Population Geography.* 2nd edition. London: Chapman.

Jurmain, R. 1999. *Stories from the Skeleton: Behavioral Reconstruction in Human Osteology.* Amsterdam: Gordon and Breach.

Kardulias, P. N. 1992. Estimating population size at ancient military sites: the use of historical and contemporary analogy. *American Antiquity* 57: 276–287.

Katzenberg, M. A. 2000. Stable isotope analysis: a tool for studying past diet, demography and life history. In Katzenberg, M. A. and Saunders, S. R. (eds.) *Biological Anthropology of the Human Skeleton.* New York: Wiley-Liss, pp. 305–327.

Katzenberg, M. A., Herring, D. A. and Saunders, S. R. 1996. Weaning and infant mortality: evaluating the skeletal evidence. *Yearbook of Physical Anthropology* 39: 177–199.

Keeley, L. H. 1996. *War Before Civilization*. Oxford: Oxford University Press.

Keenleyside, A. 2003. An unreduced dislocated mandible in an Alaskan eskimo: a case of altrusim or adaptation? *International Journal of Osteoarchaeology* 13: 384–389.

Kerley, E. R. 1965. The microscopic determination of age in human bone. *American Journal of Physical Anthropology* 23: 149–163.

Kidane, A. 1989. Demographic consequences of the 1984–1985 Ethiopian famine. *Demography* 26: 515–522.

Kimbel, W. H., Johanson, D. C. and Coppens, Y. 1982. Pliocene hominid cranial remains from the Hadar Formation, Ethiopia. *American Journal of Physical Anthropology* 57: 453–499.

Kimbel, W. H., Johanson, D. C. and Rak, Y. 1994. The first skull and other new discoveries of *Australopithecus afarensis* at Hadar, Ethiopia. *Nature* 368: 449–451.

Kirk, D. 1996. Demographic transition theory. *Population Studies* 50: 361–387.

Kitch, M. 1992. Population movement and migration in pre-industrial rural England. In Short, B. (ed.) *The English Rural Community*. Cambridge: Cambridge University Press, pp. 62–84.

Klein, R. G. and Cruz-Uribe, K. 1984. *The Analysis of Animal Bones from Archaeological Sites*. Chicago: University of Chicago Press.

Knodel, J. 1978. Natural fertility in pre-industrial Germany. *Population Studies* 32: 481–510.

Kolb, C. C. 1985. Demographic estimates in archaeology: contributions from ethnoarchaeology on Mesoamerican peasants. *Current Anthropology* 26: 581–599.

Kolman, C. J., Centurion-Lara, A., Lukehart, S. A., Owsley, D. W. and Tuross, N. 1999. Identification of Treponema pallidum subspecies pallidum in a 200-year old skeletal specimen. *Journal of Infectious Diseases* 180: 2060–2063.

Komar, D. 2003. Lessons from Srebrenica: the contributions and limitations of physical anthropology in identifying victims of war crimes. *Journal of Forensic Sciences* 48: 713–716.

Konigsberg, L. W. and Frankenberg, S. R. 1992. Estimation of age structure in anthropological demography. *American Journal of Physical Anthropology* 89: 235–256.

2002. Deconstructing death in paleodemography. *American Journal of Physical Anthropology* 117: 297–309.

Konigsberg, L. W., Frankenberg, S. R. and Walker, R. B. 1997. Regress what on what? Paleodemographic age estimation as a calibration problem. In Paine, R. R. (ed.) *Integrating Archaeological Demography: Multidisciplinary Approaches to Prehistoric Population.* Carbondale: Southern Illinois University, pp. 64–88.

Konigsberg, L. W. and Herrmann, N. P. 2002. Markov chain Monte Carlo estimation of hazard model parameters in paleodemography. In Hoppa, R. D. and Vaupel, J. W. (eds.) *Paleodemography. Age Distributions from Skeletal Samples.* Cambridge: Cambridge University Press, pp. 222–242.

Konomi, N., Lebwohl, E., Mowbray, K., Tattersall, I. and Zhang, D. 2002. Detection of mycobacterial DNA in Andean mummies. *Journal of Clinical Microbiology* 40: 4738–4740.

Kósa, F. 1989. Age estimation from the fetal skeleton. In İşcan, M. Y. (ed.) *Age Markers in the Human Skeleton.* Springfield: Thomas, pp. 21–54.

Kramer, C. 1982. *Village Ethnoarchaeology. Rural Iran in Archaeological Perspective.* New York: Academic Press.

Kramer, K. L. and Boone, J. L. 2002. Why intensive agriculturalists have higher fertility: a household energy budget approach. *Current Anthropology* 43: 511–517.

Kreager, P. 1997. Population and identity. In Kertzer, D. I. and Fricke, D. (eds.) *Anthropological Demography.* Chicago: University of Chicago Press, pp. 139–174.

Krings, M., Stone, A., Schmitz, R., Krainitzki, H., Stoneking, M. and Pääbo, S. 1997. Neandertal DNA sequences and the origin of modern humans. *Cell* 90: 19–30.

Krings, M., Capelli, C., Tshentscher, F., Geisert, H., Meyer, S., von Haeseler, A., Grossschmidt, K., Possnert, G., Paunovic, M. and Pääbo, S. 2000. A view of Neandertal genetic diversity. *Nature Genetics* 26: 144–146.

Krogman, W. M. and İşcan, M. Y. 1986. *The Human Skeleton in Forensic Medicine.* 2nd edition. Springfield: Thomas.

Laluela-Fox, C., Sampietro, M. L., Caramelli, D., Puder, Y., Lari, M., Calafell, F., Martínez-Maza, C., Bastir, M., Fortea, J., de la Rasilla, M., Bertranpetit, J. and Rosas, A. 2005. Neandertal evolutionary genetics: mitochondrial DNA data from the Iberian peninsula. *Molecular Biology and Evolution* 22: 1077–1081.

Langford, C. 2002. The age pattern of mortality in the 1918–19 influenza pandemic: an attempted explanation based on data for England and Wales. *Medical History* 46: 1–20.

Larsen, C. S. 1997. *Bioarchaeology*. Cambridge: Cambridge University Press.

Larsen, C. S. and Milner, G. R. (eds.) 1994. *In the Wake of Contact: Biological Responses to Conquest*. New York: Wiley-Liss.

Larsen, C. S., Shavit, R. and Griffin, M. C. 1991. Dental caries evidence for dietary change: an archaeological context. In Kelley, M. A. and Larsen, C. S. (eds.) *Advances in Dental Anthropology*. New York: Wiley-Liss, pp. 179–202.

Laslett, P. 1969. Size and structure of the household in England over three centuries. *Population Studies* 23: 199–223.

1972. Mean household size in England since the sixteenth century. In Laslett, P. (ed.) *Household and the Family in Past Time: Comparative Studies in the Size and Structure of the Domestic Group*. Cambridge, Cambridge University Press, pp. 125–158.

Lassen, C., Hummel, S. and Herrmann, B. 1996. PCR based sex identification of ancient human bones by amplification of X- and Y-chromosomal sequences: a comparison. *Ancient Biomolecules* 1: 25–33.

Leader-Williams, N. 1988. *Reindeer on South Georgia*. Cambridge: Cambridge University Press.

Le Blanc, S. 1971. An addition to Naroll's suggested floor area and settlement population relationship. *American Antiquity* 36: 210–211.

LeBras, H. and Wachter, K. W. 1978. Living forbears in stable populations. In Wachter, K. W., Hammel, E. A. and Laslett, P. (eds.) *Statistical Studies of Historical Social Structure*. New York, Academic Press, pp. 163–188.

Lee, R. B. 1972. Population growth and the beginnings of sedentary life among the !Kung Bushmen. In Spooner, S. (ed.) *Population Growth: Anthropological Implications*. Cambridge, MA: MIT Press, pp. 329–342.

1979. *The !Kung San*. Cambridge: Cambridge University Press.

Leslie, P. H. 1945. On the use of matrices in certain population mathematics. *Biometrika* 33: 183–212.

1948. Some further notes on the use of matrices in population mathematics. *Biometrika* 35: 213–245.

Lewis, E. G. 1942. On the generation and growth of a population. *Sankhya* 6: 93–96.

Lieberman, D. E. 1994. The biological basis for seasonal increments in dental cementum and their application to archaeological research. *Journal of Archaeological Science* 21: 525–539.

Lietman, T., Porco, T. and Blower, S. 1997. Leprosy and tuberculosis: the epidemiological consequences of cross-immunity. *American Journal of Public Health* 87: 1923–1927.

Lieverse, A. R. 1999. Diet and the aetiology of dental calculus. *International Journal of Osteoarchaeology* 9: 219–232.

Liversidge, H. M. and Molleson, T. I. 1999. Developing permanent tooth length as an estimate of age. *Journal of Forensic Sciences* 44: 917–920.

Liversidge, H. M., Dean, M. C. and Molleson, T. I. 1993. Increasing human tooth length between birth and 5.4 years. *American Journal of Physical Anthropology* 90: 307–313.

Lockwood, C. A. and Tobias, P. V. 2002. Morphology and affinities of new hominin cranial remains from Member 4 of the Sterkfontein Formation, Gauteng Province, South Africa. *Journal of Human Evolution* 42: 389–450.

Lovejoy, C. O., Meindl, R. S., Pryzbeck, T. R., Barton, T. S., Heiple, K. G. and Kotting, D. 1977. Paleodemography of the Libben Site, Ottawa, Ohio. *Science* 198: 291–293.

Lovejoy, C. O., Meindl, R. S., Pryzbeck, T. R. and Mensforth, R. P. 1985. Chronological metamorphosis of the auricular surface of the ilium: a new method for the determination of adult skeletal age at death. *American Journal of Physical Anthropology* 68: 15–28.

Lowe, J. C. and Morydas, S. 1975. *The Geography of Movement*. Boston: Houghton-Mifflin.

Lucy, D., Aykroyd, R. G., Pollard, A. M. and Solheim, T. 1996. A Bayesian approach to adult human age estimation from dental observations by Johanson's age changes. *Journal of Forensic Sciences* 41: 189–194.

Luongo, G., Perotta, A., Scarpati, C., De Carolis, E., Patricelli, G. and Ciarallo, A. 2003. Impact of the AD 79 explosive eruption on Pompeii, II. Causes of death of the inhabitants inferred by stratigraphic analysis and areal distribution of the human casualties. *Journal of Volcanology and Geothermal Research* 126: 169–200.

Lyman, R. L. 1987. On the analysis of vertebrate mortality profiles: sample size, mortality type, and hunting pressure. *American Antiquity* 52: 125–142.

Lynnerup, N. 1998. *The Greenland Norse: a Biological-Anthropological Study*. Meddelelser om Grønland, Man and Society 24. Copenhagen: The Commission for Scientific Research in Greenland.

McDaniel, A. 1992. Extreme mortality in nineteenth century Africa: the case of Liberian immigrants. *Demography* 29: 581–594.

McElroy, A. and Townsend, P. K. 1996. *Medical Anthropology in Ecological Perspective*. Boulder: Westview Press.

McKeown, T. 1976. *The Modern Rise of Population*. New York: Academic Press.

McKern, T. W. and Stewart, T. D. 1957. *Skeletal Age Changes in Young American Males*. Natick: Quartermaster Research and Development Command.

McKinley, K. 1971. Survivorship in gracile and robust australopithecines: a demographic comparison and a proposed birth model. *American Journal of Physical Anthropology* 34: 417–426.

McNeil, W. H. 1979. *Plagues and Peoples*. London: Penguin.

Maharatna, A. 1996. *The Demography of Famines. An Indian Historical Perspective*. Delhi: Oxford University Press.

Mann, A. 1975. *Some Paleodemographic Aspects of the South African Australopithecines*. Philadelphia: University of Pennsylvania.

Manning, P. and Griffiths, W. S. 1988. Divining the unprovable: simulating the demography of African slavery. *Journal of Interdisciplinary History* 19: 177–201.

Maresh, M. M. 1955. Linear growth of long bones of extremities from infancy through adolescence. *American Journal of Diseases of Children* 89: 725–742.

Maresh, M. M. and Deming, J. 1939. The growth of long bones in 80 infants. *Child Development* 10: 91–100.

Margerison, B. J. and Knüsel, C. J. 2002. Paleodemographic comparison of a catastrophic and attritional death assemblage. *American Journal of Physical Anthropology* 119: 134–143.

Marsden, P. and West, B. 1992. Population change in Roman London. *Britannia* 23: 133–140.

Martin, D. L. and Frayer, D. W. (eds.) 1997. *Troubled Times: Violence and Warfare in the Past*. Amsterdam: Gordon and Breach.

Martin, P. S. 1973. The discovery of America. *Science* 179: 969–974.

Masset, C. 1976. Sur la mortalité chez les anciens Indiens de l'Illinois. *Current Anthropology* 17: 128–132.

Mays, S. 1993. Infanticide in Roman Britain. *Antiquity* 67: 883–888.

  1996. Healed limb amputations in human osteoarchaeology and their causes: a case study from Ipswich, U.K. *International Journal of Osteoarchaeology* 6: 101–113.

  2003. Comment on 'A Bayesian approach to ageing perinatal skeletal material from archaeological sites: implications for the evidence for infanticide in Roman Britain' by R. L. Gowland and A. T. Chamberlain. *Journal of Archaeological Science* 30: 1695–1700.

Mays, S. and Cox, M. 2000. Sex determination in skeletal remains. In Cox, M. and Mays, S. (eds.) *Human Osteology in Archaeology and Forensic Science*. London: Greenwich Medical Media, pp. 117–130.

Me-Bar, Y. and Valdez, F. 2004. Recovery time after a disaster and the ancient Maya. *Journal of Archaeological Science* 31: 1311–1324.

Meindl, R. S. and Lovejoy, C. O. 1985. Ectocranial suture closure: a revised method for the determination of skeletal age at death based on the lateral-anterior sutures. *American Journal of Physical Anthropology* 68: 57–66.

Meindl, R. S. and Russell, K. F. 1998. Recent advances in method and theory in paleodemography. *Annual Review of Anthropology* 27: 375–399.

Meindl, R. S., Lovejoy, C. O. and Mensforth, R. P. 1983. Skeletal age at death: accuracy of determination and implications for paleodemography. *Human Biology* 55: 73–87.

Meindl, R. S., Lovejoy, C. O., Mensforth, R. P. and Walker, R. A. 1985a. A revised method of age determination using the os pubis, with a review and tests of accuracy of other current methods of pubic symphyseal aging. *American Journal of Physical Anthropology* 68: 29–45.

Meindl, R. S., Lovejoy, C. O., Mensforth, R. P. and Carlos, L. D. 1985b. Accuracy and direction of error in the sexing of the skeleton: implications for paleodemography. *American Journal of Physical Anthropology* 68: 79–85.

Meltzer, D. J. 1995. Clocking the first Americans. *Annual Review of Anthropology* 24: 21–45.

Mensforth, R. P. and Lovejoy, C. O. 1985. Anatomical, physiological, and epidemiological correlates of the aging process: a confirmation of multifactorial age determination in the Libben skeletal population. *American Journal of Physical Anthropology* 68: 87–106.

Miles, A. E. W. 1963. The dentition in the assessment of individual age in skeletal material. In Brothwell, D. R. (ed.) *Dental Anthropology*. Oxford: Pergamon, pp. 191–209.

   1989. *An Early Christian Chapel and Burial Ground on the Isle of Ensay, Outer Hebrides, Scotland with a Study of the Skeletal Remains*. Oxford. British Archaeological Reports, British Series 212.

   2001. The Miles method for assessing age from tooth wear revisited. *Journal of Archaeological Science* 28: 973–982.

Milner, G. R. and Larsen, C. S. 1991. Teeth as artifacts of human behavior: intentional mutilation and accidental modification. In Kelley, M. A. and Larsen, C. S. (eds.) *Advances in Dental Anthropology*. New York: Wiley-Liss, pp. 357–378.

Milner, G. R., Humpf, D. A. and Harpending, H. C. 1989. Pattern matching of age at death distributions in paleodemographic analysis. *American Journal of Physical Anthropology* 80: 49–58.

Mineau, G. P., Bean, L. L. and Skolnick, M. 1979. Mormon demographic history II: the family cycle and natural fertility. *Population Studies* 33: 429–446.

Moch, L. P. 1992. *Moving Europeans: Migration in Western Europe since 1650*. Bloomington: Indiana University Press.

Molleson, T., Cruse, K. and Mays, S. 1998. Some sexually dimorphic features of the human juvenile skull and their value in sex determination in immature skeletal remains. *Journal of Archaeological Science* 25: 719–728.

Moore, P. S., Marfin, A. A., Quenemoen, L. E., Gessner, B. D., Ayub, Y. S., Miller, D. S., Sullivan, K. M. and Toole, M. J. 1993. Mortality rates in displaced and resident populations of central Somalia during 1992 famine. *The Lancet* 341: 935–938.

Moorrees, C. F. A., Fanning, E. A. and Hunt, E. E. 1963a. Formation and resorption of three deciduous teeth in children. *American Journal of Physical Anthropology* 21: 205–213.

 1963b. Age variation of formation stages for ten permanent teeth. *Journal of Dental Research* 42: 1490–1502.

Naroll, R. 1962. Floor area and settlement population. *American Antiquity* 27: 587–589.

Nemeskéri, J., Harsányi, L. and Acsádi, G. 1960. Methoden zur diagnose des lebensalters von skelettfunden. *Anthropologischer Anzeiger* 24: 70–95.

Nettle, D. 1999. Linguistic diversity of the Americas can be reconciled with a recent colonization. *Proceedings of the National Academy of Sciences of the USA* 96: 3325–3329.

Newell, C. 1988. *Methods and Models in Demography*. London: Belhaven.

Nolan, J. 1998. The Newcastle Infirmary at the Forth, Newcastle upon Tyne. Volume I: The Archaeology and History. Unpublished report by Northern Counties Archaeological Services for Tyne and Wear Development Corporation.

Nordberg, H. 1963. *Biometrical notes: the information on ancient Christian inscriptions from Rome concerning the duration of life and the dates of birth and death*. Helsinki.

Notestein, F. 1945. Population – the long view. In Schultz, T. W. (ed.) *Food for the World*. Chicago: University of Chicago Press, pp. 36–57.

Olshansky, S. J., Carnes, B. A. and Cassel, C. 1990. In search of Methuselah: estimating the upper limits to human longevity. *Science* 250: 634–640.

Ortner, D. J., Butler, W., Cafarella, J. and Milligan, L. 2001. Evidence of probable scurvy in subadults from archaeological sites in North America. *American Journal of Physical Anthropology* 114: 343–351.

Ortner, D. J. and Ericksen, M. F. 1997. Bone changes in the human skull probably resulting from scurvy in infancy and childhood. *International Journal of Osteoarchaeology* 7: 212–220.

Ortner, D. J., Kimmerle, E. H. and Diez, M. 1999. Probable evidence of scurvy in subadults from archaeological sites. *American Journal of Physical Anthropology* 108: 321–331.

Ortner, D. J. and Mays, S. 1998. Dry bone manifestations of rickets in infancy and early childhood. *International Journal of Osteoarchaeology* 8: 45–55.

Ortner, D. J. and Putschar, W. G. J. 1985. *Identification of Pathological Conditions in Human Skeletal Remains*. Washington DC: Smithsonian Institution Press.

Orton, C. 2000. *Sampling in Archaeology*. Cambridge: Cambridge University Press.

Otterbein, K. F. 2000. Killing of captured enemies: a cross-cultural study. *Current Anthropology* 41: 439–443.

Ovchinnikov, I. V., Götherström, A., Romanova, G. P., Kharitonov, V. M., Lidén, K. and Goodwin, W. 2000. Molecular analysis of Neandertal DNA from the northern Caucasus. *Nature* 404: 490–493.

Owsley, D. W. and Jantz, R. L. 1985. Long bone lengths and gestational age distributions of post-contact Arikara Indian perinatal infant skeletons. *American Journal of Physical Anthropology* 68: 321–328.

Paine, R. R. 1989. Model life tables as a measure of bias in the Grasshopper Pueblo skeletal series. *American Antiquity* 54: 820–824.

Parker, G. 1972. *The Army of Flanders and the Spanish Road, 1567–1659*. Cambridge: Cambridge University Press.

Parker Pearson, M. and Thorpe, I. J. N. (eds.) 2005. *Warfare, Violence and Slavery in Prehistory*. British Archaeological Reports, International Series, 13/4.

Pavelka, M. S. M. and Fedigan, L. M. 1991. Menopause: a comparative life history perspective. *Yearbook of Physical Anthropology* 34: 13–38.

Pennington, R. and Harpending, H. 1988. Fitness and fertility among Kalahari !Kung. *American Journal of Physical Anthropology* 77: 303–319.

Pettitt, P. B. 1999. Disappearing from the world: an archaeological perspective on Neanderthal extinction. *Oxford Journal of Archaeology* 18: 217–240.

Phenice, T. W. 1969. A newly developed visual method of sexing the os pubis. *American Journal of Physical Anthropology* 30: 297–301.

Pianka, E. R. 1978. *Evolutionary Ecology*, 2nd edition. New York: Harper and Row.

Piontek, J., Jerszyńska, B. and Segeda, S. 2001. Long bones growth variation among prehistoric agricultural and pastoral populations from Ukraine (Bronze Era to Iron Age). *Variability and Evolution* 9: 61–73.

Plane, D. A. and Rogerson, P. A. 1994. *The Geographical Analysis of Population, With Applications to Planning and Business*. New York: Wiley.

Post, J. B. 1971. Ages at menarche and menopause: some mediaeval authorities. *Population Studies* 25: 83–87.

Postgate, N. 1994. How many Sumerians per hectare? Probing the anatomy of an early city. *Cambridge Archaeological Journal* 4: 47–65.

Pressat, R. 1985. *The Dictionary of Demography*. Oxford: Blackwell.

Preston, S. H. 1983. An integrated system for demographic estimation from two age distributions. *Demography* 20: 213–226.

Price, T. D., Bentley, R. A., Lüning, J., Gronenborn, D. and Wahl, J. 2001. Prehistoric human migration in the *Linearbandkeramik* of Central Europe. *Antiquity* 75: 593–603.

Pusch, C. M., Broghammer, M., Nicholson, G. J., Nerlich, A. G., Zink, A., Kennerknecht, I., Bachman, L. and Blin, N. 2004. PCR-induced sequence alterations hamper the typing of prehistoric bone samples for diagnostic achondroplasia mutation. *Molecular Biology and Evolution* 21: 2005–2011.

Radlauer, D. 2002. An engineered tragedy: statistical analysis of casualities in the Palestinian-Israeli conflict, September 2000 – September 2002. Available at: www.ict.org.il/articles/articledet.cfm?articleid=439

Rafi, A., Spiegelman, M., Stanford, J., Lemma, E., Donoghue, H. and Zias, J. 1994. DNA of *Mycobacterium leprae* detected by PCR in ancient bone. *International Journal of Osteoarchaeology* 4: 287–290.

Rainio, J., Lalu, K. and Penttilä, A. 2001. Independent forensic autopsies in an armed conflict: investigation of the victims from Racak, Kosovo. *Forensic Science International* 116: 171–185.

Ramirez Rozzi, F. V. and Bermúdez de Castro, J. M. 2004. Surprisingly rapid growth in Neanderthals. *Nature* 428: 936–939.

Relethford, J. H. 1994. Craniometric variation among modern human populations. *American Journal of Physical Anthropology* 95: 53–62.

Renfrew, C. 1973. *Before Civilisation*. London: Cape.

Resnick, D. 2002. *Diagnosis of Bone and Joint Diseases*. 4th edition. London: Saunders.

Reynolds, J., Weir, B. S. and Cockerham, C. C. 1983. Estimation of the coancestry coefficient: basis for a short-term genetic distance. *Genetics* 105: 767–779.

Richards, L. C. and Miller, S. L. J. 1991. Relationship between age and dental attrition in Australian aboriginals. *American Journal of Physical Anthropology* 84: 159–164.

Richards, M., Côrte-Real, H., Forster, P. et al. 1996. Paleolithic and Neolithic lineages in the European mitochondrial gene pool. *American Journal of Human Genetics* 59: 185–203.

Richardson, A. 2000. The numerical basis of Roman camps. *Oxford Journal of Archaeology* 19: 425–437.

Rick, J. 1987. Dates as data: an examination of the Peruvian preceramic radiocarbon record. *American Antiquity* 52: 55–73.

Roberts, C. 1986. Leprosy and leprosaria in Medieval Britain. *MASCA Journal* 4: 15–21.

   2000a. Trauma in biocultural perspective: past, present and future work in Britain. In Cox, M. and Mays, S. (eds.) *Human Osteology in Archaeology and Forensic Science.* London: Greenwich Medical Media, pp. 337–356.

   2000b. Did they take sugar? The use of skeletal evidence in the study of past disability in past populations. In Hubert, J. (ed.) *Madness, disability and social exclusion. The archaeology and anthropology of 'difference'.* London: Routledge, pp. 46–59.

Roberts, C. and Cox, M. 2003. *Health and Disease in Britain from Prehistory to the Present Day.* Stroud: Sutton.

Roberts, C. and Manchester, K. 1995. *The Archaeology of Disease.* Stroud: Sutton.

Roberts, G. W. 1952. A life table for a West Indian slave population. *Population Studies* 5: 238–242.

Roberts, L., Lafta, R., Garfield, R., Khudhairii, J. and Burnham, G. 2004. Mortality before and after the 2003 invasion of Iraq: cluster sample survey. *The Lancet* 364: 1857–1864.

Robling, A. G. and Stout, S. D. 2000. Histomorphometry of human cortical bone: applications to age estimation. In Katzenberg, M. A. and Saunders, S. R. (eds.) *Biological Anthropology of the Human Skeleton.* New York: Wiley-Liss, pp. 187–213.

Roff, D. A. 1992. *The Evolution of Life Histories. Theory and Analysis.* New York: Chapman and Hall.

Rogers, A. 1988. Age patterns of elderly migration: an international comparison. *Demography* 25: 355–370.

Rogers, A. R. 1995. Genetic evidence for a Pleistocene population explosion. *Evolution* 49: 608–615.

Rogers, T. L. 2005. Determining the sex of human remains through cranial morphology. *Journal of Forensic Sciences* 50: 493–500.

Roper, D. C. 1979. The method and theory of site catchment analysis: a review. In Schiffer, M. B. (ed.) *Advances in Archaeological Method and Theory* Vol. II. New York: Academic, pp. 119–140.

Rösing, F. W. 1983. Sexing immature human skeletons. *Journal of Human Evolution* 12: 149–155.

Ruff, C. B. 1981. A reassessment of demographic estimates for Pecos Pueblo. *American Journal of Physical Anthropology* 54: 147–151.

Saller, R. 1994. *Patriarchy, Property and Death in the Roman Family.* Cambridge: Cambridge University Press.

Sarkar, N. K. 1951. A note on abridged life tables for Ceylon, 1900–1947. *Population Studies* 4: 439–443.

Sattenspiel, L. and Harpending, H. 1983. Stable populations and skeletal age. *American Antiquity* 48: 489–498.

Saunders, S. R. and Hoppa, R. D. 1993. Growth deficit in survivors and non-survivors: biological mortality bias in subadult skeletal samples. *Yearbook of Physical Anthropology* 36: 127–151.

Saunders, S.[R.], Hoppa, R.[D.] and Southern, R. 1993. Diaphyseal growth in a nineteenth century skeletal sample of subadults from St Thomas' Church, Belleville, Ontario. *International Journal of Osteoarchaeology* 3: 265–281.

Schact, R. M. 1981. Estimating past population trends. *Annual Review of Anthropology* 10: 119–140.

Scheidel, W. 1996. Measuring sex, age and death in the Roman Empire. *Journal of Roman Archaeology Supplementary Series* 21: 1–184.

Scheuer, [J.]L. and Black, S. 2000a. Development and ageing of the juvenile skeleton. In Cox, M. and Mays, S. (eds.) *Human Osteology in Archaeology and Forensic Science.* London: Greenwich Medical Media, pp. 9–21.

2000b. *Juvenile Developmental Osteology.* London: Academic Press.

Scheuer, J. L., Musgrave, J. H., and Evans, S. P. 1980. The estimation of late fetal and perinatal age from limb bone length by linear and logarithmic regression. *Annals of Human Biology* 7: 257–265.

Schiffer, M. B. 1976. *Behavioral Archeology.* New York: Academic Press.

Schultz, M. 2001. Paleohistopathology of bone: a new approach to the study of ancient diseases. *Yearbook of Physical Anthropology* 44: 106–147.

Schutkowski, H. 1993. Sex determination of infant and juvenile skeletons. I. Morphognostic features. *American Journal of Physical Anthropology* 90: 199–205.

Schwarz, C., Davidson, G., Seaton, A. and Tebbit, V. (eds.) 1990. *Chambers English Dictionary*. Edinburgh: W. and R. Chambers Ltd.

Scott, S. and Duncan, C. J. 1998. *Human Demography and Disease*. Cambridge: Cambridge University Press.

Scott, S., Duncan, C. J. and Duncan, S. R. 1996. The plague in Penrith, Cumbria, 1597/8: its causes, biology and consequences. *Annals of Human Biology* 23: 1–21.

Scrimshaw, N. S. 1987. The phenomenon of famine. *Annual Reviews of Nutrition* 7: 1–21.

Scrimshaw, S. C. M. 1984. Infanticide in human populations: societal and individual concerns. In Haufstater, G. and Hardy, S. B. (eds.) *Infanticide: Comparative and Evolutionary Perspectives*. New York: Aldine, pp. 439–462.

Sealy, J. 2001. Body tissue chemistry and palaeodiet. In Brothwell, D. R. and Pollard, A. M. (eds.) *Handbook of Archaeological Sciences*. Chichester: Wiley, pp. 269–279.

Seaman, J., Leivesley, S. and Hogg, C. 1984. *Epidemiology of Natural Disasters*. Basel: Karger.

Seielstad, M. T., Minch, E. and Cavalli-Sforza, L. L. 1998. Genetic evidence for a higher female migration rate. *Nature Genetics* 20: 278–280.

Sellen, D. W. and Mace, R. 1997. Fertility and mode of subsistence: a phylogenetic analysis. *Current Anthropology* 38: 878–888.

Serre, D., Langaney, A., Chech, M., Teschler-Nicola, M., Paunovic, M., Mennecier, P., Hofreiter, M., Possnert, G. and Pääbo, S. 2004. No evidence of Neandertal mtDNA contribution to early modern humans. *PLoS Biology* 2: 0313–0317.

Shahar, S. 1993. Who were old in the Middle Ages? *Social History of Medicine* 6: 313–341.

Sharpe, F. R. and Lotka, A. J. 1911. A problem in age distribution. *Philosophical Magazine* 6: 435–438.

Shaw, B. D. 1996. Seasons of death: aspects of mortality in Imperial Rome. *Journal of Roman Studies* 86: 100–138.

Shennan, S. 2000. Population, culture history, and the dynamics of culture change. *Current Anthropology* 41: 811–835.

2001. Demography and cultural innovation: a model and its implications for the emergence of modern human culture. *Cambridge Journal of Archaeology* 11: 5–16.

2002. *Genes, Memes and Human History. Darwinian Archaeology and Cultural Evolution.* London: Thames and Hudson.

Sheridan, R. B. 1985. *Doctors and Slaves: a Medical and Demographic History of Slavery in the British West Indies 1680–1834.* Cambridge: Cambridge University Press.

Sherwood, R. J., Meindl, R. S., Robinson, H. B. and May, R. L. 2000. Fetal age: methods of estimation and effects of pathology. *American Journal of Physical Anthropology* 113: 305–315.

Short, R. V. and Balaban, E. (eds.) 1994. *The Differences Between the Sexes.* Cambridge: Cambridge University Press.

Sief, D. 1990. Explaining biased sex ratios in human populations. *Current Anthropology* 31: 25–48.

Signoli, M., Seguy, I., Biraben, J.-N. and Dutour, O. 2002. Paleodemography and historical demography in the context of an epidemic: plague in Provence in the eighteenth century. *Population* 57: 829–854.

Siler, W. 1979. A competing-risk model for animal mortality. *Ecology* 60: 750–757.

1983. Parameters of mortality in human populations with widely varying life spans. *Statistics in Medicine* 2: 373–380.

Skinner, G. W. 1997. Family systems and demographic processes. In Kertzer, D. I. and Fricke, T. (eds.) *Anthropological Demography.* Chicago: University of Chicago Press, pp. 53–95.

Smith, B. H. 1989. Dental development as a measure of life history in primates. *Evolution* 43: 683–688.

1991. Standards of human tooth formation and dental age assessment. In Kelley, M. A. and Larsen, C. S. (eds.) *Advances in Dental Anthropology.* New York: Wiley-Liss, pp. 143–168.

Smith, B. H. and Tompkins, R. L. 1995. Toward a life history of the hominidae. *Annual Review of Anthropology* 24: 257–279.

Smith, B. H., Crummett, T. L. and Bradt, K. L. 1994. Ages of eruption of primate teeth: a compendium for ageing individuals and comparing life histories. *Yearbook of Physical Anthropology* 37: 177–232.

Smith, P. and Kahila, G. 1992. Identification of infanticide in archaeological sites: a case study from the late Roman-early Byzantine periods at Ashkelon, Israel. *Journal of Archaeological Science* 19: 667–675.

Smith, T. E. 1960. The Cocos-Keeling Islands: a demographic laboratory. *Population Studies* 14: 94–130.

Snow, D. R. 1996. Mohawk demography and the effects of exogenous epidemics on American Indian populations. *Journal of Anthropological Archaeology* 15: 160–182.

Sokal, R. R., Oden, N. L. and Wilson, C. 1991. Genetic evidence for the spread of agriculture in Europe by demic diffusion. *Nature* 351: 143–145.

Solheim, T. 1989. Dental root translucency as an indicator of age *Scandinavian Journal of Dental Research* 97: 189–197.

Sorg, M. H., Andrews, R. P. and İşcan, M. Y. 1989. Radiographic ageing of the adult. In İşcan, M. Y. (ed.) *Age Markers in the Human Skeleton*. Springfield: Thomas, pp. 169–193.

Spiegel, P. B. and Salama, P. 2000. War and mortality in Kosovo, 1998–99: an epidemiological testimony. *The Lancet* 355: 2204–2209.

Stearns, S. C. 1992. *The Evolution of Life Histories*. New York: Oxford University Press.

Steele, J., Adams, J. and Sluckin, T. 1998. Modelling paleoindian dispersals. *World Archaeology* 30: 286–305.

Stewart, T. D. 1970. Identification of the scars of parturition in the skeletal remains of females. In Stewart, T. D. (ed.) *Personal Identification in Mass Disasters*. Washington: Smithsonian Institution, pp. 127–135.

Stiner, M. C. 1991. An interspecific perspective on the emergence of the modern human predatory niche. In Stiner, M. C. (ed.) *Human Predators and Prey Mortality*. Boulder: Westview Press, pp. 150–185.

Stone, A. C., Milner, G. R., Pääbo, S. and Stoneking, M. 1996. Sex determination of ancient human skeletons using DNA. *American Journal of Physical Anthropology* 99: 231–238.

Stone, A. C. and Stoneking M. 1999. Analysis of ancient DNA from a prehistoric Amerindian cemetery. *Philosophical Transactions of the Royal Society B*, 354: 143–149.

Storey, G. R. 1997. The population of ancient Rome. *Antiquity* 71: 966–978.

Storey, R. 1985. An estimate of mortality in a Pre-Columbian urban population. *American Anthropologist* 87: 519–535.

Stringer, C. B., Dean, M. C. and Martin, R. D. 1990. A comparative study of cranial and dental development within a recent British sample and among Neandertals. In Rousseau, C. J. (ed.) *Primate Life History and Evolution*. New York: Wiley-Liss, pp. 115–152.

Stuart-Macadam, P. L. 1989. Nutritional deficiency diseases: a survey of scurvy, rickets and iron-deficiency anemia. In İşcan, M. Y. and Kennedy, K. A. R. (eds.) *Reconstructing Life from the Skeleton*. New York: Wiley-Liss, pp. 210–222.

Stuart-Macadam, P. and Kent, S. (eds.) 1992. *Diet, Demography and Disease: Changing Perspectives on Anemia*. New York: Aldine de Gruyter.

Suchey, J. M., Wisely, D. V., Green, R. F. and Noguchi, T. T. 1979. Analysis of dorsal pitting in the os pubis in an extensive sample of modern American females. *American Journal of Physical Anthropology* 51: 517–540.

Suchey, J. M., Wisely, D. V. and Katz, D. 1986. Evaluation of the Todd and McKern-Stewart methods for aging the male os pubis. In Reichs, K. (ed.) *Forensic Osteology: Advances in the Identification of Human Remains*. Springfield: Thomas, pp. 33–67.

Sumner, W. M. 1989. Population and settlement area: an example from Iran. *American Anthropologist* 91: 631–641.

Sunderland, E. P., Smith, C. J. and Sunderland, R. 1987. A histological study of the chronology of initial mineralization in the human deciduous dentition. *Archives of Oral Biology* 32: 167–174.

Sussman, R. W. 1972. Child transport, family size, and increase in human population in the Neolithic. *Current Anthropology* 13: 258–259.

Sutherland, L. D. and Suchey, J. M. 1991. Use of the ventral arc in pubic sex determination. *Journal of Forensic Sciences* 36: 501–511.

Taber, R. D. and Dasmann, R. F. 1957. The dynamics of three natural populations of the deer *Odocoileus hemionus columbianus*. *Ecology* 38: 233–246.

Taylor, G. M., Rutland, P. and Molleson, T. 1997. A sensitive polymerase chain reaction method for the detection of *Plasmodium* species DNA in ancient human remains. *Ancient Biomolecules* 1: 193–203.

Thomas, M., Gilbert, P., Cuccui, J., White, W., Lynnerup, N., Titball, R. W., Cooper, A. and Prentice, M. B. 2004. Absence of *Yersinia pestis*-specific DNA in human teeth from five European excavations of putative plague victims. *Microbiology* 150: 341–354.

Thornton, R. 1997. Aboriginal North American population and rates of decline, ca. 1500–1900. *Current Anthropology* 38: 310–315.

Tilly, C. 1978. Migration in modern European history. In McNeill, W. H. and Adams, R. S. (eds.) *Human Migration: Patterns and Policies*. Bloomington: Indiana University Press, pp. 48–72.

Tobias, P. V. 1991. *Olduvai Gorge Volume IV. The Skulls, Endocasts and Teeth of Homo habilis*. Cambridge: Cambridge University Press.

Todd, T. W. 1920. Age changes in the pubic bone. I. The white male pubis. *American Journal of Physical Anthropology* 3: 285–334.

1924. Cranial suture closure: its progress and age relationship. *American Journal of Physical Anthropology* 7: 325–384.

Tomasson, R. F. 1977. A millennium of misery: the demography of the Icelanders. *Population Studies* 31: 405–427.

Torroni, A., Neel, J. V., Barrantes, R., Schurr, T. G. and Wallace, D. C. 1994. Mitochondrial DNA 'clock' for the Amerinds and its implications for timing their entry into North America. *Proceedings of the National Academy of Sciences of the USA* 91: 1158–1162.

Trinkaus, E. 1995. Neanderthal mortality patterns. *Journal of Archaeological Science* 22: 121–142.

Trivers, R. L. and Willard, D. E. 1973. Natural selection of parental ability to vary the sex ratio of offspring. *Science* 179: 90–92.

Twigg, G. 1984. *The Black Death: a Biological Reappraisal*. London: Batsford.

Tyrrell, A. J. and Chamberlain, A. T. 1998. Non-metric trait evidence for modern human affinities and the distinctiveness of Neanderthals. *Journal of Human Evolution* 34: 549–554.

Ubelaker, D. H. 1974. Reconstruction of demographic profiles from ossuary skeletal samples. A case study from the Tidewater Potomac. *Smithsonian Contributions to Anthropology* 18: 1–79.

1992. North American Indian population size: changing perspectives. In Verano, J. W. and Ubelaker, D. H. (eds.) *Disease and Demography in the Americas.* Washington DC: Smithsonian Institution Press, pp. 169–195.

Underwood, J. C. E. (ed.) 2004. *General and Systematic Pathology.* 4th edition. Edinburgh: Churchill Livingstone.

Vallois, H. V. 1937. La durée de la vie chez l'homme fossile. *L' Anthropologie* 47: 499–532.

Van Gerven, D. P. and Armelagos, G. J. 1983. 'Farewell to paleodemography?' Rumors of its death have been greatly exaggerated. *Journal of Human Evolution* 12: 353–360.

Verano, J. W. and Ubelaker, D. H. (eds.) 1992. *Disease and Demography in the Americas.* Washington DC: Smithsonian Institution Press.

Vita-Finzi, C. and Higgs, E. S. 1970. Prehistoric economy in the Mount Carmel area: site catchment analysis. *Proceedings of the Prehistoric Society* 36: 1–37.

Waldron, T. 1994. *Counting the Dead: The Epidemiology of Skeletal Populations.* New York: Wiley-Liss.

Walker, P. L. 1997. Wife beating, boxing and broken noses: skeletal evidence for cultural patterning of interpersonal violence. In Martin, D. L. and Frayer, D. W. (eds.) *Troubled Times: Violence and Warfare in the Past.* Amsterdam: Gordon and Breach, pp. 145–179.

Walker, P. L. and Cook, D. C. 1998. Brief communication: gender and sex: vive la différence. *American Journal of Physical Anthropology* 106: 255–259.

Walker, P. L., Dean, G. and Shapiro, P. 1991. Estimating age from tooth wear in archaeological populations. In Kelly, M. A. and Larsen, C. S. (eds.) *Advances in Dental Anthropology,* New York: Wiley, pp. 169–178.

Walker, P. L., Johnson, J. R. and Lambert, P. M. 1988. Age and sex biases in the preservation of human skeletal remains. *American Journal of Physical Anthropology* 76: 183–188.

Warrick, G. 2003. European infectious disease and depopulation of the Wendat-Tionontate (Huron-Petun). *World Archaeology* 35: 258–275.

Watkins, S. C. and Menken, J. 1985. Famines in historical perspective. *Population and Development Review* 11: 647–675.

Watts, E. S. 1990. Evolutionary trends in primate growth and development. In Rousseau, C. J. (ed.) *Primate Life History and Evolution.* New York: Wiley-Liss, pp. 89–104.

Weale, M. E., Weiss, D. A., Jager, R. F., Bradman, N. and Thomas, A. G. 2002. Y chromosome evidence for Anglo-Saxon mass migration. *Molecular Biology and Evolution* 19: 1008–1021.

Weaver, D. S. 1980. Sex differences in the ilia of a known age and sex sample of fetal and infant skeletons. *American Journal of Physical Anthropology* 52: 191–195.

Weidenreich, F. 1939. The duration of life of fossil man of China and the pathological lesions found in his skeleton. *Chinese Medical Journal* 55: 34–44.

Weiss, K. M. 1972. On the systematic bias in skeletal sexing. *American Journal of Physical Anthropology* 37: 239–250.

1973. Demographic models for anthropology. *Memoirs of the Society for American Archaeology* 27 (*American Antiquity* 38(2): 1–186).

White, T. D. and Johanson, D. C. 1982. Pliocene hominid mandibles from the Hadar Formation, Ethiopia: 1974–1977 collections. *American Journal of Physical Anthropology* 57: 501–544.

Whittaker, D. 2000. Ageing from the dentition. In Cox, M. and Mays, S. (eds.) *Human Osteology in Archaeology and Forensic Science.* London: Greenwich Medical Media, pp. 83–99.

Whyte, I. D. 2000. *Migration and Society in Britain 1550–1830.* London: Macmillan.

Wich, S. A., Utami-Atmoko, S. S., Mitra Setia, T., Rijksen, H. D., Schürmann, C., van Hoof, J. A. R. and van Schaik, C. P. 2004. Life history of wild Sumatran orangutans (*Pongo abelii*). *Journal of Human Evolution* 47: 385–398.

Wiessner, P. 1974. A functional estimator of population from floor area. *American Antiquity* 39: 343–349.

Williams, J. T. 1993. Origin and population structure of the Icelanders. *Human Biology* 65: 167–191.

Wilson, C. 1984. Natural fertility in pre-industrial England. *Population Studies* 38: 225–240.

Wiseman, T. P. 1969. The census in the first century B.C. *Journal of Roman Studies* 59: 59–75.

Wittwer-Backofen, U., Gampe, J. and Vaupel, J. W. 2004. Tooth cementum annulation for age estimation: results from a large known-age validation study. *American Journal of Physical Anthropology* 123: 119–129.

Wood, B. A. 1991. *Koobi Fora Research Project.* Vol. IV. *Hominid Cranial Remains.* Oxford: Clarendon Press.

Wood, J. B. 1996. *The King's Army.* Cambridge: Cambridge University Press.

Wood, J. W. 1994. *Dynamics of Human Reproduction. Biology, Biometry, Demography.* New York: Aldine de Gruyter.

Wood, J.[W.] and DeWitte-Aviña, S. 2003. Was the Black Death yersinial plague? *The Lancet Infectious Diseases* 3: 327–328.

Wood, J. W., Holman, D. J., Weiss, K. M., Buchanan, A. V. and LeFor, B. 1992a. Hazards models for human population biology. *Yearbook of Physical Anthropology* 35: 43–87.

Wood, J. W., Milner, G. R., Harpending, H. C. and Weiss, K. M. 1992b. The osteological paradox: problems of inferring prehistoric health from skeletal remains. *Current Anthropology* 33: 343–370.

Wood, J. W., Holman, D. J., O'Connor, K. A. and Ferrell, R. J. 2002. Mortality models for paleodemography. In Hoppa, R. D. and Vaupel, J. W. *Paleodemography. Age Distributions from Skeletal Samples.* Cambridge: Cambridge University Press, pp. 129–168.

Wrigley, E. A. (ed.) 1966. *An Introduction to English Historical Demography.* London: Weidenfeld and Nicolson.

Young, A. 1982. The anthropologies of illness and sickness. *Annual Review of Anthropology* 11: 257–283.

Young, D. A. and Bettinger, R. L. 1995. Simulating the global human expansion in the Late Pleistocene. *Journal of Archaeological Science* 22: 89–92.

Zar, J. H. 1999. *Biostatistical Analysis.* 4th edition. London: Prentice Hall.

Ziegler, P. 1991. *The Black Death.* Stroud: Sutton.

Zink, A.[R.], Reischl, U., Wolf, H., Nerlich, A. G. and Miller, R. L. 2001. *Corynebacterium* in ancient Egypt. *Medical History* 45: 267–272.

Zink, A. R., Reischl, U., Wolf, H. and Nerlich, A. G. 2002. Molecular analysis of ancient microbial infections. *FEMS Microbiology Letters* 213: 141–147.

Zink, A. R., Sola, C., Reischl, U., Grabner, W., Rastogi, N., Wolf, H. and Nerlich, A. G. 2004. Molecular characterisation of *Mycobacterium tuberculosis* complex in ancient Egyptian mummies. *International Journal of Osteoarchaeology* 14: 404–413.

Zubrow, E. 1975. *Prehistoric Carrying Capacity: a Model.* Menlo Park: Cummings Publishing Company.

1989. The demographic modelling of Neanderthal extinction. In Mellars, P. and Stringer, C. (eds.) *The Human Revolution: Behavioural and Biological Perspectives on the Origin of Modern Humans.* Edinburgh: Edinburgh University Press, pp. 212–231.

INDEX